# INSTRUCTIONAL DESIGN

*and*

# TECHNOLOGY-BASED LEARNING STRATEGIES APPLICATIONS

Ernesto Gonzalez

ISBN 978-1-957582-40-5 (paperback)
ISBN 978-1-957582-41-2 (digital)

Printed in the United States of America

WESTPOINT
PRINT AND MEDIA

# Dedication

*"To my Family"*

# Acknowledgement

*First, I would like to thank my professors in the Instructional Design and Technology Education Specialist Degree program at Keiser University. I would also like to thank the many people who have helped me learn and practice both the art and science of pedagogy throughout the years.*

*This book would not have been possible without the higher education institutions that allowed me to develop and test insight-related ideas in curriculum design projects, workshops, and consulting engagements over the last thirty-one years. Especially, Florida National University, I owe an enormous debt of gratitude for allowing me to grow as a professional in education and those who gave me detailed and constructive comments on one or more sections, including Ileana Torres, who supported me on the writing style of it.*

*Finally, I want to thank my family for tolerating my incessant disappearance into my home office and their giving-up moments to let me focus on this endeavor. Lifelong significant others make both the journey and destination worthwhile.*

# Contents

# Foreword

The author is Ernesto Gonzalez, and he has dedicated most of his professional life to higher education institutions. There are different reasons for writing a book about instructional design and technology. Usually, there are personal and professional excuses for making contributions in this subject. At least in the author's case, there are both. He grew up in an endearing family where his mother was a professor. It seems to be inherited, so that is one personal reason why he feels passion for education. His sensibility for providing human beings with the knowledge to succeed in life is another motivation for being an educator.

It is a responsibility to educate people. People rely on educators their intellectual capabilities to operate as reasonable beings. People expect to be equipped with the tools needed to develop their cognitive skills for their survival and development. Because of it, the author thinks that educators must dedicate time and effort to be better knowledge and life skill providers from a pedagogical standpoint. Educators face new experiences every time they teach. Even though an educator repeats the same subject, each is a unique experience because learners are always different. It is an ongoing learning process; it makes this experience more exciting, challenging, and demanding for educators.

He feels proud of having multicultural education experience from where he has learned many things related to human being behaviors. He offers his retrospective journey and gives it away for others to learn from his experience. Many people can ask him: Why did you become an education specialist after having a doctoral degree and working as an educator for so many years? Aren't you supposed to have enough experience in instruction gained from practice? The answer is no. Never is enough to learn because there is always room for knowledge, and his desire for digging deeper into the education and pedagogy world has not been satisfied so far. Now, he holds a terminal degree and can learn and contrast his basic instructional design foundation, supported by technology applications, which did not happen many years ago. Society demands quality of education, and educators should be prepared to face higher quality education standards. It is then his professional excuse for evolving in this field.

Instructional design, pedagogy, and teaching as a profession go hand. Instructional design is then part of the teaching profession, and those who teach with a more substantial pedagogical background will satisfy learners' learning demands without limits. "What is past is prologue" (William Shakespeare), and higher education is living those words. Education has a history of effective practices, and we look ahead to the next century and beyond. Educators will continue to build on a legacy in the making.

# Introduction

This material is a compilation of instructional design and technology work in the higher education context. The content covers different applications of pedagogy principles and instructional strategies and methods to suggest curriculum design improvements. It also analyzes legal issues in higher education related to instruction, the instructional design profession, its current situation, and professional development in the instructional design and technology field. Avoiding actual academic program titles and the higher education institutions for anonymity purposes, the author shows real applications as examples for those who engage in curriculum design endeavors. Since the author has worked for higher education institutions for many years, his accumulated knowledge and experience from participating in curriculum design projects has been the primary motivational source for creating this book.

The book aims to put together several research papers written by the author during his educational journey within the Instructional Design and Technology Education Specialist Degree program. As mentioned above, it is a compilation of applied work to share with instructional designers, academic program directors, professors, instructors, and future professionals in education. There are instructional design and technology applications from the author's perspectives due to the skills acquired from his 31-years' teaching and education leadership experience and the knowledge and skills gained within the graduate degree program.

The book has four sections, and each section contributes to different instructional design and technology problems identified from analyzing case studies related to education and instruction and researching instructional design as a profession. As a result, readers can also see examples of designed technology-based lesson plans and instructional design products after diagnosing academic programs and identifying gaps from curriculum design theory. In all cases, there are suggestions for improvements to reinforce knowledge acquisition. In other words, to make the learning experience for learners more solid.

Section I reveals the implications of technological advancements on global education and training from the author's sight. This section describes the impact of emerging technologies on education and training. It reflects educational technology as the general point within emerging technologies, technology-based instruction, learning environments, digital technology, and their implications for education and training. There are special applications of technologies to education classified as the most suitable aid for acquiring knowledge. We can mention eLearning, video-assisted learning, adaptive learning technologies, and artificial intelligence.

Section II is dedicated to legal issues analysis in higher education. By analyzing different real case studies and lawsuits, the author learned how technology is used in education. As we all know, technology offers advantages and disadvantages, and the ethical and legal side are undoubtedly part of the disadvantages. From the content of this section, we learn that the application of technology on education and instruction may have undesirable consequences if we unknown potential unethical and illegal practices from its implementation.

Section III is the more extensive part of the book. It is dedicated to curriculum design projects by the author in the content of higher education academic programs. The projects hold performance analysis, needs analysis, job analysis, and training design, all pillars for an accurate instructional design product and improvements. It also contributes to other instructional design projects such as instructional plans for using technology, multimedia-based online lesson design, performance intervention design, and training evaluation plans.

In contrast to section III, sections IV and V are focused on instructional design and technology as a profession. Section IV offers an overview of the instructional design job market and the instructional design valued skills for employers. After reading this section, readers can realize how demanding the instructional design field is nowadays and will be in the future as information technology applications evolve.

The nucleon of section V is the instructional design professional development for educators and instructional design professionals. Since the knowledge acquisition and learning skills will require instructional designers to keep alongside new instructional design models, e-learning development, learners' and industry learning expectations, media, and technology, this section shows professional development through different works. For instance, there is a project that analyzes professional development policies. A second project offers a personal, professional development project and one more contribution to technology-based learning through professional development training.

# Section I

## Advancements in technologies on education

# Implications of the Advancement in Technologies on Global Education and Training

Increased diverse student population (ethnicity, age, and professional background) in a globalized world demands from educational institutions leaders how to address teaching and learning missions by focusing on holistic student access to education. U.S. college enrollments will drop by 10% approximately by the late 2020s. Currently, there are more than 350 languages spoken in United States homes. Also, minority students count today for half of all high school students graduates in the United States (Educause, 2020).

Indeed, there is a diverse population with various needs to satisfy. Diversity is also reflected in the learning needs of students. For example, 13% of K-12 students receive special education services, which more than them have learning disabilities or speech and language impairments (National Center for Education Statistics, 2018).

Consequently, diverse classroom composition reflects that heterogeneous composition. As a response to the challenges mentioned above, educational institutions will have to rethink their academic offerings to accommodate teaching and learning content and delivery to the changing global environment. Some emerging responses, such as micro-degree competencies, focused on developing learners' specific skills to apply to new contexts, other options for online learning, standards-based credentialing, and collaboration and partnerships with other educational institutions and professionals' organizations (Engelbert, 2020).

In addition, online education shows ongoing opportunities to achieve educational goals, mainly for those non-traditional students, which demands from educational institutions the design and implementation of new models for online degree and non-degree programs. In parallel to the situation described above, technology and its application to education is a trendy topic. It will continue to be present as technology continues to grow.

This work aims to describe the impact of emerging technologies on education and training. It reflects educational technology as the general point within emerging technologies, technology-based instruction, learning environments, digital technology, and their implications for education and training.

## Educational Technology

Educational technology plays the role of facilitating the learning experience and improving learners' performance by creating, implementing, and managing adequate technological processes and resources (AECT, 2020). It integrates specialized tools into education and training to provide a better teaching and achieve higher learning outcomes. Different is the reason why educational technology offers an advantage for teaching and learning.

Educational technology allows instructors to offer multimedia to tackle diverse learning styles supported by videos, animations, and others and enables instructors to create online courses to learn from anywhere and anytime. Moreover, educational technology makes it possible to have all learners stay connected and develop a learning-based collaborative approach. Also, it not only offers the advantage of teaching and learning online, but it is implemented to support offline teaching-learning.

In conclusion, the appropriate use of educational technology makes the learning process more fun, engaging; students can learn better, remember better, and transfer new knowledge or developed skills to new content better (Bui, 2020).

## Emerging Technologies for Education and Training

As mentioned previously, educational technology refers to the applications of advanced information technology through the internet to education and training. However, it is essential to highlight digital technologies as a critical element for supporting teaching and learning. Through internet-connected computers and mobile devices such as tablets and smartphones, both instructors and students have access to instructional content within the academic program in which they participate. Via these electronic devices, all stakeholders have access to information, streaming videos, interactive games, simulation games, online communication, social media, and collaboration tools.

For example, Generation Z (Gen Z) and Millennial learners prefer using electronic devices more than other generations. Generation Z learners show more varied preferences for different social media platforms, online and visual and video sites, and tools for learning than Millennials. Concretely, Generation Z learners prefer YouTube (82%). Instagram (70%), Snapchat (69%), Twitter (43%). However, Millennials prefer Facebook (43%, 34& Gen Z). Regarding Online Visual and Video Sites, Gen Z likes watching movies online (43%), visiting video sharing sites (66%), playing online games (53%), and sharing pictures (66%). Millennials do not show preferences in this category. Finally, when it comes to mentioning Tools for learning, Gen Z prefers YouTube (55%), In-person group activities (57%), and Learning apps and interactive sites (47%). On the contrary, Millennials continue to prefer using books (60% compared to Gen Z -47%) (Pearson, 2018).

Those technologies used to support learning have altered existing cultural, social, economic, and political patterns by extending native peoples from their origin land, changing the way individuals experienced the world, and establishing a course for the future (Maloy et al., 2021). As a response, digital technologies have found an application in the educational context. For example, from 2010 to 2020, many digital elements are integrated into teaching and learning, such as iPad,

Instagram, Digital music outsells CDs, MOOCs, Game-based learning, Digital textbooks, Open Education Sources, and Flipped classrooms. Also, adaptive technologies, digital badges, wearable technologies, augmented, mixed, and virtual reality, and virtual and remote laboratories (Maloy, 2021).

The development of internet capabilities is paramount when explaining how emerging technologies integrate into instruction. Web 2.0 and Web 3.0 show how the internet has evolved to promote interaction and collaboration among instructors and learners. Because they include blogs, wikis, podcasts, social bookmarking and networking tools, inquiry-based educational websites photo-sharing websites widely used for teaching and learning in educational institutions (Richardson, 2011), emerging technologies have a great impact on learning. The following emerging technologies are classified as the most suitable aid for teaching and learning nowadays (Bui, 2020; Engelbert, 2020).

## Emerging Technologies

### eLearning

It is education and training delivered electronically. It is presented by different modalities (hybrid, blended, and distance learning, but the distinction is just based on time (synchronous, asynchronous, place, and platform made, such as mobile, face-to-face, Web). It is characterized by functional architectures that use several collaborative and interactive functional entities and elements and technics that use the technology designed or selected to achieve learning outcomes. However, special attention must be given to the design aspect of the instruction delivered through eLearning (Reiser & Dempsy, 2018).

### Video Assisted Learning

Students learn through computer screens supported by animated videos, improving students' learning outcomes and reducing instructors' workload (Bui, 2020).

## Adaptive Learning Technologies

It allows instructors to evolve away from content delivery in the form of lectures during class and toward the role of the leader during active learning assignments, discussions, and other exercises. It provides students with all the instructional resources online to support the learning experience and provides instructors with the learning data needed for more informed advisors or coaches (Engelbert, 2020).

## Blockchain Technology

It is used in open Massive Open Online Courses (MOOCs). Also, it is used to verify skills and knowledge through ePortfolios. It benefits education by providing encrypted data storage that can be distributed across computers in the system more secured (Bui, 2020).

## Artificial Intelligence (AI)

It refers to the notion that machines can carry out tasks intelligently. AI can automate basic activities in an education setting, such as grading multiple-choice and fill-in-the-blank questions. Through AI, students can be helped by AI tutors when instructors are too busy attending other activities. Also, students can get feedback and monitor the student progress (Bui, 2020). On the other side, AI can identify suspicious test behaviors among students and flag them for monitoring. However, there is a delicate balance between these emergent technologies, ethics, privacy because it has access to student data which is still a sensitive topic (Engelbert, 2020).

## Analytics

This technology allows educators to monitor student progress by measuring and reporting learning outcomes through the Web. It provides instructors with data to gather valuable information from students' progress and allows instructors to know what portions of knowledge need reinforcement. Also, what portions of the instruction are not delivered appropriately and require enhancement to increase the quality of teaching. Moreover, learning analytics offers essential information at the institutional level residing in registrar records, student information systems, financial systems, and research units. However, it brings some questions about student privacy, ethical considerations standpoints, and data quality. Some information from students that impact student progress cannot be part of the institutional data generated by analytics— for example, family responsibilities or work schedules (Engelbert, 2020).

## Gamification

Gamification is known as the most suitable educational technology trend. It turns to learn into a fun and engaging experience. Students learn and practice while having an enjoyable experience which results in a positive learning environment for them.

## Immersive Learning with Extended Reality

Extended reality includes virtual reality and augmented reality. Augmented reality focuses on physical objects with virtual content. *Virtual reality* is a more immersive experience that allows manipulations of virtual objects› interactions within a virtual environment. This technology finds applications in the higher education context because the applications are included in the curriculum offering a high learning potential. It also provides accessibility to learners with disabilities (Bui, 2020; Engelbert, 2020).

## STEM

Emerging technologies bring many benefits to those STEM (science, technology, engineering, art, and math) academic programs. It allows students to solve real-world problems with creative design and hands-on learning activities.

## Social Media

Many educational institutions are incorporating social media as a communication tool to encourage interaction among learners. Students can share instructional material, engage in study groups, and watch videos. Social media networks are indispensable nowadays and allow both at work and at home to connect individuals with other people. For instructional designers, social media offers a huge potential from a design standpoint. It can be included in supportive, dialogic, and exploratory meaningful strategies (Brown & Green, 2016) and can open classroom experiences, making the experience more learner centered (Reiser & Dempsey, 2018).

Engelbert (2020) conducted a study to evaluate the impact of emerging technology and its impact on education (see Figure 1). Engelbert interviewed 130 international panelists evaluated the impact of each technology or practice across several dimensions, using a five-point scale (o = low; 4 = high). The results offered the following conclusions. Even though *the cost* is one of the most critical indicators for implementing technologies, this study showed that *learning impact* and *support for equity and inclusion* rated high across dimensions except the artificial intelligence and extended reality dimension.

Cost-saving is found to be a pragmatic reason to use emerging technologies (Backhouse, 2013). The two factors, *learning impact* and *support for equity and inclusion*, rated high in instructional design, which means that instructional designers will play a relevant role in using these technologies to produce relevant knowledge and skills development for learners. It also shows a sensitive perception for making the use of these technologies accessible to all.

**Figure 1**

*Impact of Emerging Technologies on Education*

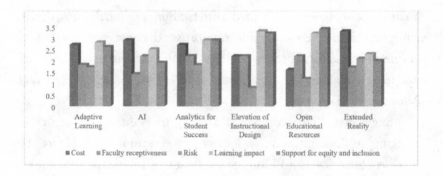

## Reasons to use Emerging Technologies

Most of the instructors who are using emerging technologies in their teaching and learning processes are motivated mainly by pedagogic reasons. By offering effective learning, social and collaborative learning, student-centered approaches, and skills development through emerging technologies, it shows a high interest in providing quality teaching and learning experience by instructors and students. Another reason for sing these technologies for teaching and learning is that they allow both instructors and students to develop their creativity, which might be more challenging to develop when both have access to primary material and tools for learning (Backhouse, 2013).

Moreover, instructors are interested in promoting social or collaborative learning, increase student engagement, facilitate new or different ways to teach better or different learning materials. Also, instructors can experience a better learning experience, better or different learning outcomes, new or improved assessment practices, to develop practical skills, and not least importantly, the possibilities of accommodating different students (accessibility). Additional reasons are facilitating personalized learning, promoting more active learning, monitoring students, promoting real-world learning, understanding complex concepts, motivating students, access experts, and supporting traditional teaching methods (Backhouse, 2013).

## Conclusions

Emerging technologies and their use for educational purposes are impressive because they renew the whole teaching and learning process. One important fact is its positive impact on those with disabilities. Emerging technologies increase the accessibility and convenience of education and professional development for all learners who desire to learn.

# Section II

## Legal issues analysis in higher education

# Legal Issues in Educational Technology

Technology allows organizations to be more efficient, increases productivity, links individuals to organizational processes, and integrates them with the external environment. Higher education institutions are part of these organizations and will continue to embrace technology for the future of education. Technology usage has become a part of human activity. Thus, educational institutions are responsible for developing and utilizing technology, both critically and rationally (Surry et al., 2011). Nevertheless, the technology itself may trigger legal problems in higher education institutions when offering distance learning instruction via technological means.

Technology applied to education encompasses people and ideas for implementing solutions to enrich the student learning process. At the same time, it implies ethical practices to improve student performance, by designing, implementing, and managing appropriate technological operations and resources (Januszewski & Persichitte, 2008).

Legal issues in technology applied to instruction are relevant, because technology has become prevalent in delivering guidance in the higher education context. Thus, there are potential legal issues in different areas involving technology use. These include accessibility policy, training and education, procurement, websites, learning management systems, classroom technologies, grievance procedures, captioning, and issues related to hacking by unauthorized individuals (Kaplin & Lee, 2014). Other potential issues such as ownership of accessibility, privacy, special education, plagiarism, copyright, and freedom of speech include the social media context, which higher education institutions should consider carefully in order to prevent legal issues (University of Washington, n.d.). As the body of federal regulations concerning online learning grows each year due to the number of students and institutions involved in online learning (Kapplin & Lee, 2014), the effort to rule out these potential issues requires more attention.

The objective of this paper is to highlight the current legal issues arising from the use of technology in higher education and their implications for ethical and administrative decision-making. Several technology-related legal issues in the higher education context, resulting from the implementation of instruction-based technology solutions to provide students with advanced means of development in learning and education are mentioned. The paper refers to legal cases regarding legal issues involving technology from lawsuits, students, faculty, or institutions that have been filed against higher education institutions.

Numerous issues related to technology enumerate possible legal areas of concern. First, the lack of training in technology adoption can result in litigation instigated by the government. Second, the use of some material from the Internet without appropriate permission violates copyright laws and intellectual property rights. Third, there are lawsuits originating from comments made or content distributed during a training session that might be discriminatory, not limited to age, race, sex, and ethnicity, trainers or employees injured during a training session due to negligence in providing a safe training environment, and injuries due to incorrect or omitted information received from training materials. Fourth, since promotion requires training, employees might feel that they are unable to advance to higher positions due to them being denied access to the necessary training, which would contribute to legal concerns (Richard & Dempsey, 2002).

On the other hand, teachers are encouraged to follow educational technology standards and performance standards to avoid legal issues arising from technology. These standards and procedures allow teachers to teach and practice technology use; apply technological resources and capabilities to enable students with diverse characteristics, backgrounds, and abilities to affirm diversity, as well as promote the safe and healthy use of these technological resources (ISTE, n.d.).

## Inaccessibility Issues for Learners with Disabilities

Disability is part of the human experience, and it does not reduce the right of individuals to make contributions to society. Higher education institutions should provide students with any disability access to distance learning technology and the possibility of participating in these programs by implementing Americans with Disabilities Act (ADA) requirements. Online courses usually use website images and graphics that are not coded with the text that can be read and interpreted by those who have a visual impairment, color blindness, seizure disorders, dyslexia, or hearing impairments. Non-compliance opens up the possibility, if not likelihood, of incurring legal problems. Then, the ADA does contribute to improving educational outcomes for individuals with disabilities as an essential component of the United States policy of ensuring equality of opportunity, independent living, economic self-sufficiency, and full participation for these people (Legal Information Institute, n.d.).

### *Harnett v. The Fielding Graduate Institute* (2006)

This case involved an online graduate program that required a 300-hour residency on campus, whereby the program accreditation requirements stipulated student–faculty on-campus contact hours. A student enrolled in this program suffering from lupus claimed that the institute lacked the interactive process required under Title III to satisfy her needs. The student was told by the institution that her needs would be accommodated by attending a face-to-face meeting using videoconferencing, being permitted to change to part-time status, and allowing her to transfer to a different group that met two miles closer to her home. The court ruled in favor of the requests made by the student for a cluster group transfer and part-time status. However, the court was concerned because there was little evidence to prove that the institution was upholding its guarantee to provide the student with an interactive learning process (Kaplin & Lee, 2014).

Title III of the ADA requires a higher education institution to make reasonable policies, practices, or procedures to satisfy students with disabilities unless the institution demonstrates that modifying these regulations would alter the nature of such rules (Legal Information Institute, n.d.).

## Accessibility Audit

The term *accessibility* means that an individual with a disability is afforded the same opportunity to obtain in an equally integrated manner, and with equal ease of use, the same information, involvement with social and technology interaction, and services as those without a disability (U.S. Department of Education, 2013). The U.S. Department of Education Office for Civil Rights (OCR) and the U.S. Department of Justice, guided by the Americans with Disabilities Act of 2008, monitor and ensure that higher education institutions follow appropriate practices that guarantee individuals with disabilities equal opportunity to contribute to society, to the same extent as those without disabilities.

Higher education institutions should conduct an audit of accessibility of information technology (IT) and develop corrective and proactive actions to address any problems related to the availability of technological platforms to support learning identified during the audit process. Higher education institutions should also set institutional standards related to accessible technology and implement methods to control compliance. In addition, higher education entities should provide training about accessibility to all individuals on campus who are responsible for creating and procuring IT and technology-related content. Moreover, institutions should design procedures for addressing accessibility within the procurement process and publicize a medium by which faculty, staff, students, and other stakeholders can report access barriers (U.S. Department of Education, n.d.).

### Settlement between Penn State University and the National Federation of the Blind

In 2013, the National Federation of the Blind (NFB) filed a complaint against Penn State University because several computers and technology-based viewers were inaccessible to blind faculty and students. As a result, the university agreed to complete the technology accessibility audit and develop a corrective strategy along with procurement procedures, replace the learning management system, and bring all university websites up to higher-level AA compliance (Penn State, n.d.).

### Accessibility Policy

This kind of legal issue relates to the lack of IT accessibility policies and procedures to be disseminated throughout the institution, including at all administrative levels.

### University of Cincinnati and Youngstown State University Complaint

A complaint was filed against two universities in Ohio. The Office of Civil Rights found that the universities failed to comply with Section 504 and Title II of the ADA due to inaccessible websites and failure to post notices of non-discrimination caused by the lack of a policy related to the issues. In both cases, the resolution agreements consisted of developing a web accessibility policy and an accompanying implementation action plan (University of Cincinnati, n.d.).

### Online Sexual Harassment

Another legal issue arising from technology in the higher education context is online sexual harassment (Kapplin & Lee, 2014). Online sexual harassment has become a problem, especially among younger generation studying at higher education institutions (Lindsay & Krysik, 2012). For example, if a student is bullied or victimized when he or she is repeatedly exposed over time to unwelcome and harmful actions on the part of one or more classmates (Olweus, 2001), it is considered a legal violation. Therefore, legal action may be taken against those who perpetrate such actions.

## Code of Conduct

Online students are required to follow the code of conduct to maintain a standard behavior of mutual respect; however, if the student resides in a different state, the institution should know how to conduct a disciplinary hearing in view of the fact that a solution is being implemented using technology.

### *Baird v. State University of New York, 2011 U.S. Dist. LEXIS 5182.*

The subject of this case was the student code of conduct in an online setting. As pointed out above, the code of conduct to ensure honesty and civil behavior in higher education institutions should be the same for both traditional and online students. If an online student fails to comply with the institutional code of conduct, an online student deserves the same due process and contractual protections as a student who attends face-to-face classes on campus. Alternatively, he or she must observe a specific code of conduct laid out especially for online students. Due process ensures that no one be denied proper proceedings that follow specific rules and principles in legal matters when it comes to depriving them of life, liberty, or property (U.S. Constitution, 1868).

Baird was an online student at Empire State University living in Maryland who was engaged in two incidents of email harassment aimed at the dean and a faculty member. He was charged with a conduct code violation. The hearing was conducted via telephone, and the institution suggested expulsion based on misconduct. Baird sued the institution by claiming racial discrimination and due process violations. Finally, the court did not find evidence of discrimination and sustained that Baird received appropriate due process, awarding a summary of judgment to the university (Kaplin & Lee, 2014).

## Procurement and Accessibility through Technology Use: Legal Implications

Various legal issue resolutions require educational institutions to establish procedures to address accessibility inside the procurement process to acquire, for example, Internet applications to support coursework. One such case consists of a complaint filed by a blind student with the Department of Justice (DOJ) in 2013 against Louisiana Tech University, which adopted an inaccessible internet-based application (MyOMLab) for various aspects of coursework. The DOJ ruled that the university must develop and implement an IT accessibility policy regulating that all web pages and instructional materials must be accessible to all (DOJ, 2013).

## Copyright and Privacy in Higher Education

### *Copyright*

There are legal issues concerning policy changes in higher education when it comes to the use of technology for reading and learning purposes as well as legal practices in electronic communication. These are the issues of copyrights and privacy.

Copyright law deals with securing author rights concerning written and other creative works. The law allows authors to control the use of their work by others. The United States Copyright Office (2009) stated that copyright literally means "the right to copy" (p. 1). Copyright law provides legal protection for original authorship, including dramatic, musical, literary, architectural, cartographic, choreographic, creations, etc. (p. 1).

Copyright issues appeared long before the digital era. However, it remained relatively static until the advent of the electronic age. Nowadays, copyright-related issues continue to impact higher education, which functions as a gatherer and disseminator of knowledge. Educators often use others' work to support student learning. Consequently, they may use copyright-protected materials and upload these to websites as well as disseminate them electronically, which in turn threatens the interests of copyright holders (Guest Jr., & Guest, 2011). However, there exists a concept of "fair use," which basically allows for the use of copyrighted materials without permission from authors when the benefits from using copyrighted material are greater than any potential harm to the creator of the work (Bays et al., 2009). The doctrine holds that the use of copyrighted work for purposes of criticism, reporting, teaching, research, or scholarships is not considered an infringement of copyright (Copyright Act, 1976).

Despite these basic doctrines, issues surrounding copyrights are considerably broad and much interpretation is left to the courts (Kaplin & Lee, 2014). Copyright issues have evolved for higher education institutions since the digital age of learning began. Thus, it is critical to have clear policies related to the use of copyrighted materials. Higher education institutions develop policies allowing flexible legal use of copyrighted materials under both fair use and the Technology, Education, and Copyright Harmonization Act (TEACH) of 2002, which further specifies copyright issues related to learning and educational use.

Bays et al. (2009) identified several common copyright misconceptions related to copyright-protected materials found on the web that can be used without any permission. Another mistake is assuming that all copyrighted materials are of equal strength and extent, when fact-intensive works receive less protection than creative works. This disparity is created by the fair use concept, which applies more to fact-intensive works that can be used in a relatively varied context than those that are classified as creative works. The lack of clarity in copyright meaning and legal support might trigger potential legal issues. To this end, faculty members must be aware of the civil and possible criminal penalties for copyright infringements (Public Law, 1992).

## Privacy in Technology Use in Higher Education

The integration of web technologies is increasingly encouraged across educational levels, from K–12 to higher education; the objective of using the latest and most advanced technology is to support teaching and learning processes to benefit students in their learning and to better suit their digital needs. However, the benefits of technology use are threatened by security issues related to different topics such as privacy, intellectual property rights, and ethical and legal issues (Ohei & Brink, 2019). Leaders should systematically consider these threats to avoid negatively impacting individuals and educate instructors on how to deal with digital media considering the immense amount of information we are bombarded with every day for which we must differentiate between useful and false content.

As mentioned above, there are issues originating from the lack of student privacy measures, which have been a massive concern for institutions of higher education long before the digital age. The predominant legal framework for dealing with student records is established by the Family Educational Rights and Privacy Act (FERPA) (1974), which offers relevant protections on student records. This Act applies to public and private institutions that receive federal funding and includes provisions requiring institutions to protect the confidentiality of student records. Moreover, since technology has changed higher education institutions' operations, FERPA has adopted several changes regarding electronic storage of information and online course delivery. Student confidential information (student personal information) is susceptible to violations when the electronic security system lacks sufficient protection against identity theft or other identity-stealing practices (Guest Jr., & Guest, 2011).

The advanced use of technology in higher education settings also impacts faculty privacy. Akin to student record confidentiality, faculty files stored in computers and email communications can be exposed but faculty privacy violation depends on the institution's computer usage policies (Kaplin & Lee, 2014).

## O'Connor v. Ortega (1987)

In *O'Connor v. Ortega* (1987), the U.S. Supreme Court ruled that public employees can reasonably expect their privacy to be respected in their offices, desks, and files after the office of a psychiatry residency program was searched. The fourth amendment generally protects citizens' expectations of privacy. However, the Court indicated the need for a case-by-case analysis to determine the application of the fourth amendment protection. If a search of such property is warranted, it would not be permissible if it is done for non-investigatory, work-related purposes, or if it fails to meet the standard of reasonableness under all circumstances (Kaplin & Lee, 2014).

## United States v. Angevine (2002)

This case relates to a situation where a professor at Oklahoma State University who pled guilty for possession of child pornography. The federal court held that a university professor had no reasonable expectation of privacy on an office computer owned by the institution. This is because the university policy clearly states that it reserves all the rights of ownership of its associated networks and the data kept on such computers.

## Legal Issues for Training and Education Using Technology

To avoid legal issues, faculty training through instructional technology must provide accessibility training for blind faculty and students to learn how to use learning management systems (LMS) for instructional purposes. For example, in 2014, the University of Montana complained about the inaccessibility of the learning management system. Blind students could not use documents, videos without captions, library database support, or web-based course self-registration. The Office of Civil Rights required the university to set a comprehensive set of steps to correct these deficiencies, which impeded students with visual impairments from learning at University of Washington, (n.d.).

Students who are blind can be affected by inaccessibility to learning aids during attempts to acquire certain knowledge. In 2015, the Massachusetts Institute of Technology (MIT) faced a lawsuit for its failure to provide online captioning, another legal issue for not taking care of individuals with disabilities. The institution was sued by the National Association of the Deaf (NAD) for the non-inclusive nature of its massive online courses; therefore, it was not in compliance with the American with Disabilities Act (ADA) and the Rehabilitation Act. The NAD alleged that students, faculty, and others who are deaf and hard-of-hearing deserve access to information on higher education institutions' online sites, notably MIT (Campus Technology, 2015).

## Social Media for Teaching and Learning: Legal Implications

Nowadays, social media tools such as Facebook, YouTube, Twitter, Instagram, and blogs have drastically changed the higher education context. The integration of these social media tools into daily practices through teaching and collaboration permits building and maintaining relationships with key stakeholders (Agozzino, 2014). Social media adoption for teaching purposes should follow several steps, including exploration, experimentation, learning, coordination, formalization, integration, and institutional absorption. However, educational leaders need to understand that these steps should be supported by consistent policies, students, and faculty members to correctly drive the legal and ethical components of the adoption, which will improve the reputation of human resource quality.

Since 86% of the adult population in the United States, ranging from 18 to 29 years, use social media regularly, the likelihood of emerging legal issues is high (Higher Education Law, 2017). Through online connections some individuals post messages or images that violate policies, codes of conduct set by colleges and universities, or take actions that deviate from professional standards. In such cases, what happens when educational institutions are made aware of these posts (Higher Education Law, 2017)? Do these actions go against the freedom of speech of individuals? Even though higher education has been a system that is supportive of freedom of speech, there are some issues of concern related to what kinds of speech are and are not protected; therefore, it remains difficult to determine exactly what speech can be prohibited or sanctioned. College and university students have an unfettered right to freedom of speech, but controversial online speech implies tangled legal protections. Thus, depending on the type of speech they face, higher education institutions can respond to online speech appropriately (Loyd, 2012).

### R.L. v. Central York School District

This is a case of a public school in Pennsylvania where the school district punished a student for a Facebook post about a bomb threat. At present, much of students' speech occurs outside of school, but in some cases the content of the speech can disrupt school activities. The York School District suspended the student mentioned in this case and the judge at the middle district of Pennsylvania found that the school district did not violate the student's first amendment rights. However, the judge agreed with the parents that the school handbook overstated its capacity to regulate student speech (Bomboy, 2018). Therefore, educational institutions must delineate what type of actions to take based on the scope of their capabilities, in order to be able to face legal demands and offer appropriate strategies that would allow them to avoid being sued.

### Shen v. Albany Unified School District (2017)

In this case, a student at Albany High School created an Instagram account with racist and derogatory messages that targeted both students and school employees. The content of the messages triggered several disruptive events at school. The school leaders expelled all students who posted on the Instagram account and suspended the ones who only followed the posts. The judge stated that the activities on Instagram were initiated by some students with the intent of creating a disturbance on the school campus; thus, the judge upheld the actions taken by the school against five students and ruled in favor of the four students who were not heavily involved with the posts on the Instagram account.

## Recognized Practices for Appropriate Use of Technology

So far, this paper has shown different angles of technology use from ethical and legal standpoints. However, it is also necessary to highlight what kind of actions should be implemented to avoid legal issues that involve students, faculty, staff, and administrators in general. In the context of higher education, educational leaders should develop the concept of digital citizenship (Ribble, 2011). The concept helps all educational stakeholders and even parents comprehend the issues that all institutional members should know about, in order to use technology appropriately. Digital citizenship is defined as the norms or standards of appropriate and responsible behavior concerning technology usage (Kentucky Department of Education, n.d.).

For employees, some of the objectives of information technology is to outline the expectations associated with increasing productivity, provide rapid access to more accurate information to speed up decision-making processes, and fulfil communication purposes among staff and students. However, these expectations might not be met if stakeholders do not understand what constitutes appropriate use of certain technological tools. For example, regarding e-mail, stakeholders must understand that the content of electronic correspondence may be subject to examination under open record laws and is not necessarily private, because e-mail addresses are provided to carry out assigned tasks.

Students should not reveal their name and personal information or establish relationships with unknown individuals. Privacy within the technological higher education context is one of the subjects of legal issues related to technology use. Privacy is not only warranted by the educational institution; we should all maintain privacy free of violations; therefore, our efforts to respect technology use are also a considerable contribution to keeping our institutions functioning within the bounds of the law. The use of technology, which encompasses computers, printers, peripheral, external hard drives, etc. are for work and learning-related purposes and not intended for personal use (Kentucky Department of Education, n.d.).

## Conclusions

Technology usage in higher education continues to increase. There is evidence of the impact of technology on student learning and student–instructor interaction for learning purposes. However, the benefits offered by technology implementation in higher education also come with negative behaviors originating from individuals who disrespect ethical standards of practices, which also applies in an on-campus context. The advantages of technology used for learning purposes should not be misunderstood and misused, in order to avoid violating individuals' fundamental rights, as mandated by the United States Constitution.

The analysis and implementation of technology in education should be based on ethical principles that guide leader behaviors in an educational institution setting (Lynch, 2015). These principles include maintaining integrity and inclusiveness, singling out the human lives and interests behind the technology, considering downstream risks for technology applications, and establishing chains of ethical responsibility and accountability (Vallor & Green, 2018). The use of these principles ensures that stakeholders view their use of technological applications with moral significance.

As higher education leaders, it is our responsibility to monitor behaviors when using technology in both online and on-campus settings to identify misconduct and work to eradicate it. It is also necessary to adhere to the rules and procedures guiding technology that can save costs associated with lawsuits filed against the institution and to prevent future damage to the students, faculty, and administrators in general, when their reputations come under question because they failed to comply with such regulations.

# Section III

## Curriculum design projects in higher education

# Instructional Design: Performance Analysis, Needs Analysis, Job Analysis, and Instructional goals

Nowadays, the rapid development of technology has impacted education tremendously. The current technological development allows knowledge in schools to be dispersed through several ways customizable to learners in their context (Park & Lou, 2017) via online learning, facilitating learning as critical to the long-term strategy of the institutions at all levels (Allen & Seaman, 2014).

However, the effectiveness of technology applications to learning requires a combination of different systemic elements. These elements are an appropriate instructional design to provide enough knowledge acquisition supported by powerful learning (Rowland & DiVasto, 2001). Instructional design creates a means for individual learning. The creation of means for learning requires specific instructional methods to match desired outcomes within given conditions. The content of the teaching will help individuals to achieve mastery in learning outcomes and improve their workplace performance (Rowland & DiVasto, 2001). As mentioned above, individuals may obtain knowledge through powerful learning.

Powerful learning is unique knowledge and skills that change predetermined thoughts and actions over time by transferring that knowledge to a wide range of contexts and circumstances. It is also considered important in achieving the capacity for superior creativity, innovation, and performance at both individual and organizational levels (Rowland & DiVasto, 2001). Instructional design based on a systemic approach provides design teams with the availability of significant resources, emphasis on try-out, revision, high front-end analysis from a defined instructional goal (Dicks et al., 2015; Smith & Ragan, 2005).

The objective of this paper is to conduct a literature review to examine and evaluate the differences between performance analysis, needs analysis, and job analysis from the Systems approach model for designing instruction given by Dick and Carey (2005). It also applies these concepts to a case study and proposes an instructional goal to cover the gap presented in the case study.

## Performance Analysis

Performance analysis aims to obtain information from a situation within a context to corroborate problems and find solutions to these problems. The performance analysis process yields a clear description of the problem in terms of a lack of success to reach planned organizational results, along with the causes of the problem and recommended cost-effective solutions (Dick et al., 2015). It determines the precise cause of the performance deficit that is preventing the institution from achieving their objectives and goals. Also, it helps define the performance required to reach the target.

Robinson and Robinson (2008) formulated a performance analysis process that is widely used in educational and business contexts. However, it can also be applied to the educational setting. The steps of the performance analysis are (1) the definition of what should be, (2) the assessment of the current performance; and (3) the identification of causes and selection of solutions. The "should" is an operational goal measured numerically to determine success. Once it is defined, the evaluator determines which assessment is appropriate for the initiate whether it is process models, competency models, or performance models.

Process models describe the workflow or procedures required to accomplish organizational goals. It is a flow of steps as individuals should perform them to achieve the desired outcome. Competency models describe the skills, knowledge, and attributes required of individuals in a specific role or job group, they perform successfully in support of the organizational goal. These models enable employees to determine strategic competencies for present and future needs in performance at a corporate level (Murphy et al., 2012). Performance models describe performance accomplishments required of individuals in a specific job if organizational goals are to be achieved.

Robinson and Robinson (2008) suggest that before beginning the assessment, it is imperative to determine how the evaluator and the client intend to use the information gathered from the assessment, the actions to be taken once the evaluation is completed, and the applications, coaching or selection, to be designed. Also, Mager and Pipe (1997) defined a 7-step model for analyzing performance problems. Their steps are (1) what is the performance problem? (2) Is it worth fixing? (3) Can fast fix be applied? (4) Are the consequences appropriate? (5) Is there a skill deficiency? (6) Are there other causes? (7) Which solutions are best? Both Robinson and Robinson (2008) and Mager and Pipe (1997) processes allow diagnosing a performance situation; however, the Mager and Pipe (1997) seems to offer more in-detail tools to find performance outcomes.

### *Modern Valley School Case Study Performance Analysis*

Modern Valley School District has a population of 130,000 students, 48 elementary schools, 21 middle schools, 16 high schools, and 29 charter schools. All the district schools have concluded a renovation of technology, increasing Internet bandwidth, access, and speed. The renovation brought 106,500 computers to the schools. The schools receive Federal Funding, and they have added a component of innovative technology use, student interaction with technology, to the teacher evaluation and observation system. The school shows a low number of teachers utilizing technology in their core content classrooms. Sheila Adams, the district assistant superintendent for technology, expressed her concerns with a lack of technology use by teachers. This situation can affect district accountability for not justifying the proper use of technology provided by the government. Also, students are acquiring the appropriate knowledge and skills to satisfy the component of innovative technology as added; therefore, students might not meet local businesses and college entry needs.

Garvin McPherney, principal of Modern Valley School, also pointed out that teachers have full access to the lab and carts; students have been given loggings, but there have been enough teachers using the technology when he walks around. He has heard from some teachers that they do not have enough time because they must catch up with everything else. Even though the school leaders have instructed teachers to use technology, he does not see that this is happening. Garvin McPherney does see some teachers using technology in non-core content courses such as arts, music, PE, and language.

As a technology coordinator, I conducted a performance analysis to identify desired and actual performance, assessed needs, to define an instructional goal to cover the gap between the desired status and the actual status. After interviewing all parties involved in the issue, teachers, district assistant, and principal, I conducted a performance analysis, and the results are summarized in Table 1 by using the Robinson and Robinson (2008) performance relationship map. The district schools are fully equipped with technology. Still, it seems that some causes are originating the gap between the desire to have a more significant number of teachers using technology in their core courses (desired status) and a low number of them using technology for the intended purpose (actual status). The causes might be focused on lack of teacher's skills in using the technology given due to lack of training support by specialists in technology and lack of follow up and measure of the technology component implementation added to the curricula.

The performance analysis indicated that these three areas may contribute to increasing the number of teachers using technology in their core content courses. However, I focused on training as one of the best solutions for a performance problem to formulate an instructional goal for that purpose.

**Table 1**

*Application of the Performance Relationship Map*

| Performance Analysis Question | Performance Analysis Answer |
|---|---|
| What is the problem that was originally voiced? | Low number of teachers using technology in their core context classroom. |
| Is the voiced problem related to a core organizational outcome? | Yes: The use of technology in Core content classroom |
| Are there operational goals established for this outcome? | Yes: More teachers using technology in core content classroom (desired status) |
| Is the operational goal being met? | No: Low number of teachers using technology in core content courses and more technology is used in non-core content classroom (actual status). |
| Is there an operational need? | Yes: More teachers using technology in core content classroom between the desired status and the actual status. |
| Have job performance standards been set for achieving the operational goal? | No: The standards are undefined before having more teachers using technology in core content courses (desired status). |
| Are job performance standards being met? | No: Performance standards are undefined (actual status). |
| Is there a job performance need? | Yes: Increase the number of teachers using technology for core content courses gap between the desired status and the actual status. |
| Are there external factors outside the control of local management that are contributing to operational and job performance needs (e.g., government regulations, corporate hiring freeze, labor contract, corporation's national contract with telephone service provider)? | No: Operational and job performance needs appear to be within the control of local management. |
| Are there internal factors within the control of local management that are contributing to job performance needs? | Yes: employee skills. |
| Are there solutions for the performance needs? | Yes: Employee skills—create training for teachers. |

*Ernesto Gonzalez*

## Needs Analysis

Needs assessment occurs before the development of the instructional goal definition, and it is part of the contextual analysis (Smith & Ragan, 2005). Needs analysis or needs assessment plays an instrumental role in the performance analysis. It is used to identify the problem to be corrected (problem model), something new to learn (innovation model), and a discrepancy between the desired status and the actual status (discrepancy model) (Smith & Ragan, 2005). The need for an assessment takes place when technologists are called to respond to a request for assistance by gathering information to assist professionals in making data-driven and responsive recommendations about how to introduce technology or solve a problem. The assessment requires information about the optimal performance, and actual performance. Feeling instructional designers want to know about how learners or job incumbents think about the topic, training about the subject, the topic priority level, and confidence around the issue. Finally, it also needs information about the causes of the actual performance (Rosset, 1995).

There are three components of needs assessment that allow identifying the discrepancy. These components are (1) the definition of the standard or goal referred to as the desired status, (2) the identification of the actual situation of the current level of performance on the standard or goal. Finally, (3) the third component is identifying the gap between the previous desired status and the actual status of the performance, which is called discrepancy (Dick et al., 2015). A needs assessment is handled to identify leading indicators as valid measures of desired results (Kaufman & Guerra-Lopez, 2013).

Both the definition of the desired and the actual status requires a detailed description to be able to provide a clear understanding and meaning of the discrepancy (Dick et al., 2015). The gap is worth to be analyzed if the divergence is negative. In other words, if the actual performance is lower or lesser than the desired standard, then there is a need of assessment. The needs of assessment are usually named based on the nature of the discrepancy, for example, lack of analytical skills needs assessment.

42

Needs assessment process implements different tools to obtain information from sources involved in the problem. These tools are interviews, employee performance observation, records and outcomes examination, group contribution, and questionnaires (Rosset, 1995).

### Modern Valley School Case Study Needs Analysis

After defining the discrepancy between greater numbers of teachers using technology in their core courses and the actual low number of them doing so, training seems to be appropriate due to technology is ever-changing, and teachers cannot get updates on technology applications as desired. Therefore, I would define a training needs assessment to provide teachers with some technology applications based on their teaching subject.

I will follow the needs assessment logic (Dick et al., 2015) via its three components: (1) scheduling one-on-one meetings with the subject matter experts (teachers) to identify actual gaps in technology applications on their teaching subject. (2) analyzing their lesson plans and lab components to identify opportunities to insert technology applications to support student learning. Also, defining with them the topics of the training. (3) explaining the gaps between specific technology applications to be used throughout the course (standards) and actual technology use performance (needs). The measures mentioned above will be used by the academic director or administrative in tracking the success of training and an instructional goal for starting the project via teacher annual evaluation, class observation, and student learning outcomes.

### Job Analysis

Job analysis is conducted after an instructional designer determined the problem or need for instruction through formal or informal needs assessment and identified the goal. It is also called instructional analysis, and it is one of the essential parts of the instructional design process. It provides information about the content and tasks considered crucial to the instructional development (Jonassen et al., 1999), determines the instructional objectives, and defines in detail the sequence of tasks and sub-tasks to identify relevant skills that might be necessary for students to perform (Dick et al., 2015). It also specifies the knowledge type to be learned (structural, declarative, and procedural), and determines instructional activities, strategies, performance assessments as well as evaluation for the knowledge to be acquired, are other functions of job analysis.

Job analysis requires the goals defined from the needs analysis and information about the learners. With that input information in hand, Morrison et al. (2006) suggested three techniques for analyzing content. These techniques are: (1) the topic analysis to create a topical outline to show the content and the structure of the content components the instructional designer will include in the instructions. Another technique is (2) the procedural analysis in which the instructional designers formulate the steps to complete a task outlined. Finally, (3) the critical analysis that identifies the knowledge and skills needed to accomplish a task or understand the described topic.

In short, the process of performance analysis, which reveals indications of a problem, is initially defined. After that, the needs assessment is conducted to determine what performance deficiencies will be addressed. Then, an instructional goal is stated. The job analysis is conducted as a further examination of the purpose to discover refined specific statements of instructional goals that learner subjects can do and the context in which they will be able to do it (Dick et al., 2015).

## Factors Impacting Instructional Design

Economic, social, cultural, political, and psychological factors affect the design and implementation of instructional design. An instructional designer should identify these factors to their application environment and determine what adjustments to make to ensure accessible instruction (Rhode, 2004).

## Psychological Factors

Instructional design requires designing with psychology in mind. Instructional designers should understand subject matter experts are aiming for providing consistent products to them. Instructional design is more effective when the designer identifies subject matter expert reactions to visual stimuli technology applications offer. Human cognition tricked on humans into believing their responses are fully thought-out and preplanned.

Human behaviors are rooted and influenced by established mechanisms that control our survival instincts. For instance, when we are exposed to a representation of food, shelter, danger, or reproduction, the brain reacts faster than conscious thought. Their reactions are called visceral instincts. There are changes in which we have an emotional response to the visual positively, so visceral reactions produce predictable results. In the instructional design context, it is recommendable using design elements that could represent any of the human brain triggers to connect with the subject matter expert (Johnson, 2019).

Cost-effective analysis is another psychological factor to consider in instructional design. This principle states that behaviors are regulated by the perceived difficulty of a task concerning the perceived reward (Croxson et al., 2010) through energy expenditure efforts. The mental activity requires frequent decisions, hunting, memorizing, learning, which drains the learner's energy until the cost of proceeding outweighs the benefit of completing a task.

Additionally, social influence comes to be part of other psychological factors used for instructional design. Principles for persuasion in the design, such as reciprocation, authority, commitment/consistency, liking, scarcity, and social proof, are used by designers to influence others toward desired actions. For example, giving away free information is used to persuade users to volunteer their contact information for follow up purposes through the reciprocity principle.

Other examples are the signs of authority or expert influence, which can increase perceived trust in the instructional designer and the progress disclosure through which the information is given to the learner or user in small bites with the option to learn more if desired. It prevents learners from being overwhelmed and lastly leads to more effective technology-based materials like websites (Nielsen & Loranger, 2006).

## Cultural Factors

Reeves and Reeves (1997) pointed out that when fundamental pedagogical values in one culture are culturally inappropriate in another, more significant challenges may emerge. The internationalization of the curricula still needs knowledge about the implications of cultural inclusivity for cognitive design or learning resources. When designing an online unit of instruction or including subjects from a diverse population, instructional designers are invited to consider design principles and methods that best match constructivist principles and avoid adopting prescriptive theories (McLoughlin & Oliver, 2000). They need to be flexible enough to ensure that the context and tasks are designed to take into consideration learners' perspectives, and that learning be socially grounded and located within communities with cultures. In other words, it is what Scheel and Branch (1993) called culturally pluralistic instruction.

## Instructional Goal that will Help Solve the Gap

As mentioned above, the definition of the instructional goal is done after analyzing performance and assessing needs. Instructional goals must be clear and concrete through which learners will demonstrate the successful completion of their instruction. Instructional designers should perform goal analysis in detail because crucial educational goals are not initially stated clear enough, and without concise descriptions of the performance, learners will develop themselves. Thus, a complete goal statement should cover: (1) the learners; (2) what learners will be able to do in the performance environment; (3) the performance environment in which the skills will apply; and (4) the instruments available to the learners as part of the performance environment (Dick et at., 2015).

I will define a clear, measurable, and achievable instructional goal for training teachers at Modern Valley School in technology use for student learning; thus, contribute to increasing the numbers of teachers using it in their core content courses.

- Goal: Teachers at Modern Valley School will be trained in new technology applications to education and use, in their core content, a more updated technology, which may facilitate student learning outcomes. Teachers will identify the appropriate technology tools (software, videos, websites, applications) that best satisfy each topic within the teaching subject and will incorporate it as part of the course syllabus.

Learners, contexts, and tools: The learners are teachers that teach core content courses. The setting is the school facility. Teachers will leverage the technological renovation made by the district and use desktop and laptop computers, tablets, and other resources available for both teachers and students.

## Conclusions

Instructional design process requires the definition of instructional goals to satisfy different problems in the educational context. Instructional goals should specify who the learners are in the instructional implementation. They should also state the actions learners will accomplish in the performance context, the performance context in which learners will apply the skills developed, and the tools or resources available for learners in the context they perform (Dick et al., 2015).

# Instructional Plan for Using Technology Innovation

Technology has become an essential part of educators' knowledge base. It has made the integration of technology more frequent to reinforce the use of appropriate methods, techniques, and materials in the process of education. Educators' technological knowledge also known as technological content knowledge (TPACK), is the knowledge acquired to integrate technology in education while teaching content to learners (Schmidt et al., 2009). However, there is no way of knowing the amount of technological knowledge that teachers should acquire and a specific method on how it should be obtained (Koehler & Mishra, 2005). The objective of this paper is to conduct a literature review to identify characteristics of goal analysis, learner characteristics, identify instructional strategies and best practices in technology integration in education, and about the skills needed to accomplish a task. Also, the paper presents a modified instructional goal for Modern Valley School case study from previous goal definition and goal analysis based on new information provided by interviewed teachers and school administrators.

## Goal Analysis

After conducting performance analysis and needs assessment, an instructional goal was identified. Each instructional goal should be clear enough to show learners' capability to achieve the goal. Goal analysis starts with identifying what learners will do if they were accomplishing the goal. The goal analysis approach will allow identifying the skills that effectively lead to the achievement of the instructional objective (Dick et al., 2015). An instructional goal must lead to the possibility to be measured to prove its effectiveness. If the goal is too general or vague, teachers or instructors will find difficulties in knowing how achievable the goal is. According to Mager (1997), these kinds of goals are called "fuzzy" goals, and there is no way to know if they have been achieved and the actions needed to make it. The process of analyzing a goal follows two steps. First, it is to classify the goal statement based on the kind of learning that will occur, and second, it is to identify the subsequent actions to follow to perform the goal (Dick et al., 2015).

The more specific and concrete the instructional goal is, the higher the likelihood of knowing its success. Goals, regardless of the context, that could be in a business or educational setting should comply with seven characteristics (Doran, 1981). These characteristics are specific, meaningful, achievable, relevant, and time bound (S.M.A.R.T.), and should lead to further readjustments to the achievement of the goal. Once the instructional goal is defined, the next step is to determine what skills must be learned to achieve it by utilizing advice from Gagne (1985) *Conditions of Learning*.

## Learners Characteristics

According to Knowles (1970), an essential factor associated with the acquisition of learning and knowledge is the importance of the experience of the learner. School teachers and university professors who have been teaching for a while should have expertise in technology to be open and willing to absorb innovations in technology for learning and teaching purposes. Learning in adulthood is a process that cannot happen in the absence of experience (Carpenter-Aeby & Aeby, 2013). Learning in adulthood, called andragogy, makes a considerable contribution to ethical practices, and has become an instructional framework to facilitate adult learning (Knowles, 1970).

Educators are adults. Thus, their knowledge is actively constructed by them, and learning is an interactive process of interpretation, integration, and transformation of their experiential world (Pratt, 1993). Since andragogy theoretical roots intertwines with Maslow hierarchy of needs, specifically, with self-actualization, a learner teacher might experience high or low levels of motivation that triggers positive and negative attitudes. It also triggers avoiding behaviors toward technology acceptance if he or she is not trained based on experiential learning. Self-actualization emphasizes on human emotions, affects, motivation, choices, and responsibility (Carpenter-Aeby & Aeby, 2013). Teachers with low motivation might show frustration and high resistance levels of integrating technology in their teaching.

There are three simultaneous processes in adult learners, based on five assumptions to consider to design, implement, and evaluate learning activities for adults. The three processes in learning are (1) the acquisition of new information, (2) the process of manipulating knowledge to make it fit new tasks, and (3) the evaluation to identify whether the way information is manipulated is adequate to the task (Carpenter-Aeby & Aeby, 2013). On the other hand, five are the assumptions from an adult's nature to consider for productive design purposes.

Teaching and learning environments are continually absorbing innovations in technology and can be used through different modalities—for instance, blended learning. Blended learning requires both face-to-face and online self-regulated learning. This modality fits adult learning very well. Adult users getting into difficulties with technology may result in abandoning the learning and eventual failure of technological applications, might experience a lack of motivation, negative attitudes, and frustration, as mentioned above. Some other learner characteristics to consider for instructional design purposes include self-regulation, computer competence, workload management, social and family, attitude toward learning modality, gender, and age (Kintu et al., 2017).

The new way of education system seems to fit adult learning education. This new model is known as competency-based education. The competency-based education focuses on both the means of delivering knowledge and the new way of thinking (Edward et al., 2018), and it depends on interaction, experience in computer usage, and motivation

(Picciano & Seaman, 2010). As mentioned in the introductory section of this paper, TPACK is needed to design technology-based instructional strategies and best practices. Therefore, the combination of knowledge, attitude, and skills, ability to perform any activity formed in the learning process of a given discipline, including educational technology (Asimov and Shchukin, 2009), contribute to competency development.

## Instructional Strategies and Best Practices

Technology use has a significant impact on student learning. Teachers should use technology in their classrooms and design learning environments and experiences that support teaching by using best practices as a set of practices correlated consistently with higher student achievement (Oliveira et al., 2012). Empirical results indicate that teacher education programs have not taught new teachers how to use technology effectively (Liu, 2012; Maddux & Cummings, 2004); thus, teachers still lack the ability and knowledge needed to teach effectively with technology.

In technology-supported learning, teachers who engage in best practices use a varied instructional delivery method to assist learners. The use of several instructional delivery methods allows educators to help motivate students, help connect students with prior and subsequent learning, and incorporate higher-level thinking and problem-solving into activities. Best practices include classroom management, setting clear course expectations, enhancing student's transferability skills, creating collaborative learning opportunities, and learner satisfaction (Stone, 2004). Also, it allows assessing student learning before, during, and after an academic session, helps teachers set expectations for completing lessons, projects, units, activities, and provides active learning opportunities to internalize learning (March & Peters, 2008).

Moreover, the use of technology alone might not create the expected effect on the learning of the students. Instead, educators need to know how to use technology-guided instruction during the teaching process. It is necessary to differentiate "media" from "method of instruction."

The use of specifics media might not contribute to learning. Media is a tool that provides knowledge using appropriate methods and techniques while teaching students. Therefore, the effective use of instructional media is more critical than just possession of them (Karatas et al., 2017).

Teachers, to attain enough experience in technology integration, may interact with mentors during training sessions to modify their pedagogical beliefs about teaching -which is called "preferred ways of teaching" (Teo at al., 2008). It is because both training and mentor guidance enhance their knowledge (Nilsson & Drie, 2010), and professional abilities in technology integration.

The use of Interactive Whiteboard (IWBs) has become a significant platform for learning between students and teachers. These devices enable users to integrate and manipulate visual multimedia resources, which can be found in several research reports focused on curricula, pedagogy, and the process of utilizing IWBs in schools (Jankowska & Atlay, 2008; Lopez, 2010; Smith et al., 2006). Also, IWBs allow an interacting process between students and teachers to confirm ideas, create confrontation, and gain consensus. Alternatively, the interaction between teachers' perceptions of information technology and andragogy is also relevant (Liang at al., 2012).

Nevertheless, a growing number of educators seek out for instructional strategies conducive to higher student performance in different subjects, for instance, the use of audio and video recordings of classroom lectures and practices such as snapshots of practice-internet, and video of inquiry-based instruction (Van Zee & Roberts, 2006). All these mentioned tools are useful as part of the development of the Virtual Learning Environment (VLE) (Keller, 1987) to motivate students, increase attention, confidence, and satisfaction through the aesthetics and navigation of the VLE space (Power & Kannara, 2016).

As commented in the learner characteristics section, Knowles (1980) and Carpenter-Aeby and Aeby (2013) offered some design elements and their instructional strategies for adult learners (See Table 1).

**Table 1**

*Design Elements of Andragogy and Strategies for Adult Learners*

| Design elements | | Strategies |
|---|---|---|
| Climate | Mutual, respectful, collaborative, informal | Assessment learning style, class agenda, structure, open atmosphere, physical structure of class (small groups, dinner, class discussion) discussions on adult learning and characteristics of adult learners. |
| Planning | Mechanism for mutual planning | Portfolio, individual conferences, group meetings, agenda |
| Diagnosis of Needs | Mutual self-diagnosis | Weekly assessment, goal setting, evaluation, group discussion/review |
| Formulation of Objectives | Mutual negotiation | Individual conferences, group needs assessment, classes 1 and 2 discussions of adult-learner characteristics and evaluation criteria |
| Design | Sequenced in terms of readiness, problem units | Class structure: attendance, discuss weekly evaluations/goal setting, review previous materials, introduce new material, small group teaching/presentation/role play, dinner theater, group presentation, class assessment, individual conferences. |
| Activities | Experiential techniques | Group and individual presentations, small groups, role playing, case studies, class discussion, practical application of assessments. |
| Evaluation | Mutual re-diagnosis of needs, mutual measurement of program | Self-evaluation, teacher-facilitators, group portfolio, weekly assessment, evaluation, goal setting. |

## Skills Needed to Accomplish a Task

The skills refer to verbal information, intellectual skills, psychomotor skills, and attitudinal skills (Dick et al., 2015).

### Verbal Information

This kind of goal requires learners to offer specific responses to specific questions. It usually is defined in terms of *state, describe, list,* and *mention.* The opportunity for the learner to convey with verbal information comes from the content of the instruction. In other words, the learner should know what to state, list, describe, or mention from the content of the instruction (Dick et al., 2015).

### Intellectual Skills

Intellectual skills require the learner to perform a cognitive activity. He or she must be able to solve a problem or develop an event with non-existing information or examples. This kind of skills is given by making discriminations, applying rules, forming concepts, solving problems, and the learners can classify subjects according to characteristics, use a standard, select a variety of rules to apply to solve specific problems (Dick et al., 2015).

### Psychomotor Skills

Psychomotor skills involve the coordination of both mental and physical activity to execute new, significant motor skills, or performance, depending on a proficient execution of physical skill (Dick et al., 2015).

### Attitudinal Skills

Attitudinal skills refer to the ability of learners to choosing to do something. These skills are defined in terms of the tendency, from learners, of making choices or decisions, and they are often long-term goals (Dick et al., 2015).

## Instructional Goal that will Help Solve the Gap

The goal analysis of the instructional goal defined for teachers at Modern Valley School to increase technology integration into the instruction of the core subject courses yielded some room for improvements. After knowing what a goal analysis means, and the perceptions teachers have about not to use technology more often in their instruction through the interview process, it was decided to modify the instructional goal to satisfy teacher and school administrators about including technology in their teaching activity for the students.

There are some observations from reading the opinion of the interviewed subjects carefully. Phrases such as "*...it is needed training to understand how to use technology in actual teaching...*"; ... "*it would be beneficial to show other teachers how to use technology successfully*" ...; ... "*teachers are confused about how to use it*"...; ... "*we need a little more time to plan and practice*"...; ... "*we need to know programs and instructional strategies*"...; ... "*how technology looks or works in the classroom*"...; ... "*there are two groups of teachers, one need more baseline help, and other teachers could jump into using more technology*"..., definitely tell us that there is lack of knowledge about technology applications for learning purposes and lack of knowledge about instructional strategies supported by technology. In all cases, there is a common denominator, lack of implementation of technological tools for teaching purposes.

As stated, the highest expectation from the school administration and the district is to use the resources assigned by the government to enhance student learning through technology. Also, there is a need identified and exposed by teachers focused on learning more about technology integration. These two factors, linked to the fact that technology came to stay forever, suggest that teachers must develop competencies rather than just knowing or developing skills in technology use. Competency-based education is ideal for adult learners. Thus, it implies knowledge acquisition and update, as well as skills development to finally gain competencies. Since the process of acquiring competencies is a long-term rather than a short-term outcome, the instructional goal will focus on knowledge acquisition and skills development to start the implementation of technology integration at the school faster and satisfy expectations of the stakeholders immediately.

From interviewing teachers and school leaders, it seems that not all teachers are placed at the same level of knowledge about technology use. Anyway, technology is updated progressively, and there are advanced research and breakthroughs that all teachers should know. Thus, it suggests concentrating on an instructional goal to help acquire knowledge about current trends in technology use for learning and higher-level cognitive domains to develop intellectual and attitudinal skills. The modified instructional goal for training teachers at Modern Valley School states as follows.

Goal: Describe current technological tools to enhance teaching and learning and recognize the information technology applications that best fit the teaching subject. Also, classify technological tools to be used for each topic within the curricula. The learners are teachers that teach core content courses. The setting is the school facility. Teachers will leverage the technological renovation made by the district and use desktop and laptop computers, tablets, and other resources available for both teachers and students.

To determine teacher knowledge level about technology applied to education, which innovative technologies, instructional strategies, and methods of support they need most, it is suggested to survey teachers for instructional goal planning and implementation purposes. Specifically, for knowing the level of knowledge teachers have about technology. See Table 2.

**Table 2**

*Technology Use in Education Survey*

1. Indicate the extent to which you used the listed learning approaches in teaching.

1 = Not used, 2 = rarely used, 3 = Sometimes used, 4 = Frequently used, 5 = Heavily used

| Learning approaches | 1 | 2 | 3 | 4 | 5 |
|---|---|---|---|---|---|
| Learning by experts | | | | | |
| Learning with others | | | | | |
| Learning through making | | | | | |
| Learning through exploring | | | | | |
| Learning through inquiry | | | | | |
| Learning by experts | | | | | |
| Learning with others | | | | | |

2. Indicate the extent to which you used the listed tools, strategies/ methods in teaching.

1 = Not used, 2 = rarely used, 3 = Sometimes used, 4 = Frequently used, 5 = Heavily used

| | 1 | 2 | 3 | 4 | 5 |
|---|---|---|---|---|---|
| Rich Media Capture Technology, | | | | | |
| Interactive whiteboard, | | | | | |
| Virtual learning environment | | | | | |
| E-Assessment to support assessing learning interactions | | | | | |
| Online social tools to support collaborative learning interactions | | | | | |
| Ludic interactions: Massive multiplayer online gaming | | | | | |
| Mobile technologies: smartphones, tablets | | | | | |
| Satellite-transmitted instruction | | | | | |

| | | | | | |
|---|---|---|---|---|---|
| Constructivist learning tools: Instant messaging, blogs, wikis, and podcasts | | | | | |
| Narrative in multimedia learning | | | | | |
| Infographic | | | | | |
| Virtual filed trips | | | | | |
| Videos for mini-lessons | | | | | |

3. Indicate the extent to which you used the listed tools, strategies/ methods in teaching.

1 = Not used, 2 = rarely used, 3 = Sometimes used, 4 = Frequently used, 5 = Heavily used

| | 1 | 2 | 3 | 4 | 5 |
|---|---|---|---|---|---|
| Active learning | | | | | |
| Student response systems | | | | | |
| Formative assessments | | | | | |
| Summative assessments | | | | | |
| E-portfolio | | | | | |
| Feedback/Self check | | | | | |
| Brainstorming | | | | | |
| Collaborative learning | | | | | |
| Discussions | | | | | |
| Peer learning | | | | | |
| Social media/learning communities | | | | | |
| Case studies | | | | | |
| Online Concept mapping | | | | | |
| Multimedia instruction | | | | | |
| Digital storytelling | | | | | |
| Experiential learning | | | | | |
| Independent study | | | | | |
| Online sign-ups | | | | | |
| Simulation games | | | | | |

## Conclusions

Instructional goal analysis is performed based on the needs assessment and the primary instructional goal definition. Goal analysis allows identifying whether the previous goal requires modification or re-elaboration. Also, it facilitates the process of identifying potential content to be delivered to satisfy verbal information, as well as intellectual skills, psychomotor skills, and attitudinal skills.

# Curriculum Design Project

Curriculum design is the way instruction is described within a class or course. In other words, it specifies what should be done and the sequence the content will follow to achieve learning goals and outcomes (Schweitzer, 2019). However, the process of designing a curriculum implies more steps, such as identifying the needs of stakeholders, developing goals and outcomes, identifying constraints, setting benchmarks, defining courses, dividing courses into units, planning units, formulating specific objectives, considering creating curriculum maps, and identifying instructional and evaluation methods (Glatthorn et al., 2016).

Before designing a new curriculum or modifying an existing one, there should be a need to justify doing so (Diamond, 2008). The institution shall find reasons to engage in curriculum design tasks in such a way that students will benefit from the new knowledge the proposed curriculum will offer them. One relevant subject marketing students must be prepared for is data analysis. Data analysis skills are very demanding nowadays due to the advent of the technology applied to business and economics. In the business world, data changes over time, and many applications and users need to access data at different points in time for problem-solving. The speedy dynamic of the decision-making process to solve problematic situations in corporations is triggered by the analysis of data generated by companies in real-time. Thus, stronger skills in this area are needed by marketing students (Wormerli & Ground, 2011).

After a deep review of the business student data analysis skills at the university, a lack of data analysis content for the marketing students' learning and preparation was found, as compared to the labor market demands in this specific subject. To satisfy the gap shown in the current bachelor's in marketing curriculum being taught, the academic department found it pertinent to expand the current data analysis subject (limited to univariate and bivariate statistical analysis) in the marketing research course to fill the gap in data analysis knowledge in which our marketing students should be trained to gain additional multivariate statistical data analysis skills and finish the degree program more prepared to satisfy their expectations and the employers'.

This curriculum design follows the technological process of curriculum planning. This model emphasizes defining learning objectives and outcomes early in the design process and then identifying what is needed to achieve these objectives and outcomes (Wulf & Schave, 1984). It is also a problem-centered curriculum design that focuses on teaching students how to look at a marketing problem in businesses from a data standpoint and requires students to contribute with a solution. Students are exposed to real marketing situations, which will help them develop data analysis skills. This design enables students to use their creativity and innovation as they are learning (Schweitzer, 2019).

## Needs

As referenced above, the inclusion of an additional unit to the current marketing research course curriculum of multivariate statistical data analysis for marketing students is demanding. Data analysis skills are in high-demand because data helps employees make better business decisions, see the business and marketing performance, improve business and marketing processes, and solve complex real business problems.

After performing an in-depth analysis of data analysis content in the bachelor's in marketing curriculum, it was realized that there is a lack of deeper data analysis content. Currently, students take Introduction to Statistics at a basic level and Marketing Research. These courses mainly cover the basic concepts of statistics, and it is limited to univariable and bivariable statistical analysis. So, it was found that it is needed to enhance the data analysis knowledge by providing students additional preparation in more complex multivariable data analysis techniques to improve their skills in data-driven-problem-solving decisions.

Another source of the need to enhance data analysis skills for marketing students comes from employment opportunities for present-day and future. Employment of market research analysts, for instance, is projected to increase 20% from 2019 to 2018, faster than the average shown for all business-related occupations. This increase will be driven by an escalating use of data and market research across industries. It will then demand increasing data analysis skills to understand customer needs and wants (United States Department of Labor, 2019).

Thus, specific topics such as multivariable techniques aimed by data processing applications for data analysis are essential for marketing students to satisfy corporate America data analysis skills expectations, and it will motivate and stimulate them to take it because of its imminent application.

## Audience

The intended audience for this seminar is marketing students who have taken all general education, lower, and upper core courses in the bachelor's degree in marketing. Senior students will acquire a deeper understanding of higher-level statistical analysis because they should already know data business and marketing processes, environment, and market dynamics. Thus, the development of their data analysis skills-based will be rapidly absorbed. This content will be offered as a learning unit as part of the data analysis subject in the current marketing research course, and delivered in five sessions for five weeks, one hour each session. It will also have the same rigor than other marketing research sub subjects in the current curriculum.

## Goals

The goal of any learning unit is a general statement, which describes the major objectives of the unit and the instructional experience (Glatthorn et al., 2016). Multivariate analysis requires more variables than are contained in univariate or bivariate data analysis designs. These variables must be analyzed together to identify in some manner composite variable or variate. The value of multivariate designs lies in the agreement that individuals in a business context generate many behaviors and react in different ways to the situations they encounter in the business environment. Also, it rests on the idea that the causes of behaviors are complex. Since business context is a network of different kinds of situations given by its open-system nature (Meyers et. al., 2016), marketing students must be prepared to navigate into the complex business environment to make decisions from manipulating complex data.

This learning unit offers theoretical basics of multivariate statistics, familiarizes marketing students with new trends in using data from a complex and multivariate reality, and allows them to gain new or advanced skills to perform a more precise data analysis. There are two learning activities that will be frequently used through the learning-by-doing approach, participation via discussions and in-class exercises. The content of the learning unit uses professionally supported measuring exercises in the center of an intensive five-week training unit covering the areas of multivariate statistical analysis, such as multivariable analysis of variance, multiple regression analysis, multilevel modeling strategies, discriminant function analysis, canonical correlation analysis, cluster, confirmatory, and path analysis, etc. The major goals defined for the *Multivariate Data Analysis Learning Unit* are described as follows:

- Unit Goal 1: Develop data analysis skills throughout the course and apply mastery of that content to real case studies and data analysis simulations.

- Unit Goal 2: Marketing students will demonstrate knowledge and skills in advanced data analysis techniques for use in their business and marketing career.

## Objectives

Learning objectives are detailed descriptions of what students must do to achieve a goal upon specific learning conditions (Diamond, 2008). Setting objectives for the subject course will lead to a successful course if the objectives are stated in performance terms, course goals linked to assessment, and supported by instructional methods that help achieve the objectives (Diamond, 2008). The purpose of any learning unit as an academic activity is to provide students with strong strategies and skills that may implement into their business and marketing environment. The *Multivariate Data Analysis Learning Unit* is a practical academic activity where the students will engage in discussions and practical exercises about data analysis multivariate techniques for problem-solving purposes. By learning new content from the unit, students will be able to do the following:

1. Demonstrate how data and data analytics can be used by managers to improve the decision-making process through datasets, simulated situations, and case studies.
2. Analyze the changing data environment in a business setting in relation to the marketing decision-making process.
3. Describe different multivariate techniques used in real business content to improve decision-making process.
4. Apply quantitative data analysis techniques in several business settings and draw reasonable contribution supported by a deeper explanation.
5. Write an insightful and detailed report from applying multivariate techniques to real situations.

## Scope and Sequence

As mentioned in the goal section, this learning unit is planned to be taught in five sessions for 5 weeks, 1 hour each session. Since this unit is part of the hybrid/blended-3-credits marketing course, the unit will follow that structure. Students will meet once a week at the university campus to receive lectures, practice exercises, and satisfy concerns related to the previous knowledge to make sure they are achieving the learning objectives. Students will spend the remaining online weekly hours in self-preparation under the guidance of the instructor. So, both students and instructor are co-responsible for learning. The scope and sequence of the seminar are shown in Table 1.

**Table 1**

*Multivariate Data Analysis Learning Unit Scope and Sequence*

| Week | Number of class meetings | Objectives covered | Activities |
|------|--------------------------|--------------------|------------|
| 1 | 1 (on-campus) on Wednesdays | 1, 2, 3 | Lecture, Class discussion, in-class exercises. Online assignment. |
| 2 | 1 (on-campus) on Wednesdays | 1, 2, 3, 4 | Online quiz, class discussion, collaborative in-class learning activities. Online assignment. |
| 3 | 1 (on-campus) on Wednesdays | 1, 2, 3, 4 | Online quiz, class discussion, collaborative in-class learning activities. Online assignment. |
| 4 | 1 (on-campus) on Wednesdays | 1, 2, 3, 4 | Online quiz, class discussion, collaborative in-class learning activities. Online assignment. |
| 5 | 1 (on-campus) on Wednesdays | 3, 4,5 | Online quiz, class discussion, collaborative in-class learning activities. Online assignment. |

## Multivariate Data Analysis Learning Unit Curriculum Map

| Week | Essential questions | Content | Skills | Assessment |
|------|---------------------|---------|--------|------------|
| 1 | What is understood by multivariate data analysis? What are the multivariate data techniques? What is the impact of data on business decision-making process? | -Role the data analysis in business nowadays -Multivariate data analysis techniques | -Students will understand the role of data analysis in business context. -Students will classify multivariate techniques based on their purpose | -Class discussion. - Week 1 assignment submission. -Quiz 1 |
| 2 | How can I compare means? | -Multivariate analysis of variance technique | -Students will understand multivariate techniques for means comparison purposes -Students will analyze business data-based business situations to come up with conclusions and decisions from applying mean comparison techniques. -Students will do extra exercises and take weekly evaluation to make sure they understood the content of the technique learned during the week. | -Class discussion and in-class exercises participation -Quiz 2 -In-class Week 1 assignment result analysis- Week 2 Assignment submission |

| | | | | |
|---|---|---|---|---|
| 3 | What are the multivariate techniques for predicting the value of a single variable? | -Multiple regression analysis | -Students will understand multivariate techniques for predicting values of a single variable<br>-Students will analyze business data-based business situations to come up with conclusions and decisions from applying predicting values of a single variable technique<br>-Students will do extra exercises and take weekly evaluation to make sure they understood the content of the technique learned during the week. | --Class discussion and in-class exercises participation<br>-Quiz 3<br>-In-class Week 2 assignment result analysis<br>Week 3 Assignment submission |
| 4 | What are the multivariate techniques for data structure analysis? | -Discriminant function analysis<br>-Cluster analysis | -Students will understand multivariate techniques for data structure analysis<br>-Students will analyze business data-based business situations to come up with conclusions and decisions from applying data structure analysis techniques.<br>-Students will do extra exercises and take weekly evaluation to make sure they understood the content of the technique learned during the week.<br>-Students will practice how to design a group project for the seminar. | --Class discussion and in-class exercises participation<br>-Quiz 4<br>-In-class Week 3 Assignment result analysis<br>-Week 4 Assignment submission |

| 5 | What are the multivariate techniques for fitting models to data? | Confirmatory factor analysis | -Students will understand multivariate techniques for fitting models and data -Students will analyze business data-based business situations to come up with conclusions and decisions from applying fitting models to data techniques. -Students will do extra exercises and take weekly evaluation to make sure they understood the content of the technique learned during the week. | -Class discussion and in-class exercises participation -Quiz 5 -In-class Week 4 assignment result analysis -Week 5 Assignment submission (case study Oral presentation via Bb) |

## Assessment

Unit assessments help strengthen learning unit delivery. Because this learning unit will be part of the marketing research course syllabus, it will use weekly quizzes to monitor student progress weekly and work proactively with those students showing difficulties in their unit goals achievement (Glatthorn, 2016). Also, the instructor will use class participation and weekly assignments as assessment tools to identify weaknesses from the delivery method and teaching effectiveness.

## Part II

The first part of the curriculum design defines the need and purpose of the curriculum, audience, consideration for funding, training, resources, audience, goals, and learning objectives of the curriculum, scope, and sequence of the content, curriculum map, and assessment. The second part serves as a comprehensive blueprint of all the elements part of the content of the units and the material needed to deliver content. These elements are course preparation material, instructional strategies and techniques, instructional materials, evaluation, and technological tools. All these elements are compressed in the lesson plans, which guide faculty to teach the content units. A lesson plan outlines teaching goals, learning objectives, and ways to achieve them. It also shows what students need to learn throughout the unit, as well as what will be done during class time and out of the class (Centre for Teaching Excellence, 2019).

The Multivariate Data Analysis Unit will require from the students to bring their personal computer and excel application to do in-class exercises (See Table 2).

**Table 2**

*Multivariate Data Analysis (MDA) Learning Unit Lesson plans*

| Week | Learning activities | L.O. | Materials needed |
|---|---|---|---|
| 1 | • **Unit introduction.** The instructor will explain the purpose of the MDA as part of the marketing research course and its importance for decision-making process. The instructor will share video 1 illustrating MDA role in business (10 min).<br>• **Ask students** their thoughts about MDA and the application in their workplace (5 min). | 1, 2, 3 | **Video 1:** *Big data, strategic decisions: Analysis to action.* https://www.youtube.com/results?search_query=multivariate+data+analysis+-for+decision+making<br>**Video 2:** *Multivariate Data Analysis Overview.* https://www.youtube.com/watch?v=uCopIs17zlo |
| | • **Lecture:** What is understood by multivariate data analysis? What are the multivariate data techniques? What is the impact of data on business decision-making process? Show video 2 and PowerPoint presentation (35 min).<br>• **Conclusions** (3 min). | | **Power Point** Presentations **Class discussion material:** Why is data important for their business? At https://www.grow.com/blog/data-important-business **Computer** and **overhead.** |

*Multivariate Data Analysis (MDA) Learning Unit Lesson plans*

| | | | |
|---|---|---|---|
| | • **Instructions for the weekly online component** (7 min): Students must read Textbook Chapter 1, do Week 1 assignment, take Week 1 Quiz online, and prepare to participate in the next class discussion.<br>• For the next class discussion, students should read a supplemental material and bring their ideas about "Why is data important for their business." | | |
| 2 | • **Class introduction**: Instructor starts the class by refreshing the last class's content. Ask students the difficulties found when reading and understanding chapter 1. Instructor goes over quiz 1 and Assignment 1results to share results and clarify wrong answers. (10 min).<br>• **Instructor starts class participation activity** by discussing about "Why is data important for their business." (20 min).<br>• **Lecture:** "How can I compare means?" This topic is covered in Chapter 1 of the Textbook. Instructor will show how to compare means by using excel tools to solve business problems. Also, instructor will show some solved problems for student reference and understanding of the technique.<br>• **Class conclusions** (3 min).<br>• **Instructions for the weekly online component** (7 min): Students must read Textbook Chapters 4 (Liner regression) and 5 (Multiple regression), do Week 2 assignment, take Week 2 Quiz online<br>• For the next class, students will discuss with peers one of week-1-assignment exercises. Instructor will select the exercise randomly at the beginning of the class next week. | 1, 2, 3, 4, 5 | **Power Point** Presentations<br><br>**Computer** and **overhead**<br><br>**Supplemental material:** **Video:** *Hypothesis test for 2 population means using excel's data analysis.* https://www.youtube.com/watch?v=_WNUfgZipww |

*Multivariate Data Analysis (MDA) Learning Unit Lesson plans*

| 3 | • **Class introduction:** Instructor starts the class by refreshing last class's content. Ask students the difficulties found when reading and understanding chapters 4 and 5. Instructor goes over Quiz 2 and Assignment 2 to share results and clarify wrong answers. (5 min).<br>•<br>• **Instructor starts class activity** by selecting randomly an exercise from week 2. Instructor asks students to pair up and share their understanding from doing the exercise (15 min). Instructor clarifies doubts and concerns about means comparison (10 min).<br>• **Lecture:** "What the multivariate techniques for predicting the value of a single variable?" This topic is covered in chapter 7 of the Textbook (Multiple regression). Instructor will show how to perform linear and regression techniques by using excel tools to solve business problems. Also, instructor will show some solved problems for student reference and understanding of the technique (20 min)<br>• **Class conclusions** (3 min). Instructor will use this video "Cluster Analysis tutorial" as a supplemental material. See Video 1.<br>• **Instructions for the weekly online component** (7 min): Students must read Textbook, chapter 7, do Week 3 assignment, take Week 3 quiz online.<br>• This week, students must purchase and play the Harvard Simulation game to practice marketing strategies through Conjoint analysis. | 1, 2, 3, 4, 5 | **Power Point** Presentations<br><br>**Computer** and **overhead**<br><br>**Harvard Simulation Game:** Access to Harvard simulation game by clicking on the link below. Enroll, download student materials, and play the simulation. https://hbsp.harvard.edu/import/634102 |

*Multivariate Data Analysis (MDA) Learning Unit Lesson plans*

| 4 | • **Class introduction**: Instructor starts the class by refreshing the previous class's content. Ask students the difficulties found when reading and understanding chapter 7 (Regression technique). Instructor goes over Quiz 3 and Assignment 3 to share results and clarify wrong answers. (5 min). <br> • **Instructor starts class activity**. Instructor asks students to pair up and share their understanding about conjoint analysis technique after performing the Harvard simulation game (10 min). The instructor clarifies doubts or concerns about the technique. <br> • <br> • **Lecture:** "What the multivariate techniques for data structure analysis? This topic is covered in Chapters 11 (Discriminant function analysis) and 15 (Cluster analysis) of the Textbook. Instructor will show how to perform discriminant and cluster analysis techniques by using excel tools to solve business problems. Also, instructor will show some solved problems for student reference and understanding of the technique (30 min) <br> • **Class conclusions** (3 min). Instructor will use this video "Cluster Analysis tutorial" as a supplemental material. See Video 1. <br> • **Instructions for the weekly online component** (7 min): Students must read Textbook, chapters 11 and 15, do Week 4 assignment, take Week 4 quiz online. | 1, 2, 3, 4, 5 | **Power Point** Presentations <br><br> **Computer** and **overhead** <br><br> **Video 1: Cluster Analysis tutorial:** https://www.youtube.com/ watch?v=3MnVCX94jJM |

*Multivariate Data Analysis (MDA) Learning Unit Lesson plans*

| 5 | • **Class introduction**: Instructor starts the class by refreshing the previous class's content. Ask students the difficulties found when reading and understanding chapters 11 and 15 (Discriminant and Cluster analysis). Instructor goes over Quiz 4 and Assignment 4 to share results and clarify wrong answers. (5 min). <br>• **Instructor starts class activity**. Instructor asks students to pair up and share their understanding about discriminant and cluster techniques (10 min). The instructor clarifies doubts or concerns about the technique. <br>• **Class conclusions** (3 min). <br>• **Instructions for the weekly online component** (7 min): Students must read Textbook, chapter 16, do Week 5 assignment, take Week 5 quiz online. <br>• Student must analyze a Harvard case study "Store24(A): Managing employee retention." In this case, students must handle an excel dataset to answer the case study questions. Students must identify what multivariate data analysis technique is the proper one(s) from the methods studied throughout the unit. Students must prepare a PowerPoint presentation based on the answers of the case study, videotape the presentation (8-min length), and submit it to the instructor through the Blackboard component. Students will receive online feedback from the instructor (see rubrics for oral presentations) immediately after submission. The instructor will use an oral presentation rubric to assess students. | 1, 2, 3, 4, 5 | **Power Point** Presentations <br><br> **Computer** and **overhead** <br><br> **Case study: "Store24(A): Managing employee retention"** at https://store.hbr.org/product/store24-a-managing-employee-retention/602096?from=quickSearch |

## Grading Rubrics for Class Participation
## (Eberly Center, 2019)

| | A (18-20 points) | B (16-17 points) | C (14-15 points) | D/R |
|---|---|---|---|---|
| **Frequency and Quality** | Attends class regularly and *always contributes* to the discussion by raising thoughtful questions, analyzing relevant issues, building on others' ideas, synthesizing across readings and discussions, expanding the class' perspective, and appropriately challenging assumptions and perspectives | Attends class regularly and *sometimes contributes* to the discussion in the aforementioned ways. | Attends class regularly but *rarely contributes* to the discussion in the aforementioned ways. | Attends class regularly but *never contributes* to the discussion in the aforementioned ways. |

## Case Studies as a Learning Strategy

Case studies present realistic, complex, dilemma, conflict, or problems, and contextually rich situations that participants in the case study analysis must discuss and find solutions (Eberly Center: Teaching Excellence & Educational Innovation, 2019).

Go to the following link and find information about case study analysis:

https://www.cmu.edu/teaching/designteach/teach/instructional strategies/casestudies.html

74

# Rubric for Classroom Discussion
# (Texas Education Agency, 2006)

### Rubric for Classroom Discussion*

Task Description: (Teacher may explain specific assignment in this space.)

| Criteria | Weight | Exemplary | Effective | Minimal | Unsatisfactory |
|---|---|---|---|---|---|
| Level of Engagement | 50% | ☐ Contributes to class activities by offering quality ideas and asking appropriate questions on a regular basis<br>☐ Actively engages others in class discussions by inviting their comments<br>☐ Constructively challenges the accuracy and relevance of statements made<br>☐ Effectively identifies and summarizes main points | ☐ Contributes to class activities by offering ideas and asking questions on a regular basis<br>☐ Often engages others in class discussions by inviting their comments<br>☐ Challenges the accuracy and relevance of statements made<br>☐ Identifies and summarizes main points | ☐ Occasionally contributes to class activities by offering ideas and asking questions<br>☐ Sometimes engages others in class discussions<br>☐ Sometimes has an understanding of main points<br>☐ Identifies and summarizes some of the main points | ☐ Fails to contribute to class activities<br>☐ Fails to invite comment/opinions from other students<br>☐ Demonstrates little understanding of main points<br>☐ Does not identify or summarize main points |
| Preparedness | 25% | ☐ Always prepared for class with assignments and required materials<br>☐ Accurately expresses foundational knowledge pertaining to issues raised during the discussion | ☐ Usually prepared with assignments and required materials<br>☐ Expresses basic foundational knowledge pertaining to class discussions | ☐ Seldom prepared with assignments and required materials<br>☐ Expresses limited foundational knowledge pertaining to class discussions | ☐ Consistently unprepared for class<br>☐ Expresses no relevant foundational knowledge |
| Attitude | 25% | ☐ Consistently positive, cooperative attitude during class<br>☐ Always supportive of other students' ideas | ☐ Usually positive and cooperative with classroom projects and discussions<br>☐ Often supportive of other students' ideas | ☐ Seldom actively participates in classroom projects and discussions<br>☐ Sometimes supportive of other students' ideas | ☐ Rarely if ever participates in classroom projects and discussions<br>☐ Occasional disruptive behavior |

Assignment Score _____ + Beyonder/Bonus _____ = Final Score _____

# Oral presentation rubric
# (ReadWriteThink, 2019)

Name: _____     Score: _____

### Oral Presentation Rubric

| | 4—Excellent | 3—Good | 2—Fair | 1—Needs Improvement |
|---|---|---|---|---|
| Delivery | • Holds attention of entire audience with the use of direct eye contact, seldom looking at notes<br>• Speaks with fluctuation in volume and inflection to maintain audience interest and emphasize key points | • Consistent use of direct eye contact with audience, but still returns to notes<br>• Speaks with satisfactory variation of volume and inflection | • Displays minimal eye contact with audience, while reading mostly from the notes<br>• Speaks in uneven volume with little or no inflection | • Holds no eye contact with audience, as entire report is read from notes<br>• Speaks in low volume and/or monotonous tone, which causes audience to disengage |
| Content/ Organization | • Demonstrates full knowledge by answering all class questions with explanations and elaboration<br>• Provides clear purpose and subject; pertinent examples, facts, and/or statistics; supports conclusions/ideas with evidence | • Is at ease with expected answers to all questions, without elaboration<br>• Has somewhat clear purpose and subject; some examples, facts, and/or statistics that support the subject; includes some data or evidence that supports conclusions | • Is uncomfortable with information and is able to answer only rudimentary questions<br>• Attempts to define purpose and subject; provides weak examples, facts, and/or statistics, which do not adequately support the subject; includes very thin data or evidence | • Does not have grasp of information and cannot answer questions about subject<br>• Does not clearly define subject and purpose; provides weak or no support of subject; gives insufficient support for ideas or conclusions |
| Enthusiasm/ Audience Awareness | • Demonstrates strong enthusiasm about topic during entire presentation<br>• Significantly increases audience understanding and knowledge of topic; convinces an audience to recognize the validity and importance of the subject | • Shows some enthusiastic feelings about topic<br>• Raises audience understanding and awareness of most points | • Shows little or mixed feelings about the topic being presented<br>• Raises audience understanding and knowledge of some points | • Shows no interest in topic presented<br>• Fails to increase audience understanding of knowledge of topic |
| Comments | | | | |

readwritethink   International Reading Association   NCTE   Copyright 2005 IRA/NCTE. All rights reserved. ReadWriteThink materials may be reproduced for educational purposes.

**Harvard Simulation game for Week 3: "Marketing
Simulation: Using conjoint analysis for business decisions"**
(Harvard Business Publishing Education, 2019).

This simulation is designed to reinforce student understanding and
use of one of the most popular market research methods in academia
and practice - conjoint analysis.

## Goal

The goal is to provide users with an appreciation of how
conjoint analysis output can be relevant in practice, and to provide a
highly interactive experience of using conjoint analysis for managerial
decision-making. The simulation, delivered entirely online, gives
students concrete exposure to key business concepts such as demand
curves, segmentation, profit functions, competitive responses, vertical
and horizontal differentiation, optimal pricing, niche vs. mass market
strategies, product portfolio management, and brand equity. In all cases,
the link to conjoint analysis and its output is made explicit. It includes
two scenarios: The Green Car exercise and the Over-the-Counter Cold
and Flu Medicine exercise. Across these two scenarios, students work
on a series of goals and face a host of competitive settings. In order to
inform their decisions in each of the settings, students have access to the
results of a conjoint analysis study. They can see these results in various
ways and can run market simulations (e.g., what would demand in units
or sales be for each product and price tested/simulated under various
conditions) (Harvard Business Publishing Education, 2019).

## Conclusions

A unit of study is an organized set of learning topics as part of
a course (Glatthorn et al., 2016), and it demands including strategies
for setting learning objectives, introducing new knowledge, monitoring

progress toward learning objectives, and determining whether learning objectives have been achieved (Marzano et al., 2001).

The curriculum design shown is the result of analyzing critical thinking skills development, especially data analysis skills in marketing students at the university. After looking at the data analysis skills that business students develop throughout the bachelor's in marketing, the in-depth Principles of Statistics course, and the current marketing research course, the academic unit identified a shortage of considerable data analysis-based-thinking skills in the curriculum. Based on the job market outlook, data analysis-based professional occupations are increasing exponentially. So, it is needed to cover the observed gap that business students have in this subject by endowing the marketing research course with more content related to data analysis. The academic unit designed a blended multivariate data analysis learning unit (five-on campus contact hours a week and online work) as part of the marketing research course to satisfy the above-described need.

# Design for an Online Lesson

This project describes a lesson content for the brand perception and positioning topic aligned with the instructional design requirements. The project covers the following aspects. It starts by defining the learning model or theory chosen and how it looks in an online setting versus a traditional instructional setting, emphasizing student support structures, activities, socialization/collaboration, feedback and instructor interaction/support, and multimedia applications. The project also describes how the constructivist learning theory components will be included in the Learning Management System (LMS) used to support the online lesson design. Moreover, it describes how the audience's specific needs (business students) are addressed through the lesson's design and how the instructional design can be assessed and modified based on changing students' needs and outcomes.

## Constructivist Learning Theory Chosen

Constructivism posits that teaching and learning processes are based on the premise of cognition as the result of the mental construction of learning. In order to promote student learning, it is necessary to create learning environments that directly challenge learners to the material being studied (Bada, 2015). This theory's implementation will allow learners to build new knowledge of what they have and learn throughout the lesson by analyzing data, creating mental models through the instruction content, and transforming data into information for decision-making purposes. Constructivist theory demands the design to create a predisposition towards learning, the sequential presentation of the material, and the evaluation of the new knowledge acquired through problem-solving (McLeod, 2019).

Considering this, the constructivist perspective applies to both the classroom environment and the online environment. Specifically, an online learning environment also offers conditions for applying constructivism to help create knowledge. Instructors and instructional designers use this perspective in an online environment because in this environment, knowledge can be shared between instructors and students in this environment. Both instructors and students can share authority. The instructor's role is also one of a facilitator or guide, and the learning process in groups count on small numbers of heterogeneous students (Tam, 2000).

There are additional benefits of using constructivism in online learning. Students can learn more when involved actively in the learning process; students own what they know. By grounding activities in an authentic, real-world context, the constructivist perspective stimulates and engages students. This perspective also helps promote social and communication skills by emphasizing collaboration and exchanging ideas when working together in the online environment (Bada, 2015).

The following chart compares the traditional constructivist classroom with an online constructivist learning environment. Essentially, the principles of constructivism are present in both environments. However, there are some differences between the two domains. These differences are given by the context (face-to-face/online), resources used (electronic-based information, collaboration, assessment resources -when referring to a fully online context), and tools used by instructors to engage and motivate students to make a meaningful constructivist online learning experience.

## Table 1

*Constructivist-based Traditional Classroom (Bada, 2015) and Online Envrionemnt Comparison*

| Traditional classroom | Online Environment |
| --- | --- |
| Curriculum emphasizes big concepts with the whole and expanding to include parts. | Curriculum emphasizes big concepts with the whole and expanding to include parts. |
| Students' questions and interest are valued during live sessions, and face-to-face discussions, debates (socialization/collaboration) | Students questions and interest are valued during discussion board, Wikis, blogs remote interactions, and face-to-face virtual discussions, debates. Community-building also helps reduce or prevent feelings of isolation and alienation that often contribute to distance education student attrition. Sense of community in an educational setting includes social community and learning community (Rovai et al., 2004). |
| Uses primary sources and manipulative sources of materials provided by textbooks, classroom equippment, Library hand-on materials, face-to-face interviews. | Uses primary sources and manipulative electronic sources of materials accessible via internet, computer software, social media platforms, video-interactive tools such as Zoom, and others. |
| Interactive learning built on what the student already knows by using classroom materials. | Interactive learning built on what the student already knows by using electronic and multimedia-based materials. It includes opportunities for reflective thought prior to participating in a discussion and post-participation review/access to written discussions. Also, reduction of nonverbal cues, such as encouraging gestures, during the communication process (Reis, n.d.). |
| Instructors play an interactive role when interacting face-to-face with students. | Instructors play an interactive role when interacting with students via social media platforms, multimdeia tools, video-interactive tools such as Zoom. The online instructor fosters a sense of community by creating a safe environment where students are not threatened when they express their ideas, promoting socialization, communicating respect for diverse perspectives and backgrounds, providing timely feedback that gives direction and keeps information flowing, responding to the educational needs of students, and maintaining an online presence (Reis, n.d.). |

| | |
|---|---|
| Students are assessed from their work, observations, standpoints, and tests applied in the live-synch classroom activities. | Students are assessed from their work, observations, standpoints, and tests via interactive quizzes, LMS test setting, video demonstrations, video-based oral presentations. |
| Knolwedge acquisition is dynamic, enriched by the experiences shared while working together in the classroom. | Knolwedge acquisition is dynamic, enriched by the experiences when interacting remotely via the LMS, social media platforms. Students are self-directed and autonomous learning which allows fostering lifelong learning by allowing greater abilities to control their own leaning process, create their learning agendas, develop their learning strategies, and establish a learning pace (Reis, n.d.). |
| Team work is predominant when interacting in the classroom environment. | Team work is predominant through virtual-sync sessions, and async interaction using discussion boards, Wikis, and others. |

## Instructional Design Structure

The design intends to satisfy learning through asynchronous and self-paced learning.

### Instructor Information

It provides information about the instructor's qualifications, which satisfy lesson content and instructional goals and learning objectives, instructor availability, office hours, and email address. The availability of the instructor in an online asynchronous learning activity reinforces psychological closeness.

### Meaningful Instructional Goal and Learning Objectives

The instructional goals and learning objectives are placed as a separate section in the lesson layout. Students will be aware of the importance of the topic and how different learning activities will satisfy the learning objectives to provide enough knolwewdge acquisition.

## Intuitive, Consistent Navigation, and Content Activities that engage the Learners

It shows intuitive and consistent navigation by following scaffolding and modeling/explaining supportive instructional strategies, sequential content activities that engage the learners. Course content is divided into Modules. Each module builds on the previous one. Thus, students must follow each module to learn the topic and obtain the practical skills to solve practical problems with collaboration and communication tools (discussion, wiki activity, videos, excel software).

The content area shows what information, concepts, rules, and principles will be presented to the learners. It gives the new content to help learners obtain the knowledge and remember it when needed in the future with learning guidance (Dick et al., 2015). It also includes the critical part of a lesson, such as goals, objectives, learning strategies, material, and assessments (Carney & Indrisano, 2013).

The content design of this project covers three elements. They are sequence, chunking, and purpose. After developing the objectives, the instructor defines the *sequence of the instruction*. This current project uses scaffolding. Scaffolding includes a sequencing method that reduces the instructor's support to learners in moving little by little from novice understanding to more sophisticated, and it increases the level of performance gradually (Reigeluth & Keller, 2009), becoming learners more independent in the learning process (Baldwin, 2016). The sequential content to obey the scaffolding method is presented through the chunking section next.

*Chunking content* is the strategy of breaking down information into pieces to allow the brain digests new information easily, because working memory holds a limited amount of information at one time (Malamed, n.d.). It defined the lesson subtopics and organized them into a logical and progressive order. In this project, the content will be organized sequentially, as follows in Table 2.

The *purpose of the lesson content* is the third element of the ID structure. This lesson aims to understand brand perception and positioning, make brand perceptual maps and positioning maps, and define marketing strategies from analyzing brand perception and positioning.

**Table 2**

*Chunked Content Sequence*

| Modules | Learning Objectives | Constructivist stages |
|---|---|---|
| 1. Antecedents of perception and positioning | LO1 | Active learning creation |
| 2. Brand perception and positioning definition | LO1 | Active learning creation |
| 3. How to analyze brand perceptions through perceptual maps? | LO2 | Mental model creation |
| 4. How to analyze positioning through positioning maps? | LO2 | Mental model creation |
| 5. Marketing strategy definition through perceptual and positioning maps. | LO2 | Transform data into information for decision-making |

*Learning goals and learning objectives* are described as follows, and they will show in CourseSites. Business students taking a strategic marketing course will be able to explain the brand perception process and brand positioning from a competitive brand in the market to design marketing strategies for their companies. As learning objectives, there are two performance objectives tentatively defined. First, after finishing the lesson content regarding brand perception and positioning, students will explain and analyze the process of brand perceptions by consumers and explain how to interpret brand positioning in the market. Second, students will be able to identify market niches from cracking brand positioning and create marketing strategies to position brands.

*Instructional strategies* describe the general components of the instructional materials and procedures used with those materials to enable students to achieve learning objectives. They include the content presented to the learner, sequencing, clustering, what learners will do with that content, and how to transfer the content to a performance context (Dick et al., 2015). In this project, several activities will support students' active learning and mental model creation and will transform data into information to transfer knowledge into practice and cover the performance gap identified in these students. They are as follows:

1.  Gaining attention through an interactive multimedia lesson content component.
2.  Informing learner of the lesson objectives through a tab created for learning objectives.
3.  Presenting stimulus material via videos and introductory PowerPoint presentation.
4.  Giving learning guidance through a multimedia-based sequential content.
5.  Providing feedback to learners by using oral presentation rubric and assessing their performance (Gagne et al., 2004) through a quiz at the end of the lesson.

## Communication, Interaction, and Collaboration

Students learn by interacting, collaborating, and communicating with the instructor, peers, and content through online learning. Students will learn the content of perception and positioning posted in each learning module built based on the scaffolding approach. Moreover, this project will use *discussion board* questions and *Blackboard Collaborate* for students to interact with each other by exchanging knowledge and real-life experiences related to brand perception and positioning. It will also enable students to interact with the instructor by a question and concern forum and receive feedback for their oral presentation through the Wikis and a quiz administered at the end of the lesson. These interactive and collaborative activities allow students to articulate and reflect on making knowledge explicit to others (dialogic).

## Online Lesson Technical Support Instructions

The online lesson uses CourseSites as the LMS to provide a learning experience. It shows clear information on how students can find help or obtain technical support when experiencing technical issues. It also informs students about accessing tutoring and other academic services such as library for research activities, Writing Lab access for personalized feedback on papers, and reports.

## Lesson Structure supported by Technology and Multimedia

The present online lesson design incorporates different multimedia tools to support learning. The *introduction* or *presentation* shows the content of new information. The introduction to the topic -under the Introduction to the Topic tab in CourseSites, offers an overview of the latest information about brand perception and positioning and their use to design marketing strategies. The introduction should illustrate pictures, gestures, objects from the real world, videos, or anything else that helps make the meaning clear (Writing@CSU, n.d.). It uses Prezi as a multimedia tool to describe the topic supported by a PowerPoint presentation.

## Students' Needs Addressed in this Project

Concretely, the present design is intended to cover the performance gap identified in business (Marketing Bachelor Program) students. From whom it has been perceived as challenging symptoms related to analyzing brand perception and positioning concepts and applications when designing marketing strategies. Students must understand the theory of brand perception and positioning to develop marketing strategies (*desired status*). Students struggle in defining marketing strategies because they do not understand these concepts theoretically and do not know how to build perceptual and positioning maps to identify potential marketing strategies from a practical standpoint (*actual status*). The performance gap identified results from the needs assessments conducted based on observed student progress compared to the desired status of knowledge in this marketing topic (Kauffman & Guerra-Lopez, 2013).

**Instructional Design Assessment**

This lesson design will follow the InTASC model (Model Core Teaching Standards), and the National Standards for Quality Inline Teaching (NSQOT) designed by the Association K-12 Online Learning. These models regulate the quality of online learning through which instructors ensure that students reach the highest quality educational goals. These standards are: Standard A (course overview and syllabus), Standard B (course content), Standard C (instructional design), Standard D (learner assessment), Standard E (accessibility and usability). Also, standard F (technology), and Standard G (lesson plan evaluation). With the Standard G, the instructor will have to review periodically the lesson content and learning objectives achievement to ensure that the content and multimedia tools still satisfy student learning.

## Conclusions

The lesson designed is based on constructivist learning theory. This learning theory is supported with meaningful online learning strategies such as scaffolding and mental models to help a technology-based combination of active, constructive, intentional, authentic, and cooperative learning. Multimedia technologies support meaningful learning when interactions among learners and learner-instructor are conceptually and intellectually engaging.

# Content Area Design Plan for an Online Lesson

Instructors design content areas for instruction after responding to the following questions: What content area will be included in the lesson plan? How will students actively engage in literacy and subject-related activities during the lesson? These answers require an in-depth analysis to define what specific content is appropriate for student learning. The content area's design derives from conducting an assessment and analysis through which instructors or course designers identify the knowledge and skills gaps (needs) between learner current performance and desired outcomes (Kauffman, 2011).

The content area chosen will define the strategies that will impact learners the most and help them succeed in their course. To craft learning strategies adequately, content area definition requires examining learners' needs and including the critical part of a lesson, such as goals, objectives, learning strategies, material, and assessments (Carney & Indrisano, 2013). Moreover, the content area also encompasses what information, concepts, rules, and principles will be presented to the learners. In other words, the content area explains what the unit is all about and how new content will be formatted to help learners obtain the knowledge and remember it when needed in the future (Dick et al., 2015).

This paper is an opportunity to plan for a final project. In the content of this paper, we mention the method of needs assessment to be used to identify learning gaps, the nature of the content, and problems with delivering the subjected content. It also remarks about how to obtain data concerning the problem, as well as the documentation to be gathered and from whom, to determine the needs to deliver this content successfully. Moreover, it shows the instructional goals of the content area and the instructional objectives.

## Needs Assessment Method

Needs assessments reveal the gaps between current and desired outcomes. The identification of needs shows the basis for justifying where we should go and the evidence for proving the meeting costs or not meeting costs the need (Kauffman & Guerra-Lopez, 2013). The present final project plans to follow the components of needs assessment logic defined by Dick et al. (2015). These components establish a standard for a goal as the desired status, determine the actual situation or existing level of performance on the standard or goal, and identify the gap between expected and actual status. The definition of the performance discrepancy results in instructional goals and learning objectives, which are the pillars for beginning this instructional lesson design. Specifically, this project uses the micro-level needs assessment approach (Kauffman & Guerra-Lopez, 2013), which identifies performance gaps at the individual, group, or department performance level.

## Nature of the content

The content to be delivered is related to brand perception and positioning to define marketing strategies. This content is a unit part of the strategic marketing course for marketing students. Brand perception and positioning is a critical subject to define marketing strategies when selling products or services. The analysis or brand perceptions and positioning allow learners to visualize how the market (consumers) perceives a brand and compares a brand with competitor brands in the market landscape.

This content area requires a foundation in consumer behavior to understand how to explain perceptions and position from a psychological standpoint to extrapolate the concepts over the marketing context. The topic of consumer behavior is taught before this content area; thus, students will follow a logical sequence to apply brand perception and positioning definitions to business and marketing situations. Students define brand perceptions and positioning by using statistical models to identify visual gaps in the market landscape and define niches to move in and create a "position" in the consumer's mind. It is difficult for students because they need to learn or refresh multivariate statistical methods to define perception and positioning. They must also use excel (as a tool) to obtain figures and graphs through which the identification of market niches is easier. The lack of skills in using excel also contributes negatively to the understanding of the topic. Therefore, this content area requires a design to overcome the mentioned difficulties to achieve the learning objectives and move on to the following content area.

## Data and Information about the Problem

The identification of the performance gap will be determined by analyzing student performance related to the topic. The academic unit in charge of the marketing academic program gathers data from learning objectives and outcomes for each course taught each period (8-weeks term). The data is kept in the grade book spreadsheets submitted by the instructors teaching that content (marketing subject) and analyzed by both instructors and department chair to identify weaknesses in specific learning objectives and outcomes associated with the content. The data analysis will be accompanied by Robinson and Robinson (2008)'s performance relationship map to clearly define the performance gaps from conducting interviews to students and the instructors who teach marketing subjects. Is there any learners' needs or characteristics in particular that will need to be thought of to best design the lesson? What is challenging about this content in particular that the design needs to account for (that you would likely learn from a needs assessment)?

## Instructional Goal and Instructional Objectives

This final project has defined the following instructional goal: Business students taking strategic marketing course will be able to explain brand perception process and brand positioning from a competitive brand in the market to design marketing strategies for their companies. As learning objectives, there are two performance objectives tentatively defined. First, after finishing the lesson on content regarding brand perception and positioning, students will **explain and analyze** the process of brand perceptions by consumers and explain how to interpret brand positioning in the market. Second, students will be able to **identify** market niches from cracking brand positioning and create marketing strategies to position brands.

## Conclusions

This paper is intended to craft a design lesson plan to teach brand perception and positioning content as part of the strategic marketing course. By gaining knowledge and skills concerning brand perception and positioning, students are equipped to analyze, interpret, and create marketing strategies to position brands in the market. This process of designing the lesson content requires a needs analysis to identify the knowledge gap in learning the brand perception and positioning content by business students and the appropriate data and information to define how much content and how it can be designed and delivered effectively.

## Appendix A. Lesson Plan Diagram

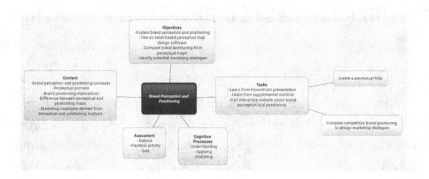

## Appendix B. Lesson Plan Flow Chart

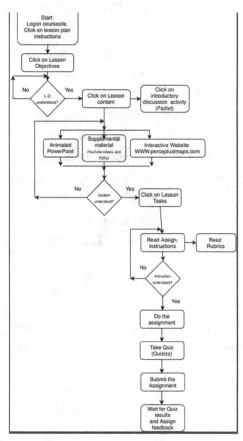

# Multimedia-Based Online Lesson Overview

Multimedia includes different technology-based tools used for reference or instruction, both in and out of the classroom, where learners engage in constructing and conveying knowledge. Learners spend time learning at home, at the workplace, or elsewhere by using different devices such as smartphones, tablets, desktop computers, and laptops. The use of these electronic devices to support knowledge acquisition and skills produces a positive impact on learning (Florida Center for Instructional Technology, n.d.). Practical impact is given when these devices incorporate attractive and exciting elements such as text, graphics, animation, sound, and video (Florida Center for Instructional Technology, n.d.) into different formats such as ebooks, films, and internet sources. These formats allow learners to develop and enhance both knowledge and linguistics, and the interaction between learners and such audiovisual materials on topics of interests makes learners more familiar with new terminology and vocabulary structures, stimulates imagination, and prepares them for analysis and interpretation (Joshi, 2012).

Multimedia when being part of the lesson, course, or program, also requires planning (Florida Center for Instructional Technology, n.d.). One of the challenges that instructional designers and teachers face when planning the use of media in instruction is the choice of the appropriate media and its application for optimizing learning. The availability of multimedia allows instructors to satisfy diverse learning objectives (e.g., related to information and general knowledge recalling, communication skills, collaboration development, and critical and creative thinking development). The identification of appropriate technology is a valuable effort that leads to satisfactory academic outcomes.

## Multimedia Online Lesson Plan

The objective of this paper is to define an initial plan for a one-week online lesson supported by multimedia elements. The topic of the lesson is related to brand perception and positioning marketing strategies for business students taking the strategic marketing course at the university level. The content of this paper covers the instructional goal, learning objectives, and the audience that receives the instruction. Also, it outlines the motivation, learning theories, and the model selected to design the instruction.

## Online Lesson Plan Structure

A lesson plan is a structure that instructional designers (IDs) and teachers design to guide students toward learning. It specifies what students will need to learn, how the topic will be taught, and how learning will be measured. The structure of the lesson plan is adapted from a variety of learning theories that best fit the needs of the learners. It also helps teachers be more productive during the instruction and provides students with a detailed outline that facilitates knowledge acquisition. The components of a lesson plan that make it most effective are lesson objectives, lesson materials, lesson procedures, evaluation or assessment methods, and lesson reflection (Stauffer, 2019). A brief overview of the lesson plan follows.

### Instructional Goal

Business students are showing difficulties in performing a perceptual and positioning analysis of brands in the market. Perceptual and positioning maps analysis constitute a source of marketing strategies design, and it is one of the main learning objectives students should achieve in the strategic marketing course. There is indeed a performance problem by students not having to learn the right type and amount of content related to the mentioned topic. Based on this evidence and problem definition, the present lesson plan follows a *content outline approach* to identify the instructional goal (Dick et al., 2015).

## Goal

The learners are business students taking an online strategic marketing course through CourseSites at the University. The setting is the online environment from home, university, or elsewhere. After studying brand perception and positioning during one week, students will be able to explain how consumers perceive different brands in the market. Students will also examine brands and different brand positions in the market by comparing competitive brand performances. The instructor will leverage multimedia resources that students can use to learn the topic of brand perception and positioning, and they use both their personal computers and computers from the university library.

## Learning Objectives

### Objective 1

At the end of the week, and from using multimedia resources, students will be able to explain the process of brand perception and positioning (behavior) to design marketing strategies.

### Objective 2

At the end of the week, and from using multimedia resources, students will be able to compare brands in the market, as required for designing marketing strategies, and in the multimedia used for learning.

## Lesson Audience

An essential step toward meaningful multimedia development is to identify the audience and the expectations of the learners, which will help find the appropriate resources to satisfy them. During the process of identifying expectations from learners through interviews, observation, and questionnaires, IDs and teachers ensure what type of multimedia resources students know better, and what they feel more comfortable using. The effort in identifying that information allows IDs and teachers to understand the skills that students have in using alternative multimedia. Designers should also consider inquiring about the infrastructure available for students in their context to prevent some conflicts given by the lack of conditions to perform the lesson. With all that said, designers will then define the proper instruction design to achieve the best learning objectives and the instructional goal (Explore Talent LMS, n.d.).

## Learning and Motivational Learning Theories

### E-learning Theory

Multimedia-based instructional designs are commonly based on e-learning theory, and this theory offers principles to guide how e-educational tools (combined use of text, visuals, and audio) can be utilized to promote active learning. However, the combination of these elements should be designed appropriately to avoid cognitive load and distractions by unrelated content such as music, unconnected videos, and graphics, among others. (David, 2015). As part of the e-learning theory contribution, there are motivational theories that add value to the instructional design chiefly when multimedia will play an essential role in learning.

### ARCS Model

Nevertheless, the lesson plan should not only be guided by learning theories to prepare effective instruction. It should also consider motivation in learning, to generate in students' positive attitudes toward knowledge acquisition by making them experience curiosity, fantasy, competition, cooperation, and at the same time, fun, challenging, and uniqueness (Gopalan et al., 2017). One well-known assumption that foothills on learner motivation is the ARCS model, which stands for *attention, relevance, confidence,* and *satisfaction.* Implementing this model helps learners develop positive attitudes toward the learning process because learners can feel comfort and satisfaction from the achievement of their expectations during these processes.

Concretely, any lesson plans should include elements that bring learners *attention* (such as multimedia animations, audio, videos), interest and the sensation of seeking to learn more. Also, the lesson plan should be *relevant*. If learners perceive that the instructional requirements based on multimedia are consistent with the instructional goal objectives and their learning styles, it will positively impact the perceptions of the subjects. Therefore, learners will feel *confident* as they will attribute their learning success to the instruction's robustness and coherency, and then, *satisfied*, if both intrinsically and extrinsically rewarding outcomes sustain their desirable learning behaviors (Keller, 2016).

## ADDIE Model

Instructional design models help organize the learning activities intended to support the instruction (Instructional Design, n.d.) and facilitate proven evaluation and measurement activities based on learners and performance, goals, and outcomes. The instructional models focus on actual performance perceived through expected behaviors in the educational and workplace context (Kurt, 2018). Among different instructional models, it is worth citing two of them, the ADDIE model, and the ARCS model.

The ADDIE approach is regularly used by corporations to train individuals for a specific job. However, it can also extrapolate to any instructional sophisticated or straightforward learning setting in which learners will learn a topic, for instance, a simple lesson for a learning unit or big corporative divisional-level training programs (Bamrara, 2018). The implementation of this model by IDs and teachers implies transitioning sequentially throughout different logical stages that allow learners to acquire knowledge and skills. These stages are analysis, design, development, implementation, and evaluation (Morrison, 2010). Further characteristics of this model are that it is flexible enough to adapt to any learning environments (McIver et al., 2015), and it allows instructors to offer feedback through the evaluation stage, which enriches the design and implementation processes (Durak & Ataizi, 2016).

IDs and teachers need to consider that the analysis stage includes needs analysis, content analysis, technical and structural analysis, and learner and environment analysis required for the design of the instruction. Once the report's outcomes are obtained, IDs and teachers question how to achieve the instructional design and learning objectives through different learning strategies supported by multimedia. IDs and teachers then develop the lesson content, including the appropriate multimedia identified in the previous stage. Next, after designers generate the content of the lesson, learners will be able to start using it for learning. IDs and teachers might use formative and summative assessments to verify instructional lesson effectiveness and implement corrective actions for improvement purposes (Durak & Ataizi, 2016).

## Diagram and Flow Chart Initial Ideas for Navigation/Organization

The LMS to be used is CourseSites (from blackboard). The layout of the lesson will include the following components: interactive introduction using Padlet, weekly assignment, interactive PowerPoint presentation with animation, learning objectives, online discussion, supplemental material bottom with YouTube videos, interactive website holding video tutorial about crafting perceptual maps, and positioning maps, rubrics bottom, interactive quiz using Quizizz as an assessment tool after learning the lesson content, activity/assignment bottom to submit the assignment with the option of reading feedback provided by the instructor as shown in the final section of the flow chart. Learners will navigate as follows:

- Log on CourseSites, go to lesson general instruction, then go to the learning objectives bottom

- Click on the introductory discussion and participate in it using Padlet.
- Click on lesson content that includes three primary sources of information about the subject to study (PowerPoint presentations, supplemental readings, and interactive websites that provide some video tutorials and excel interface for practice purposes)
- Click on assignment tasks and read the assignment instructions and rubrics, do the assignment and submit it through a submission link.
- Click on weekly discussion by using Schoology online discussion tool.

After submitting the assignment, learners will take an interactive quiz (using Quizizz) as a lesson assessment. Appendices A and B show both the lesson plan diagram and the lesson plan flow chart, respectively.

## Conclusions

This paper was intended to design a lesson plan which included multimedia support to teach students how to analyze, explain, and compare brands in the marketplace to identify marketing strategies in the business context. By acquiring knowledge related to brand perception and positioning, students are equipped to analyze brands and compare competitor brands in a specific market. This initial lesson plan defined one instructional goal and two learning objectives derived from a gap performance identified in students who were unable to explain brand perceptions and positioning to design marketing strategies. The audience for this lesson is business students taking the strategic marketing course in which they should be able to understand and apply strategic concepts to design marketing strategies. The preliminary lesson plan (lesson overview) design was thought based on the Addie and ARCS models of learning and motivational theories, respectively. Both models are a strong foundation for designing effective multimedia-based instruction.

## Appendix A. Lesson Plan Diagram

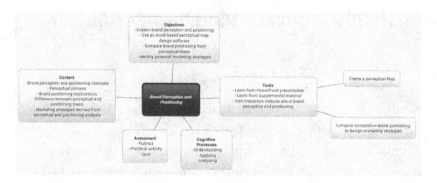

## Appendix B. Lesson Plan Flow Chart Very good flowchart! Detailed and graphically complete, demonstrating the main components of the lesson.

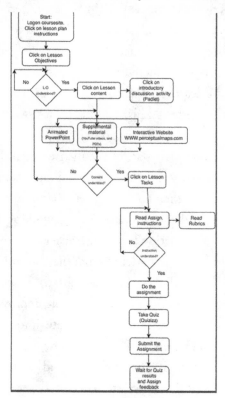

# Needs Analysis and Learner Analysis

Needs analysis and learner analysis are two processes performed before designing instruction to satisfy learners' performance in their work environment or educational setting, attitudes toward task performance, knowledge acquisition, and skills development. These processes are part of the instructional design process, and they are needed to identify what learners need to change and help produce the desired change (Brown & Green, 2016).

Needs analysis provides data about the causes of the gaps identified through the needs assessment (Kaufman & Guerra-Lopez, 2013); therefore, needs analysis allows identifying the need to improve learners' attitudes toward task performance, knowledge of a particular content subject, e.g., increasing productivity. On the other hand, learner analysis allows determining learners' approach to the instruction by defining prerequisite of knowledge, skills, and attitude toward the task. Both needs analysis and learner analysis go hand in hand, even though they are performed separately. As part of the instructional design approach, they belong to different steps. Instructional designers usually start with needs analysis first and then go for learner analysis after; however, they can conduct both studies simultaneously if working in teams. They both also generate information from the learners and their surrounding context, which is paramount to define what they can and will do through the instructional design (Brown & Green, 2016).

This paper outlines the process of implementing needs analysis and learner analysis to gather the appropriate information to design the Business and Management Lesson Unit within the SLS (College Learning Skills) course. SLS course is offered to freshmen business students at university. It allows students to develop competence in orientation to college, study and survival, time management skills, life planning, critical, and experiential learning skills. Thus, this course's context is ideal for developing systems thinking skills for business students. This paper is structured in two parts. Part I describes the performance analysis and learner analysis processes before designing the lesson unit content. Part II shows some specific examples of questions/ data to collect information on the learner and needs of the academic unit at the university.

## Part I: Processes for Conducting Needs Analysis and Learner Analysis

### Needs Analysis Process

As mentioned in the introductory section, both needs analysis and learner analysis help determine what is needed to propitiate a change related to attitudes, knowledge, and skills in learners based on what they need to perform better. Needs analysis and learner analysis also identify critical needs that have a significant financial impact, affect safety, or disrupt the work or educational environments, set priorities for defining an intervention, and contributes to baseline data to assess the intervention effectiveness (Morrison et al. (2006).

Needs analysis provides information about the change requested by learners, who are requesting the change, the context where the change will occur, and whether the instruction designed for learners is the appropriate means for bringing about the desired change. Mager (1988) recommends 12 steps when conducting a performance analysis. These steps are mentioned below.

1. Describe the person or people.
2. Describe what learners are doing that causes the learner to say there is a problem.
3. Describe what learners should be doing.

4. Determine the costs of the discrepancy between what they do and what they should or desire to do in terms of aggravation, frustration, turnover, scrap, insurance rates, time, money, and customers lost, equipment damage, accidents, and so on.
5. Stop, if the estimated cost is low because the identified problem is not impacting the rest of the context.
6. If the cost is excellent, determine whether the target individuals know how to do what is expected of them.
7. If they could do what is expected of them, they already know how to do it. So, determine the consequences and obstacles of performing should be identified by inquiring: What happens to the performers if they do it right? What happens to them if they do it wrong? And What are obstacles to performing as desired?
8. If individuals could not do it, then determine whether they can simplify the task to allow them to perform it, whether they ever knew how to do it if they often used the skills. If they do not do it often and are used to know-how, they need a job aid. Also, designers can make inquiries about whether learners have the potential to learn to do it.
9. Draft potential solutions from the outcomes obtained in previous steps.
10. Determine the cost of implementing potential solutions.
11. Compare the cost of the solutions to the cost of the problem.
12. Select the solutions less expensive than the problem itself and practical to apply.

## Learner Analysis Process

Learner analysis facilitates the process of instructional design. Instructional designers will understand the professors' target audience and determine in advance what learners can potentially develop based on their level of skills, knowledge, beliefs, and attitudes identified through the process (Bransford et al., 2000). In addition to needs analysis, Mager (1988) also recommends the following procedure to analyze learners:

1.  Keep all the information gathered from learners in a working document. Since learning analysis is a working document only in possession of the instructional designer, it is unnecessary to organize the content into specific categories.
2.  Instructional designers should write down everything they know about the target audience. The process of gathering information from learners can start by asking trigger questions, such as: Why are they taking this course? Do they want to be in this course? What training and experience do they have concerning the subject matter?
3.  Describe the range of characteristics whenever possible as learners are, not as the instructional designer would like them to be. The instructional designer should also describe people, not institutions or policies, and the differences and similarities among the learners.

Mager (1988) also recommends gathering information about the target audience based on age range, sex distribution, nature and range of educational background, reasons for attending the course, learners' attitudes about the class, biases, prejudices, beliefs, hobbies; other spare-time activities, and interests in life. Besides, Mager (1988) contemplates the following learner characteristics: needs-gratifiers; physical characteristics, reading ability, terminology, or topics to be avoided, organizational membership, and specific prerequisite and entry-level skills already learned.

## Part II: Questions and Data for Analysis Purposes

This section shows questions and data collection sources on the learner and needs of the organization, which is necessary for gathering information to start thinking on the instruction design content.

### Questions for instructional designers:

- Are first-year business students learning business and management from a systems approach?
- What are first-year business students doing to learn business and management from a system's approach?
- Will a systems approach cause student frustration when taking core business courses?
- Do first-year business students know how to analyze business and management from a system's approach? Why?
- What happens to the first-year business students if they know how to analyze business and management from a system's approach? What happens if they study business and management without knowing how to do it from a system's approach? What are the obstacles first-year business students face when analyzing business and management from a systems approach?
- Can the process of learning business and management from a system's approach be included in the SLS course? Did first-year business students ever know how to analyze business and management from a systems approach? Do they have the potential to learn to study business and management from that approach?
- Is the inclusion of the business and management from a system's approach topic the solution? What is the cost of including the subject as part of the SLS course? Is the cost of this solution high or low compared to the cost of the problem?

## Data About the Target Audience

Data about the target audience (first-year business students) will be obtained using demographics kept in the University Campus Database System, and by interviewing current freshmen business students enrolled in the SLS course. For example, data about age and sex. Data from interviewing students will refer to the reasons for attending the course, attitudes about course attendance, learning business and management expectations, and hobbies. As well as data will refer to learners' interests, terminology to be avoided, organizational membership students belong to, whether they need gratifiers, and their familiarity with Learning Management Systems (LMS), e.g., Blackboard, their technology usage skills, and mobile learning experience.

Physical characteristics will be determined by observing the student and reading ability (e.g., student's behavior during class time, the final grades). Specific prerequisites will be identified by reviewing their scores earned in the university entry tests, remedial taken, English Composition I and II, obtained from the institution registration office and the department chairs.

## Conclusions

Both needs analysis and learner analysis are an essential component in the instructional design process. Both analyses aim to provide valuable information for the design process because they identify learning gaps and learners' perceptions and attitudes toward learning. Once instructional designers know the outcomes of performing needs analysis and learner analysis, they are equipped to design the instruction to satisfy learners' knowledge and skills shortage.

# Task Analysis Paper

Task analysis is the process of identifying the content and sequence to teach specific content. After conducting a needs analysis, instructional designers define an instructional goal to cover the gap between the desired performance and the actual performance. To achieve an instructional goal, designers, along with the learners' characteristics previously identified and the information gathered from learners, define the appropriate content or tasks to be part of the instruction (Brown & Green, 2016).

The composition of freshmen business students at the university is diverse, 68% female and 37% male. They are working professionals with family responsibilities; some of them have more than one job, and they are predominantly Hispanic. Because of the work schedule and time constraints, they require specific yet high-quality instruction to succeed in the job market.

This paper describes the task to complete the Business and Management Lesson Unit's content within the SLS (College Learning Skills) course. Next, it shows an analysis of the task to be performed to carry out the lesson unit's instructional goal. Finally, it shows the entry and subordinate skills of the task learners will complete through the lesson.

## Broad Level Task to Complete Through the Business and Management Lesson Unit

The outcomes of the needs analysis performed on current business students showed that they started taking business-content-based courses without a generalized business and management comprehension. The results also show that they lack knowledge about the systems' thinking approach as desired, which is essential in understanding the business and management context. Therefore, they unknow the interconnection among business and management elements to make efficient and effective management decisions to solve business problems.

Since the lesson content is about understanding the composition of a business and the management function, there is an instructional goal. First-year business students will be able to describe the business and management components as a system. They will also explain how these components interact with each other in the real-world context from a holistic perspective. Instructors will deliver the lesson in one out of eight weeks of the SLS course length. So, the time frame to achieve this instructional goal is one week. Students will leverage the instructors' instructional resources and use the equipment installed in the university for learning purposes.

## Task Analysis Overview for Content Identification

Task analysis helps determine the type of content and skills to include in the lesson unit. It will allow developing the knowledge of how the instructional process is accomplished. This paper will follow the Dick et al. (2015), Gagne (1985), and Morrison et al. (2006) approaches. Once identified the instructional goal (as mentioned in the previous section of this paper) from the needs and learner analysis, the definition of the Business and Management lesson content will use the topic or hierarchical analysis (Gagne, 2006; Morrison et al., 2006).

The topic analysis is a technique that provides two types of information: (1) the content that will make up the content of the instruction and (2) the structure of the content components. As a result, the topic analysis technique will generate an outline that starts with the central topic and identifies the main topic's subordinated information (Morrison et al., 2006). Each subordinated knowledge associated with the main subject will show the subordinated skills students must have to meet the instructional goal (Dick et al., 2015).

Some of the questions to identify content components from the topic analysis technique are the following:

1.  What exactly would newcomer business students be doing if they demonstrated that they already could perform a description of the business and management components as a system and explain how these components interact with each other in the real-world context from a holistic perspective? (it should match the instructional goal)
2.  What are business and management?
3.  What are the components of a business? What is management? What are the functions of management?
4.  What is a system thinking approach? Are businesses a system? Is management a system?
5.  Should the decision-making process be developed in a business/management context? Explain.

## Entry and Subordinate Skills of the Broad Level Task

### Entry Skills

For the business and management lesson unit content, the skills depend on knowledge of a business's basic concepts and management that freshman business students should already know before they begin the instruction. First-year business students must master them to learn new skills (Dick et al., 2015). However, it is expected that freshmen students have minimum knowledge about business and management because they should have working experience in for-profit or not-for-profit organizations. Some of them might have managerial experience. There is also the case that some might not have any working or management experience, yet they must have heard about business and management. Therefore, freshmen business students should have some intellectual skills related to the subject in question.

## Subordinate Skills

It is possible to identify subordinate skills by answering questions such as What must the student already know how to do, the absence of which would make it impossible to learn these subordinate skills? (Gagne, 1985). As described in the previous section, and based on the needs analysis, the business and management lesson unit should cover the following subordinate skills. (1) Freshmen business students must understand these two areas as a system for decision-making purposes. (2) First-year business students must know about business as a value-creation process, business industry, social values and culture, ethics in business and management, business functions (operations, accounting, finance, marketing, operations, human resources, and customer service). (3) Moreover, they must know management functions (planning, organizing, leading, and controlling). All these elements will be presented under a business and management systems approach.

A graphical representation of the entry and subordinate skills based on the topic analysis is shown in Figure 1. It shows how the instructional designer identifies the subordinate skills a business student must learn to achieve a higher-level intellectual skill.

## Additional Tasks to be Performed by First-year Business Students

1. Visit University Library for information gathering.
2. Meet peers for teamwork assignments.
3. Learn how to use electronic databases.

## Conclusions

The task analysis process is essential for designing instruction. It is performed after defining the instructional goal derived from needs analysis and learner analysis. Task analysis provides enough information to plan high-quality learning if instructional designers use different techniques to elaborate learning content to cover the performance gap.

**Figure 1.**

*Entry and subordinate skills*

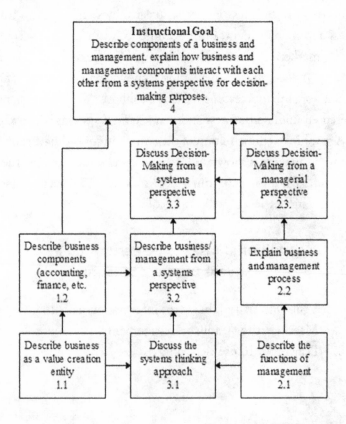

**Instructional Goal**
Describe components of a business and management. explain how business and management components interact with each other from a systems perspective for decision-making purposes.
4

Discuss Decision-Making from a systems perspective
3.3

Discuss Decision-Making from a managerial perspective
2.3.

Describe business components (accounting, finance, etc.
1.2

Describe business/management from a systems perspective
3.2

Explain business and management process
2.2

Describe business as a value creation entity
1.1

Discuss the systems thinking approach
3.1

Describe the functions of management
2.1

# Instructional Design: Introduction to Business and Management Lesson Unit

The primary purpose of a curriculum is to help students learn. Making changes to a curriculum help business students be aware of the changing world. One source of motivation for learning is understanding how things are going, which makes room for new topics relevant today (Chalk, 2020).

This paper presents the preliminary ideas about including a lesson unit into the College Study Skills (SLS) course to cover the nature of business and management. The proposed lesson is intended to show business students taking the SLS course an in-depth view and angles of the business and management theory and practice to reinforce their motivations toward their program degree in business. The paper informs about the rationale for choosing that lesson and the unit's main components such as needs and tasks analyses, events of instruction, and learner and instructional design (project) evaluation. It also describes two technologies to be incorporated into the lesson's content to support its success.

## Rationale for Choosing Introduction to Business and Management Lesson Unit

Business students at the university start taking business-content-based courses without being introduced to the business and management world as students need to. Therefore, students start dealing with technical content taken in 8-week-based terms without understanding the business components and the connection with other business courses as a system approach. After having in-class conversations with students and discussing real-world case studies for solving-problem, we identified a gap between a desired and actual business and management mindset comprehension. The identified gap impedes the appropriate skills development in decision making and solving business students' problems as required by the dynamic business world.

Business students have access to technology. Instructors are called for creating learning situations in which students can evaluate easily if they hold a comprehensive view of the business and management activity before going into specific course content. Students will be able to enrich their past and present experiences with a higher learning ability if they visualize the business context as part of a system approach. Also, instructors will adapt teaching and learning practices to meet the needs of business students and business program goals, as well as learning objectives (Nkana, 2020).

As mentioned in the introductory section, all freshmen students at the university take the required SLS course (College Study Skills). This course develops students' skills to be competent in orientation to college, study and survival skills, time management, life planning skills, critical thinking, and experimental learning. The academic unit decided to include a lesson into the SLS content for freshmen business students to involve and prepare them for the business and management context and its understanding from a system perspective before taking specific business courses. This unit's inclusion into the SLS course will positively impact business students because it will help business students learn, think, and practice business and management accordingly within an 8-week course (Brown & Green, 2016).

## Components of the Business and Management Lesson Unit

The proposed lesson unit will cover introductory topics related to a business's composition as an organization and processes under a systems perspective. These topics are business industry, values and culture, ethics, economics in business, types of business and entrepreneurial activity, business creation, and business operations such as management, human resources, marketing, finance, and accounting.

## Technologies incorporated into the Lesson Unit

All courses taught at the university use an Learning Management System (LMS) for administering and supporting course delivery. Since the LMS offers multiple opportunities for using technology-based tools for meaningful online learning, this unit will incorporate numerous business industry practices-based videos, and external videos embedded within the LMS presentations to show different business and management components, interactive PowerPoint presentations, and wikis for student-student, student-instructor interaction, and collaborating work.

## Needs Analysis and Learner Analysis

Needs analysis and learner analysis are two processes performed before designing instruction to satisfy learners' performance in their work environment or educational setting, attitudes toward task performance, and knowledge acquisition, and skills development. These processes are part of the instructional design process, and they are needed to identify what learners need to change and help produce the desired change (Brown & Green, 2016).

Needs analysis allows identifying the need to improve learners' attitudes toward task performance, knowledge of a particular content subject, e.g., increasing productivity. On the other hand, learner analysis allows determining learners' approach to the instruction by defining prerequisite of knowledge, skills, and attitude toward the task. Both needs analysis and learner analysis go hand in hand, even though they are performed separately. As part of the instructional design approach, they belong to different steps. Instructional designers usually start with needs analysis first and continue with earner analysis; however, they can conduct both studies simultaneously if working in teams. They also generate information from the learners and their surrounding context, which is paramount to define what they can and will do through the instructional design (Brown & Green, 2016).

## Part I: Processes for Conducting
## Needs and Learner Analyses

### Needs Analysis Process

As mentioned in the introductory section, both needs analysis and learner analysis help determine what is needed to propitiate a change related to attitudes, knowledge, and skills in learners based on what they need to perform better. They also identify critical needs that have a significant financial impact, affects safety, or disrupts the work or educational environments, and set priorities for defining an intervention and contributes to baseline data to assess its effectiveness (Morrison et al., 2006).

Needs analysis provides information about the change requested by learners, who is requesting the change, the context where the change will occur, and whether an instruction is the appropriate means for bringing about the desired change. Mager (1988) recommends 12 steps when conducting a performance analysis. These steps are outlined below.

1. Describe the person or people.
2. Describe what learners are doing that causes the learner to say there is a problem.
3. Describe what learners should be doing.
4. Determine the costs of the discrepancy between what they do and what they should or desire to do in terms of aggravation, frustration, turnover, scrap, insurance rates, time, money, customers lost, equipment damage, accidents, and so on.

5. Stop if the estimated cost is low because the identified problem is not impacting the rest of the context.

6. Determine whether the target individuals know how to do what is expected of them, if the cost is excellent.

7. If learners could do what is expected of them, they already know how to do it. So, determine the consequences and obstacles of performing by inquiring what happens to the performers if they do it right. What happens to them if they do it wrong? What are obstacles to performing as desired?

8. If individuals could not do what was expected of them, then determine whether they can simplify the task to allow them to perform it; or decide whether or not they ever knew how to do it and often used the required skills. If they know how to perform the task, but often do not use the required skills, they need a job aid. Also, designers can make inquiries about whether learners have the potential to learn how to do the tasks.

9. Draft potential solutions from the outcomes obtained in previous steps.

10. Determine the cost of implementing potential solutions.

11. Compare the cost of the solutions to the cost of the problem.

12. Select the solutions that are less expensive than the problem itself and which are practical to apply.

## Learner Analysis Process

Learner analysis facilitates the process of instructional design. Instructional designers will understand learners' target audience and determine in advance what learners can do based on their level of skills, knowledge, beliefs, and attitudes identified through the process (Bransford et al., 2000). In addition to needs analysis, Mager (1988) also recommends the following procedure to analyze learners:

1.  Keep all the information gathered from learners in a working document. Since learning analysis is a working document only in possession of the instructional designer, it is unnecessary to organize the content into specific categories.
2.  Instructional designers should write down everything they know about the target audience. The process of gathering information from learners can start by asking trigger questions, such as: Why are they taking this course? Do they want to be in this course? What training and experience do they have concerning the subject matter?
3.  Describe the range of characteristics whenever possible the learners show, not as the instructional designer would like them to be. The instructional designer should also describe people, not institutions or policies, and the differences and similarities among the learners.

Mager (1988) also recommends gathering information about the target audience based on age range, sex distribution, type and range of educational background; reasons for attending the course, learners' attitudes about the class, biases, prejudices, beliefs, hobbies, other spare-time activities, and interests in life. Moreover, Mager (1988) contemplates the following learner characteristics: needs-gratifiers; physical characteristics, reading ability, terminology, or topics to be avoided, organizational membership, and specific prerequisite and entre-level skills already learned.

## Part II: Questions and Data for Analysis Purposes

This section shows some questions and data collection sources on the learner and needs of the organization.

## Questions

- Are first-year business students learning business and management from a system's approach?
- What are first-year business students doing to learn business and management from a system's approach?
- Will a systems approach cause student frustration when taking core business courses?
- Do freshmen business students know how to analyze business and management from a systems approach? Why?
- What happens to the freshmen business students if they know how to analyze business and management from a systems approach? What happens if they study business and management without knowing how to do it from a systems approach? What are the obstacles first-year business students face to analyzing business and Management from a systems approach?
- Can the process of learning business and management from a systems approach be included in the SLS course? Did first-year business students ever know how to analyze business and management from a systems approach? Do they have the potential to learn to study business and management from that approach?
- Is the inclusion of the business and management from a systems approach topic the solution? What is the cost of including the subject as part of the SLS course? Is the cost of this solution high or low as compared to the cost of the problem?

## Data About the Target Audience

Data about the target audience (first-year business students) will be obtained using demographics kept in the University Campus Database System, and by interviewing current freshmen business students enrolled in the SLS course. Data about demographics refer to age and sex. The composition of freshmen business students at the university is diverse, 68% female and 37% male. They are working professionals with family responsibilities, and some of them have more than one job. Because of the work schedule and time constraints, thus, they require specific yet high-quality instruction to succeed in the job market.

Data from interviewing students will refer to the reasons for attending the course, attitudes about course attendance, expectations about learning business and management, and hobbies. First-year business students attend business programs because they like the business world and plan to be a business owner in the future. They prefer attending classes physically through a hybrid/blended modality supported by an LMS, e.g., Blackboard. They are motivated to learn about business and management to practice the managerial skills in their businesses.

Moreover, data will also show their additional interests, terminology to be avoided when learning the terminology, organizational membership they aspire, need gratifiers, their technology usage skills, and mobile learning experience. Physical characteristics will be determined by observing the student and reading ability. Specific prerequisites will be identified by reviewing their scores earned in the university entry tests, remedial courses taken, English Composition I and II courses.

## Task Analysis

Task analysis is the process of identifying the content and sequence to teach specific content. After conducting a needs analysis, instructional designers define an instructional goal to cover the gap between the desired performance and the actual performance. To achieve an instructional goal, designers, along with the learners' characteristics previously identified and the information gathered from learners, define the appropriate content or tasks to be part of the instruction (Brown & Green, 2016).

## Broad Level Task to Complete Through the Business and Management Lesson Unit

The outcomes of the needs analysis performed on current business students showed that they started taking business-content-based courses without a generalized business and management comprehension. The results also show that they lack knowledge about the systems thinking approach as desired, which is essential in understanding the business and management context. Therefore, they unknow the interconnection among business and management elements to make efficient and effective management decisions to solve business problems.

Since the lesson content is about understanding the composition of a business and the management function, there is an instructional goal. First-year business students will be able to describe the business and management components as a system. They will also explain how these components interact with each other in the real-world context from a holistic perspective. Instructors will deliver the lesson in one out of eight weeks of the SLS course length. So, the time frame to achieve this instructional goal is one week. Students will leverage the instructors' instructional resources and use the equipment installed in the university for learning purposes.

## Task Analysis Overview for Content Identification

Task analysis helps determine the type of content and skills to include in the lesson unit. It will allow developing the knowledge of how the instructional process is accomplished. This paper will follow the Dick et al. (2015), Gagne (1985), and Morrison et al. (2006) approaches. Once identified the instructional goal (as mentioned in the previous section of this paper) from the needs and learner analysis, the definition of the Business and Management lesson content will use the topic or hierarchical analysis (Gagne, 2006; Morrison et al., 2006).

The topic analysis is a technique that provides two types of information: (1) the content that will make up the content of the instruction and (2) the structure of the content components. As a result, the topic analysis technique will generate an outline that starts with the central topic and identifies the main topic's subordinated information (Morrison et al., 2006). Each subordinated knowledge associated with the main subject will show the subordinated skills students must have to meet the instructional goal (Dick et al., 2015).

Some of the questions to identify content components from the topic analysis technique are the following:

1. What exactly would newcomer business students be doing if they demonstrated that they already could perform a description of the business and management components as a system and explain how these components interact with each other in the real-world context from a holistic perspective? (It should match the instructional goal).
2. What is the definition of business and definition of management?
3. What are the components of a business? What are the functions of management?
4. What is a system thinking approach? Are businesses a system? Is management a system?
5. Should the decision-making process be developed in a business/management context? Explain.

## Entry and Subordinate Skills of the Broad Level Task

### Entry Skills

For the business and management lesson unit content, the skills depend on knowledge of a business's basic concepts and management that freshman business students should already know before they begin the instruction. First-year business students must master them to learn new skills (Dick et al., 2015). However, it is expected that freshmen students have minimum knowledge about business and management because they should have working experience in for-profit or not-for-profit organizations. Some of them might have managerial experience. There is also the case that some might not have any working or management experience, yet they will have heard about business and management. Therefore, freshmen business students will have a basic understanding of business and management including 1) basic conceptual understanding of the two categories and 2) basic conceptual or experiential understanding of how these work in an actual enterprise.

## Subordinate Skills

It is possible to identify subordinate skills by answering questions such as: What must the student already know how to do, the absence of which would make it impossible to learn these subordinate skills? (Gagne, 1985). As described in the previous section, and based on the needs analysis, the business and management lesson unit should cover the following subordinate skills: freshmen business students must have to understand these two areas as a system for decision-making purposes. First-year business students must know about business as a value-creation process, business industry, social values and culture, ethics in business and management, business functions (operations, accounting, finance, marketing, operations, human resources, and customer service). Moreover, they must know management functions (planning, organizing, leading, and controlling). All these elements will be presented under a business and management systems approach. Not every student will have all of these understandings to the same level. Still, the instructors should look for a general sense of these items and ask about their experiences or knowledge of these concepts in a survey or introductory session to get a sense of the class's level.

A graphical representation of the entry and subordinate skills based on the topic analysis is shown in Figure 1. It shows how the instructional designer identifies the subordinate skills a business student must learn to achieve a higher-level intellectual skill.

## Additional Tasks to be performed by First-year Business Students

1. Visit University Library for information gathering.
2. Meet peers for teamwork assignments.
3. Learn how to use electronic databases.

**Figure 1.**

*Entry and subordinate skills*

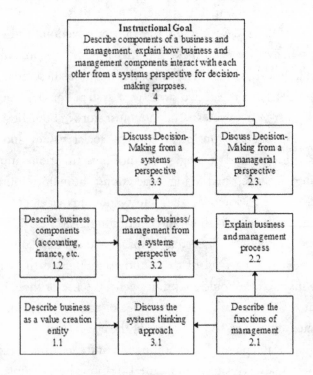

## Events of Instruction

Events of instruction show the order of the activities within a lesson unit. The events are certain activities that offer an expected performance in a specific order. However, to design events of instruction, it is necessary to define learning objectives and performance objectives. Learning objectives describe a performance an instructor wants students to do after completing the lesson unit (Brown & Green, 2016). After examining the subordinate skills shown in Figure 1, the next section shows the learning outcomes and performance objectives defined for the Business and Management Lesson Unit. The lesson is intended to provide students with the knowledge about business's components and management functions, all from system's thinking approach.

## Learning Outcomes

1.  First-year business students will be able to mention a business's component as a unit of value creation.
2.  First-year business students will be able to define the management and decision-making process through management functions.
3.  First-year business students will explain business, management, and decision making from a system perspective.

## Performance/Learning Objectives

Performance objectives, called behavioral objectives by Mager (1987), also learning/instructional objectives by Dick et al. (2015), define what a student will be able to do by using skills and knowledge when he or she completes a set of instructional materials. Performance objectives derive from the entry and subordinate skills identified previously upon the task analysis process completion (Dick et al., 2015), and they have three parts. The first part describes what the learner will be able to do;

in other words, the behaviors (B) or actions learners perform to acquire knowledge or skills from the skills identified during the task analysis process. The second part defines the prevailing conditions (CN) within learners who perform the actions or behaviors. Finally, the third part sets the criteria (CR) to evaluate student performance (Dick et al., 2015; Mayer, 1984).

## Performance Objectives for Learning Outcome 1

1.1. From Q/A activity (CN), describe a business as an economic and social (organization) value creation unit by mentioning the financial, tangibles/intangibles, and human resources used to generate revenues; the costs incurred during the business operations; the impact of business outcomes on individuals, local, regional, and global economy; as well as, the effect on society, the business environment, its impact on business outcomes, and its role from an ethical and social responsibility standpoint (B). Students will name at least three elements that characterize a business as an economic and social value creation unit, as stated in the instructional material shared during the lesson development (CR).

1.2. Given a business description (CN), describe the accounting, operations, marketing, and finance components/functions through which a business operates; describe how these functions relate with each other. Also, identify the organizational processes that keep linking these components, such as informational, communication, negotiation, and leadership (B). Students will identify and describe the four elements/functions of a business and the four organizational processes stated in the instructional material (CR).

## Performance Objectives for Learning Outcome 2

1.1. When asked either orally or in writing (CN), students describe management's concept; the seventeen managerial roles performed by those who oversee human, financial, and tangible/intangible resources; and management subsystem as part of an organization system (B). The student should mention that management is the process of achieving goals and objectives through human, financial, and tangibles/intangibles resources. They should also identify at least ten managerial roles and management as a subsystem (CR).

1.2. When asked either orally or in writing (CN), students mention the four management functions (planning, organizing, leading, and controlling). Students should also describe each function; the decision-making process as part of the management activity and the management cycle from performing the four functions sequentially (B). Students should name and describe the content of the four functions of management (planning, organizing, leading, and controlling), and define the decision-making process (CR).

## Performance Objective for Learning Outcome 3

2. Given a case study showing the four management functions performed by managers and decisions made to solve problems from a systems approach (CN), students (individually and in-groups) will identify and describe each management function throughout the case study. Students should identify managers' decisions; comment about the effectiveness of these decisions from a system's approach (B). Students should work collaboratively to identify management functions and explain whether their decisions were from a system approach or not (CR).

# Why are selected objectives appropriate?

The performance objectives are shown in the previous section derived from the instructional goal and learning objectives defined to cover the performance gap identified through the needs and tasks analyses performed. These performance objectives are supported by the data gathered from interviewing freshmen business students and analyzing senior business students' performance taking core business courses. The content of the performance objectives directs us to create an instruction capable of supporting the business students' population in gaining the skills needed from performing the tasks already identified (Brown & Green, 2016). The structure of these performance objectives follows the three elements (condition, behavior, and criteria) that performance objectives should hold, as required by the Mayer's model (Mayer, 1984). It makes performance objectives measurable.

## Events of Instruction

Events of instruction are the order or continuum of the lesson's learning activities to be taught to achieve performance objectives, as Smith & Ragan (2005) suggested. These events are introduction, body, conclusion, and assessment. The Business and Management lesson unit is structured in three parts to satisfy three learning outcomes with their corresponding performance objectives, and it will be delivered in one week. There are approximately ten business students enrolled in the SLS course, which will take this lesson. See Table 1.

## Table 1.

*Events of instruction for the Business and Management Lesson Unit*

| Learning activities | Performance objectives |
|---|---|
| **Part I: Business as Value creation and its components (Monday/Tuesday)** **Learning outcome**: Freshmen business students will be able to describe business's components as a unit of value creation. **Introductory discussion**: Instructor posts a discussion board thought-provoking question: *Have you ever learned what is a business and its value creation?* Perform a pre-test to understand what students already know about the lesson content. | |
| **Activities**: **1.1.** Watch the video about business value creation: https://www.youtube.com/watch?v=nyl-4LkV30g Watch instructor lecture: Business and resources, business and economy, business social responsibility. Participate in a discussion board question about the topic above. | **Performance Objective 1.1.** From Q/A activity (CN), describe a business as an economic and social (organization) value creation unit by mentioning the financial, tangibles/intangibles, and human resources used to generate revenues; the costs incurred during the business operations; the impact of business outcomes on individuals, local, regional, and global economy. Moreover, the effect on society, the business environment, its impact on business outcomes, and its role from an ethical and social responsibility standpoint (B). Students will name at least three elements that characterize a business as an economic and social value creation unit as stated in the instructional material shared during the lesson development (CR). |

| | |
|---|---|
| **1.2.**<br>Watch the video about<br>business functions:<br>https://www.youtube.com/<br>watch?v=Ffam2HWSaTw<br>Watch instructor lecture about<br>business processes, communication,<br>negotiation, and information.<br>Do the exercise about business functions<br>and submit the contribution.<br>Feedback to students.<br>Take Quiz | **Performance Objective 1.2.**<br>Given a business description (CN),<br>describe the accounting, operations,<br>marketing, and finance components/<br>functions through which a business<br>operates; describe how these functions<br>relate with each other. Also, identify the<br>organizational processes that keep linking<br>these components, such as informational,<br>communication, negotiation, and leadership<br>(B). Students will identify and describe<br>the four elements/functions of a business<br>and the four organizational processes<br>stated in the instructional material (CR). |
| **Part II: Management functions<br>and decision-making process<br>(Wednesday/Thursday)**<br>**Learning outcome:** Freshmen business<br>students will be able to describe the<br>management and decision-making<br>process through management functions. | |
| **Activities:**<br>**2.1.**<br>Watch the video about Concept of<br>Management: https://www.youtube.<br>com/watch?v=_OBqwhYLEJo<br>Watch the video about Management<br>as a system: https://www.youtube.<br>com/watch?v=8EhnIJf9KTw<br>Watch instructor lecture:<br>Seventeen managerial roles.<br>Participate in a discussion board<br>question about the topic above. | **Performance Objective 2.1.**<br>When asked either orally or in writing<br>(CN), students describe management's<br>concept; the seventeen managerial roles<br>performed by those who oversee human,<br>financial, and tangible/intangible resources;<br>and management subsystem as part of<br>an organization system (B). The student<br>should mention that management is the<br>process of achieving goals and objectives<br>through human, financial, and tangibles/<br>intangibles resources. They should also<br>identify at least ten managerial roles and<br>management as a subsystem (CR). |

| | |
|---|---|
| **2.2.**<br>Watch the video about Management functions: https://www.youtube.com/watch?v=aWV8w-coyhM<br>Watch the video about decision-making process: https://www.youtube.com/watch?v=XtMMX4jZs2k<br>Answer key questions and submit the answers.<br>Feedback to students.<br>Take Quiz | **Performance Objective 2.2.**<br>When asked either orally or in writing (CN), students mention the four management functions (planning, organizing, leading, and controlling). Students should also describe each function; describe the decision-making process as part of the management activity and describe the management cycle from performing the four functions sequentially (B). Students should name and describe the content of the four functions of management (planning, organizing, leading, and controlling), and define the decision-making process (CR). |
| **Part III: Systems approach applied to business and management context (Friday to Sunday)**<br>**Learning outcome:** Freshmen business students will discuss business, management, and decision making from a system perspective. | |
| **Activities:**<br>**3.1.**<br>Watch the video about systems approach: https://www.youtube.com/watch?v=2cYncmhKLUc<br>Watch instructor lecture about the application of systems approach to business and management.<br>Read the material related to business and management as a system.<br>Discuss the mini case about business and management as a system individually.<br>Discuss in-groups the answers for the case study questions and post your group comments on the Wiki created by the instructor. Comments on other groups' contribution.<br>Provide feedback to students.<br>Take Quiz | **Performance objective 3:**<br>Given a case study showing the four management functions performed by managers and decisions made to solve problems from a systems approach (CN), students (individually and in-groups) will identify and describe each management function throughout the case study. Students should identify managers' decisions; comment about the effectiveness of these decisions from a system' s approach (B). Students should work collaboratively to identify management functions and explain whether their decisions were from a system approach or not (CR). |

| **Conclusions:** Perform a post-test to understand what students learned after taking the one-week lesson about business and management. Both instructor and students will post comments by expressing their perceptions about the opportunity of learning business and management before going into business core courses. | |
|---|---|

## Formative and Summative Assessment

Assessment is an essential part of the instructional design process. It measures the success of learners and instructional design products (e.g., degree programs, projects) at different stages, and it helps ensure that the instruction created meets the needs of learners. Evaluation implies the "identification, clarification, and application of defendable criteria to determine an evaluation object's value, quality, utility, effectiveness, or significance in relation to those criteria (Worthen et al., 2004, p. 5). Consequently, a proper evaluation system provides an instructional designer with the data to determine the success level of what is evaluated (Brown & Green, 2016).

Learner evaluation has the purpose of measuring the level of success reached by learners when the instruction progresses and when it finishes. As stated above, the instructor verifies whether the learner is able to meet instructional goal and learning objectives. Once instructional designers define the instructional goals and learning outcomes, the evaluation of the learner begins to determine the change in knowledge, skill, or attitude in learners. Evaluation should have validity if the intended outcomes of instruction were met. Also, it should be reliable. An evaluation is reliable if its results are similar when conducted on multiple occasions. In all cases, learner can be evaluated before instruction begins, during instruction, and at the end of the instruction (Brown & Green, 2016).

# Evaluating the Learner

## Task A: Instructional Strategies for a Performance Objective

Instructional activities have the purpose of helping students learn. Students participate in learning activities to gain knowledge and skills to be able to apply to new contexts. There are multiple learning activities such as lectures, presentations, practices, demonstrations, questions/answers, problem-based activities, simulations and games activities, just-in-time teaching activities (Brown & Green, 2016). Others can be mentioned, such as identifying similarities and differences, summarizing and note-taking, reinforcing effort and providing recognition, nonlinguistic representations, cooperative learning, and generating and testing hypothesis (Dean et al., 2012; Marzano et al., 2001).

Gagne (1985) presented nine events of instruction in a specific order through which learners are meant to become interested, engaged, and invested in the learning topic, so that learners can learn effectively (Center of Innovative Teaching and Learning, n.d.). These events are: (1) gain the learner's attention, (2) inform learners of the objectives, (3) stimulate recall of prior learning, (4) present the stimulus, (5) provide guidance for the learners, (6) elicit learner performance, (7) provide feedback, (8) assess learner performance, and (9) enhance retention and transfer. For the Business and Management Lesson Unit, below find the instructional strategies using Gagne's events of instructions for two performance objectives (1.1. and 1.2.) as an example.

The following performance objectives belong to learning outcome 1 (see previous section Events of Instruction for the Business and Management Lesson Unit).

## Performance Objective 1.1.

From Q/A activity (CN), describe and give examples of a business as an economic and social (organization) value creation unit by mentioning the financial, tangibles/intangibles, and human resources used to generate revenues; the costs incurred during the business operations; the impact of business outcomes on individuals, local, regional, and global economy. As well as the effect on society, the business environment, its impact on business outcomes, and its role from an ethical and social responsibility standpoint (B). Students will name at least three elements that characterize a business as an economic and social value creation unit, as stated in the instructional material shared during the lesson development (CR).

## Performance Objective 1.2.

Given a business description (CN), describe the accounting, operations, marketing, and finance components/functions through which a business operates; describe how these functions relate with each other. Also, identify the organizational processes that keep linking these components, such as informational, communication, negotiation, and leadership (B). Students will identify and describe the four elements/ functions of a business and the four organizational processes stated in the instructional material (CR). See Table 1.

# Table 1

*Instructional Strategies for Performance Objective (PO) 1.1 and 1.2.*

| Event of Instruction | Objective of this activity | Instructor's performance | Student Performance | When this event can be skipped |
|---|---|---|---|---|
| **Gaining the learner's attention**: Ask a thought-provoking question. | Capture student's attention | Instructor will design a question and post it on Blackboard course within the lesson Unit (Part I): *Have you ever learned what a business is and its value creation? Ask students their take on it.* (PO 1.1/1.2) | Students will read the question and answer it. They will use the discussion board question created to write and post their contributions. | |
| **Inform students of the objectives**: Explain learning objectives of the lesson. | Help students understand what they expect from the lesson's content from learning standpoint. | Instructors will describe the learning outcomes of the learning experience by using a video presentation (Visual/audio). (PO 1.1/1.2) | Students will watch the video and get back to the instructor through an email, confirming their understanding of the lesson's purpose. | |
| **Stimulate recall of prior learning**: Perform a pre-test. | Identify freshmen business students current knowledge about business and management from Systems Thinking approach. | Instructor will create a pre-test and apply it to students. The assessment tool will be posted on Bb course. (PO 1.1/1.2) | Students will take the pre-test assessment via Bb course. | Freshmen business students are supposed to know just a little about business and management. Instructors might skip this event. However, a pre-test will help identify student perspectives of a company and management from a system perspective. It will also help emphasize this subtopic to ensure student systems approach comprehension. |
| **Present the learning content** | Present Part I lesson content to students. Inform students about business as a value creation and its components. | Instructor will ask students to do the following activities. Watch the video about business value creation (PO 1.1): https://www.youtube.com/watch?v=nyl-4LkV30g | • Students will watch the videos to learn about the topics presented in Part I. (PO 1.1/1.2). | |

133

| | | | | |
|---|---|---|---|---|
| | | Watch instructor lecture: Business and resources, business and economy, business social responsibility. **(PO 1.1)** Participate in the discussion board question about the topic above. **(PO 1.1.)** Watch the video about business functions **(PO 1.2):** https://www.youtube.com/watch?v=Ffam2HWSaTw<br>• Watch instructor lecture about business processes, communication, negotiation, and information. **(PO 1.2)**<br>• Do the exercise about business functions and submit the contribution. **(PO 1.2)** | • Students will post their comments on the discussion board question after watching the lesson material requested by the instructor. Students will elaborate on video guides created by the instructor. **(PO 1.1).**<br>• Students will do an exercise about business functions as requested. Students will submit their contributions through a Safe Assign link on Bb course **(PO 1.2).** | |
| **Provide guidance for learning** | Make students' learning experience simple by providing clear guidance for confusion-free learning activities performance | Instructor will prepare **(PO 1.1/1.2):**<br>• Instructions for watching the videos (video guides).<br>• Instructions for students to elaborate their thoughts from watching and analyze the video content.<br>• Create the discussion board question tab on Bb course.<br>• Ask students to read peers' contributions.<br>• Create instructions to participate seamlessly in the discussion activity.<br>• Elaborate an exercise about business functions.<br>• Set the exercise content on Bb course.<br>• Prepare instructions for submitting the exercise. | Students will **(PO 1.1/1.2):**<br>• Read the instructions to watch the videos (video guides).<br>• Read the instructions and follow them through to elaborate on the video content.<br>• Post their responses (contributions) in the discussion board question as instructed.<br>• Read peer's contributions and learn from their thoughts.<br>• Do the exercise about business functions.<br>• Submit their assignment by the deadline as requested. | |

| Elicit performance | Allow giving time to students to study and practice | Instructor will set the deadlines for every activity (watching videos, preparing discussion board contribution, and submitting the exercise. This lesson's Part I will be performed during the first two days of the week (the lesson is a one-week lesson). | Students will perform the requested activities, participate, and submit their contributions by the deadline set by the instructor. | |
| --- | --- | --- | --- | --- |
| Provide timely feedback | Let students know how they are doing correctly and what to improve upon | Instructor will provide students immediate feedback for Part I based on the contributions made through the discussion board question (rubrics), written assignment (rubrics), and Quiz Part I. | Students will receive feedback from the instructor related to their contributions made through the discussion board question, written assignment, and Quiz Part I. | |
| Assess performance | Test student's understanding and progress. | Instructor will design a quiz within the Bb course that covers Part I. Design includes instructions to take the quiz, type of questions, allotted time, and submission instructions. | Students will take the Quiz Part I as instructed. | |
| Enhance retention | Apply the knowledge to real-world situations | Instructor will use videos and real-world cases (assignment exercise) to deliver the content. These are interactive learning activities to enhance retention. | Students will interact with videos and real-world situations (assignment exercise) to learn and practice themselves. | Instructor might skip this event. However, it will be kept. Since it is one-week lesson delivered in three parts, students must retain all concepts and their interaction to visualize business and management as part of a system. It will be achieved through the videos, real-world case to stimulate cognition and memory, ask students about an example or talk to someone who is an expert in between sessions, coming prepared to discuss that next time. |

**Task B: Assessments of Learning for Instructional Activities**

Learner evaluation has the purpose of determining the level of success of a learner and an instruction. The evaluation outcomes provide instructors with appropriate data to determine the level of performance acquired by learners or the instruction's level of success (Brown & Green, 2016).

Learners can be evaluated before the instruction begins, during the instructions, and when the instruction finishes. The business and management lesson unit is a one-week lesson within the eight-week SLS course freshmen students take. Thus, it will not require a summative assessment. This lesson plans to implement two types of formative evaluations, a pre-post test and quizzes. The pre-post test identifies what the business student knows about the systems approach (pre) and how he/she will know about this subject after taking the lesson (post). Also, three quizzes are corresponding with each part, which students will take during the lesson length.

The pre-post test is based on the 20-item Systems Thinking Scale (STS) developed by Frances Payne Bolton School of Nursing (n.d.) adapted to business and management context. The content of the scale (items) will be included in the instruction to provide students with the system's thinking when studying business and management. See Table 2.

**Table 2.**

*Systems Think Statements*

| Instructions:<br>Please read each statements and place an "x" in the answer box, referring to the systems thinking approach. | Answer box |
|---|---|
| 1 | I seek everyone's view of the situation within the company. | |
| 2 | I look beyond a specific event in my company to determine the cause of the problem. | |
| 3 | I think understanding how the chain of events occur in my company is crucial. | |
| 4 | I include people in my work unit to find a solution. | |

| 5 | I think recurring patterns are more important than any one specific event. | |
| 6 | I think of the problem at hand as a series of connected issues within the company. | |
| 7 | I consider the cause and effect that is occurring in a situation within the company. | |
| 8 | I consider the relationships among coworkers in the work unit. | |
| 9 | I think that systems are constantly changing. | |
| 10 | I propose solutions that affect the work environment, not specific individuals. | |
| 11 | I keep in mind that proposed changes can affect the whole system. | |
| 12 | I think more than one or two people are needed to have success. | |
| 13 | I keep the mission and purpose of the organization in mind. | |
| 14 | I think small changes can produce important results. | |
| 15 | I consider how multiple changes affect each other. | |
| 16 | I think about how different employees might be affected by the improvement. | |
| 17 | I try strategies that do not rely on people's memory. | |
| 18 | I recognize system problems are influenced by past events. | |
| 19 | I consider the past history and culture of the work unit. | |
| 20 | I consider that the same action can have different effects over time, depending on the state of the system. | |

As mentioned above, there are three quizzes during the lesson length that will measure how students learn from each part. This paper only shows the quiz covering Part I as example. See Table 3.

## Table 3.

*Part I Quiz example*

| 1. | Free enterprise is a system of business in which individuals decide what to produce and how to produce it. | T F |
| 2. | Business is the organized effort of individuals to produce and sell, for a profit, the products and services that satisfy society's needs. | T F |
| 3. | The ability to produce a specific product more efficiently than any other nation is called comparative advantage. | T F |

## Evaluating the Instructional Design

The objective of this section is to define a system for evaluating the quality and effectiveness of the instructional design before, during, and after the design for the Business and Management Lesson Unit. Thus, the content shows a pre-assessment tool to assess the design of the lesson unit itself and will follow with the formative assessment instruments to evaluate the lesson unit during the implementation. Finally, it also informs on how the lesson unit in question will be evaluated after implementation. In other words, the summative assessment is conducted to measure the lesson unit efficiency and effectiveness.

## Pre-assessment of the Design Itself

Pre-assessment is well-known as an instructors' tool about what students know regarding the subject to learn and what they can do before instruction. It also identifies learners' interests and learning styles (Seth Warner, 2005). However, the notion of pre-assessment may be extended to instructional design as a product or project. Each instructional project is different and unique, and instructional designers should verify whether the instruction is well-conceived to start implementation. Thus, it is necessary to look at the design and its elements as an instructional product.

Pre-assessment of an instruction design (product) will help measure accurate instruction content, offer instructional designers what will be expected of the design content, and give future lesson designs (Seth Warner, 2005). For this particular instructional project evaluation, the pre-assessment will perform when this instruction design (Business and Management Lesson Unit) is finished to evaluate whether the instruction holds its components.

Pre-assessment of the Business and Management Lesson Unit will evaluate critical components such as clear learning objectives, intuitive eLearning navigation, relevant multimedia, and feedback system (Pappas, 2016). It should also consider accessibility (lesson content supported by several abilities and senses), aesthetic-usability effect (how learners perceive aesthetic design as easy to use), chunking (a combination of multiple units into logical chunks), consistency (standard in design, presentation, language, and experience within the lesson unit). Moreover, pre-assessment will verify hierarchy (the order of the components on the screen are presented within the lesson), legibility (easy reading of the text on the screen, font size, color, contrast), and readability (how the learner can understand the content) (Ferriman, 2020). This lesson unit will consider peers and various content and technology experts to perform the pre-assessment process.

Based on instructional design practice theory (Seth Warner, 2005), the results obtained from comparing pre-assessment and summative assessment show how effective an instructional design is. Therefore, in addition to evaluating the critical components of an instructional design mentioned in the previous paragraph, the pre-assessment will also incorporate the four training evaluation levels: learner's reaction, learning, behavior, results (Kirkpatrick, 1994), and return on investment (ROI) as an additional level of Kirkpatrick's model (Phillips, 1991).

ROI has transformed somewhat into a fifth level and is becoming more commonly used, particularly by institutions and businesses. There are many ways to express the levels, but here is one:

Level 1 – did participants enjoy or like the training?

Level 2 – to what degree did participants actually learn from the training?

Level 3 – did participants take the training back into the workplace?

Level 4 – did participants continue to demonstrate the learning over time?

Level 5 – to what degree did the training make a difference in ROI?

The fifth level is used to estimate the potential profit from conducting a training program (lesson unit in this case). Even though the ROI is measured in monetary terms of projected profit and costs, this study considers that in educational settings, the benefits or impact of a lesson unit can be measured using intangible indicators related to learners within a learning context. The expenses for teaching a lesson unit will produce learners' attitudes and behaviors in other ways (Diem, n.d.). For example, learners taking this lesson will be able to rationalize and transfer their knowledge to new business subject contents afterwards in their junior and senior years, resulting in skilled and prepared business students ready to make better decision-making processes with a systems approach. Thus, the time and effort spent by both instructors and business students will cost-effectively accomplished that end (Kirkpatrick & Kirkpatrick, 2016). Therefore, it is relevant to find the appropriate instructional material and compare the expenditure to the lesson unit's learning outcomes in terms of instructional achievement to identify the added value.

The fifth training evaluation levels will also be part of the summative assessment tool to evaluate the effectiveness of the Business and Management Lesson Unit (instruction product). In brief, the Kirkpatrick model will be used for the pre-assessment (as a pretest). Also, after follow-up assessment, as a summative assessment tool (posttest) to contrast and gather conclusions about the instruction effectiveness. See Table 1.

**Table 1.**

*Pre-assessment evaluation tool check list*

| | Instructional Design Critical Components | Yes | No |
|---|---|---|---|
| 1. | Is the content presented in a way that does not require the learners to rely solely on one ability or sense? (accessibility) | | |
| 2. | Can the learner perceive more aesthetic designs as easier to use an understand than those that do not take aesthetics into account? | | |
| 3. | Is the content combined in multiple logical chunks? (chinking) | | |
| 4. | Is there a standard in design, language, presentation, and overall learner experience? (Consistency) | | |
| 5. | Are the components on the screen presented and viewed by the learner? (Hierarchy) | | |
| 6. | Is the text easy to read on the screen (Legibility) | | |
| 7. | How well the learner can understand the content (Readability) | | |
| 8. | Would it be the content of the lesson useful, likeable, interesting for learners? (Reaction) | | |
| 9. | Would learners learn with the content of the lesson? (Learning) | | |
| 10. | Can learners apply what they learn from the lesson content to exercises, case studies? (Behavior) | | |
| 11. | Can this lesson contribute to business and management understanding from a system thinking approach? (Results) | | |
| 12. | Can this lesson make a difference in an intangible/learning profit? (ROI) | | |
| 13. | Have this lesson defined how to measure reaction, learning, behavior, and results? | | |

## Formative Assessment During Implementation

Instructional designers use formative assessment throughout the design process to gather data to provide feedback about the process development. The data obtained by designers (feedback) allows improvements to the instruction before it is totally designed. The data can be shared with co-workers teaching a similar subject to indicate how the process is going (Brwon & Green, 2016).

This Business and Management Lesson Unit will use the Gooler (1980) model for formative assessment. This model focuses on practical procedures that might enhance the likelihood of effective formative evaluation implemented as part of an instructional development effort. It follows eight steps: (1) purpose, (2) audience, (3) issues, (4) resources, (5) evidence, (6) data gathering techniques, (7) analysis, and (8) reporting. The purpose of the evaluation is to identify the instruction's purpose, whether related to the materials, time, or satisfy administrative requirements. The audience is defined by defining the target recipients of the evaluation results. The definition of the questions/objectives of the evaluation reveals the issues. The resources relate to the declaration of what is needed in terms of tangible or intangibles required to evaluate.

Moreover, evidence will show the data or information required to answer the evaluation questions. Data-gathering techniques define the methods needed to collect the evidence necessary to analyze it after. Finally, reporting specifies to whom and when the results of the evaluation will be reported.

## Summative Assessment After Implementation

As a complement to formative evaluation, instructional designers also perform the summative assessment. Summative evaluation is conducted after the lesson unit has been implemented, and the data obtained from this evaluation allows measuring the level of effectiveness of the instruction. As mentioned in the pre-assessment section above, the Business and Management Lesson Unit will conduct summative assessments when students take lower and upper-level courses. The purpose of this is to verify how they perceive and apply in their decision-making processes business and management concepts from a systems perspective. The summative assessment will follow the Kirkpatrick model as a posttest.

This Lesson Unit proposes conducting a longitudinal evaluation of freshmen students (for the first cohort) throughout their transition to senior business students as an after-follow-up assessment to measure their progress. Successive freshmen business students will be only assessed (posttest) when they finish their senior year to graduate. Since the business program director controls all first-year business students by name and identification number, he will follow up on these students and interview them to gather the data for analysis, conclusions, and suggestions to the lesson content for improvement purposes. The degree of learning will also be able to be determined, as well as whether any of the course content has been retained, applied, or transferred. See Table 2.

**Table 2.**

*Summative Assessment Tool Check List*

| 14. Instructional Design Critical Components | Yes | No |
| --- | --- | --- |
| 1. Was the content of the lesson useful, likeable, interesting for learners? (Reaction) | | |
| 2. Did learners learn with the content of the lesson? (Learning) | | |
| 3. Did learners apply what they learn from the lesson content to exercises, case studies? (Behavior) | | |
| 4. Did this lesson contribute to business and management understanding from a system thinking approach? (Results) | | |
| 5. Did this lesson measure reaction, learning, behavior, and results? | | |

## Conclusions

Based on the actual performance shown in business students and characterized by difficulties in integrating business and management components as part of the business systems, the academic unit suggested the inclusion of a lesson unit into the SLS course to help business students understand the nature of business before gaining in-depth specific knowledge through each business course. Consequently, it impacts students' skills in decision-making to solve real-world business problems easier.

Both needs analysis and learner analysis are an essential component in the instructional design process. Both analyses aim to provide valuable information for the design process because they identify learning gaps and learners' perceptions and attitudes toward learning. Once instructional designers know the outcomes of performing needs analysis and learner analysis, they are equipped to design the instruction to satisfy learners' knowledge and skills shortage.

The task analysis process is essential for designing instruction. It is performed after defining the instructional goal derived from needs analysis and learner analysis. Task analysis provides enough information to plan high-quality learning if instructional designers use different techniques to elaborate learning content to cover the performance gap.

This paper aimed to visualize the business and management lesson plan's organization, which is structured by three elements: condition, behavior, and criteria. These three elements allow understanding the content and measuring the performance objectives, specifically through the criteria element. Moreover, the content of the instruction helps achieve performance objectives. Finally, a lesson is more effective if it has an introduction, body, conclusion, and assessment.

This paper also offered details about the Events of instruction for two performance objectives to achieve within the Business and Management lesson unit. Also, it shows two evaluation tools as part of the formative assessment component of the unit. It aimed to visualize the system designed to evaluate the Business and Management Lesson Unit. The evaluation system is defined by pre-assessment, formative evaluation (while teaching the lesson), and summative assessment after being delivered.

# Performance Intervention Design

The acquisition of learning and knowledge by adult learners is mainly associated with the experience of the learner. Teachers and instructors as adultu learners with vast experience in teaching and technology use should be open and willing to embrace technology-based innovations for teaching and learning (Knowles, 1970). Thus, teachers and instructors as an adult cannot learn in the absence of experience (Carpenter-Aeby & Aeby, 2013). Their knowledge is dynamically constructed through an interactive process of interpretation, integration, and transformation of experiential reality (Pratt, 1993).

The theoretical foundation of andragogy interlaces with Maslow's needs of self-actualization. When a teacher is motivated to teach, it triggers positive attitudes toward learning. Self-actualization, as a need, focuses on human beings' emotions, and affects motivation, choices, and responsibility (Carpenter-Aeby & Aeby, 2013). Those learners who show low motivation levels might display frustration and resistance at being challenged to integrate technology in their teaching.

When designing training for adult learners, it would be pertinent to consider the three simultaneous processes in adult learners. Carpenter-Aeby and Aeby (2013) suggest that these three processes are (a) the acquisition of new information, (b) the manipulation of knowledge to make it fit new tasks, and (c) the evaluation of the way information is manipulated to the task. Carpenter-Aeby and Aeby (2013) described the process as aligned with the new competency-based model of education. This model emphasizes the means of delivering knowledge to learners (Edward et al., 2018), supported by interaction, experience in computer use, and motivation (Picciano & Seaman, 2010).

Educators understand that learners' characteristics will impact how fast and how well overall learning occurs (Ahn Farzan & Brusilovsky, 2006). Each learner has different features, and they can learn in various educational settings. In any case, knowledge content could be adapted to individual characteristics through the e-learning system to be perceived more as usable than non-adaptive e-learning system. If learners understood e-learning as highly usable, it would determine higher satisfaction, engagement, and motivation levels (Alshammari et al., 2015). Moreover, other learners' characteristics that yield higher levels of the mentioned outcomes are the goals of the learner, experience and learning style (Henze & Nejdl, 1999; Surjono & Maltby, 2003), and background and preferences (Papadimitriou & Gyftodimos, 201

Nakic et al. (2015) showed that the adaption to learning systems is successful when learning styles, cognitive styles, background knowledge, preferences (for specific learning materials), and motivation as characteristics of learners can be adapted. Learners with different expertise and motivation should be treated differently. Learners with more favorable aspects such as higher prior knowledge, more complex epistemological beliefs, more positive attitudes toward mathematics, and better cognitive strategy use, are more eager to display a more adaptive example utilization behavior, report less cognitive load, and can solve more problems correctly than those learners with less favorable characteristics (Flores et al., 2012). Moreover, learners with different prior knowledge benefit differently in technology-based systems (Chen, 2008).

Different factors impact learner's performance. These factors are economic, social, cultural, political, curricular, and psychological (Rhode, 2014). Psychological factors such as anxiety, worry, nervousness, motivational, and reactions to visual stimuli of technology application affect learner's knowledge comprehension. For instance, when an individual has an emotional response to the visual positively, there will be visceral reactions that produce predictable results. It is recommendable that the training content uses design elements that could represent any of the human mind triggers to connect with the learner (Johnson, 2019).

Another psychological factor is a cost-effective analysis. Behaviors are regulated by the perceived difficulty of a task concerning the reward to be granted (Croxson et al., 2010) through energy expenditure efforts given by mental activity. The mental activity requires frequent decisions, memorizing, analyzing, and learning until the cost of proceeding is greater than the benefits of completing the task. Political factors as funding might affect the success of the training. Cultural factors include knowledge, beliefs, customs, art, morals, law, other capabilities, and habits of a person as a member of a group. However, motivational factors are paramount. The motivation level of learners contributes to positive achievement. The training design must trigger high-performance levels in learners, recognition, advancement (Herzberg et al., 1959), and the sense of competence they are developing as professionals (Vallerand & Losier, 2001) to increase positive attitude and behaviors toward learning.

### Concord High School Case Study

This case study posits that teachers at Concord High School are not adequately using the district's LMS. A Learning Management System (LMS) is an online software used to administer (plan execute, documenting, tracking, recording, enhancing, and assessing) a specific learning process over the internet. Organizations use it for training and learning purposes (Sharma, 2015). Based on the school's need performance outcomes, it reveals that there are teachers who are not using the LMS to the capacity that the district desires. Leaders say that teachers are not using it because teachers do not take the time to do so. Also, teachers are leaving the school and district because they do not want to engage with the system. With a foundation of computer skills, these teachers might have more confidence in integrating technology in the classroom. These teachers can help others (less skilled) motivate to change perceptions from novice teachers (Ramorola, 2013).

On the other hand, there are teachers considered novices that have a minimum or no familiarity with the LMS. Some of them are not growing and still struggle with some of the basic elements such as uploading documents to it. The perception from teachers might be given by a lack of motivation to use the LMS. More teachers are frustrated, and there is an undertone of dissatisfaction among faculty concerning the LMS. Teachers feel frustrated to implement technology because they are unsure of how to use it, and they have a curriculum to teach (Niekerk & Blignaut, 2014), which holds them back from dedicating time to learn and use LMS. The perception of negative attitudes from both more experienced and less experienced teachers in technology use (toward using the LMS) is impacting negatively technology-based learning and resources allocated to the institution for that purpose.

Despite the pessimistic feelings that teachers have about adopting the LMS, many feel comfortable with technology in general. 60–70% of the teachers are willing to use the LMS if it is needed, even though there is a portion of them who are struggling with basic features of the LMS. Thus, it seems that there is a high percentage of technology acceptance, which opens a window of hope to improve technology use by teachers.

This paper aims to design a performance improvement plan for increasing the use of the LMS by the Concord High School for teaching and student learning support. Based on the performance analysis outcomes conducted by school leaders, which yielded some opportunities for improvement since the LMS provided by the district was not being used effectively, there is an imminent urge for training teachers to help increase LMS usability. The next sections cover the following content: instructional design models, performance improvement goal statement, behavioral or performance objectives, the role of different stakeholders to support the plan, and materials to support the implementation of the program.

## Instructional Design Models

Instructional design models (IDM) provide frameworks to organize the process of creating all the activities related to instruction (Instructional Design, n.d.). Instructional design models are learner-and-performance centered goals and outcomes to facilitate reliable measurement and evaluation activities. They focus on real-world performance through behaviors that will be expected of them in the real world (Kurt, 2018). There are different IDMs, for instance, the Addie model and the ARCS model.

### ADDIE Model

This model stands for analysis, design, development, implementation, and evaluation to build practical training and performance. This model is easy to apply, flexible, and systematic, and it allows turning back to previous phases (Durak & Ataizi, 2016; Vejvodova, 2009). The *analysis* phase includes needs analysis, analysis of learners, content analysis, technical analysis, structural analysis, and analysis of the learning environment. The stage of *design* responds to the questions of how to carry out the objectives and strategies identified from the analysis phase. The *development* phase is the one that prepares the elements determined in the design phase, including the platform (LMS) to be used. In the *application* phase, learners start using the prepared design. Finally, the *evaluation* phase defines the training criteria, including all course work assigned to learners (Durak & Ataizi, 2016).

### ARCS Model

The conceptual foundation of this model rests on human motivation. Motivation moves toward a goal or acquires a new behavior by rewarding positive behaviors related to the desired one. Motivation refers to those things that describe the direction, magnitude, and persistence of responses (Keller, 1983). This model stands for attention, relevance, confidence, and satisfaction. The *attention* incorporates curiosity and arousal, interest, and other related areas like sensation seeking. *Relevance* refers to learners› perceptions; that is, that the instructional requirements be consistent with goals and outcomes, their learning styles, and past experiences. *Confidence* stands for the effects of positive expectancies and attributions for success. Finally, *satisfaction* includes a mix of intrinsically and extrinsically rewarding outcomes, sustaining desirable learning behaviors (Keller, 2016).

## Performance Improvement Plan Goal Statement

Increase the LMS usage provided by the LCPS to Concord High School (CHS) for the student work completion by training both novices and experts or advanced expert teachers in LMS use from June 2 to December 15, 2020. The learners are teachers who are not using the LMS to the capacity that the district desires. Also, teachers are leaving the school and district because they do not want to engage with the system. Moreover, there are teachers considered novices that have a minimum or none familiarity with the LMS. Some of them are not growing and still struggle with some of the basic elements such as uploading documents to it. Teachers will leverage the LMS provided by the district and use the current equipment installed in CHS. Other free resources are available for teachers to learn and practice LMS for course content administration and delivery purposes.

### Entry Skills

The skills depend on knowledge of the basic concepts of an LMS that teachers must already know or be able to acquire before they begin the instruction. Learners must already master them to learn the new skills included in the instruction (Dick et al., 2015). Since almost all the teachers already know the LMS as a tool, teachers should have some intellectual skills related to the LMS. Learners should already understand the concept of an LMS, features (LMS instructor, course content, offline content, announcements, collaborate, discussions, grading, tests, and assignments, push notifications, grading center, evaluation center, and course design –layout). They should also know about the LMS impact on facilitating students to learn in an organized manner from diverse technological resources, the advantages it offers for tracking course performance and progress, and engaging students.

## Subordinate Skills

Gagne (1985) suggests that subordinate skills can be identified by asking the following question: What must the learner already know how to do, the absence of which would make it impossible to learn this subordinate skill? As mentioned in the introduction section, when it refers to the characteristics of learners at Concord High School -based on the performance analysis, the training or performance improvement plan should emphasize the following subordinate skills that teachers must have in order to use the LMS effectively. Teachers must know how to set up the LMS features, such as those mentioned in the entry skills section. In other words, teachers must know how to set up an assignment, choose the assignment to design, and upload different types of documents, including PowerPoint presentations. Further, how to attach web-related links, set up tests, select the type of test to be used, set up and download the grade book for reporting and analysis purposes. Moreover, he/she should master how to use the retention center, send notifications to students when delaying work submissions, post announcements, create hyperlinks, design effective communications, and post them to engage students, as well as, how to design and perform class discussions and create virtual sessions for discussions and oral presentation purposes.

## Performance Objectives

Performance objectives, also called behavioral objectives (Mager, 1987), learning objectives, or instructional objectives (Dick et al., 2015) emphasize on describing what the learner will be able to do when he/she completes a unit of instruction. They derive from the skills identified in the instructional analysis. Performance objectives should consider three elements: conditions (CN), behavior (B), and criteria (CR) to be able to guide the learner to do an action towards developing skills (Dick et al., 2015).

**Performance objectives for LMS usability**

*Objective 1:*

At the end of the LMS training (December 15, 2020) (CN), teachers will be able to list all the benefits of the LMS and describe the LMS features that support an online course component (B) to visualize all the LMS spectrum (CR).

*Objective 2:*

By the end of the LMS training (December 15, 2020) (CN), teachers will be able to set up their courses in the LMS (B) to support student work completion (CR).

*Objective 3:*

During the LMS training, teachers will be able to measure their level of motivation and satisfaction with the knowledge and skills acquired for each section of the LMS.

## Stakeholders Role in Developing and Implementing the Plan

Stakeholders will be able to provide ideas and help create potential solutions when facing a critical situation in the educational setting. Stakeholders should be involved in the training process to increase the overall chance of training success through final execution. Instructional designers (IDs) should work in their instructional design project very close with stakeholders by informing them of the training updates and any information regarding the progress of the performance implementation plan. Stakeholders can contribute to positive communication when they are engaged, and it allows preventing unforeseen problems with the implementation process (Leonard, 2012).

The performance analysis conducted in Concord High School revealed that the school leadership is sensitive to the lack of usage of LMS provided by the district. They recognize that the school district has equipped Concord High School with computer labs or laptop carts to provide the means for integration. However, they are aware that equipment support does not necessarily indicate that technology is being integrated into learning (Ramorola, 2013). It seems that school administrators have not taken sufficient actions to propitiate enough conditions to take teachers into a higher level of involvement with the LMS usage. The fact that teachers are experiencing dissatisfaction with technology usage indicates that school leadership support is not enough. Teachers have not been involved in the process of technology integration. They have not been provided by structured procedures to guide them on the path to implementation (Ramorola, 2013). Then, the role of the ID is critical in articulating a practical LMS training involving school administrators to provide teachers with resources (time, flexible schedule to combine with training sessions, training program schedule throughout the academic year to help assimilate the change).

## Technology use in the design and development of the training

Technology has proved to be a critical support to deliver innovative, engaging, and practical training opportunities. Technology for learning offers ease of use, dissemination of information, learning retention, and the ability to reinforce student learning, and it can positively impact teaching productivity. Since learning supported by technology allows teachers to complete training materials anytime and anywhere, this training will use LMS already installed in Concord High School for professional development.

The most potent influence on using instructional technologies is not the technology itself, but the content of what is delivered with that technology, with the support of information obtained from using the technology (Beach, 2016). Through the LMS, teachers will acquire knowledge from the LMS features and external support materials such as videos, research-and-industry-based reports, learning tools, and the skills and subskills needed to enrich their teaching and impact student learning. The LMS will provide teachers self-paced, directed learning from home, or work further on the scheduled on-campus training sessions. It will motivate teachers because they can work at their own pace and learn from discovering technology use by themselves.

# Training Evaluation Plan

Evaluation of training programs plays an essential role in verifying whether the needs for improvement are covered from what was identified through the needs assessment and analysis stages. Training program evaluation focuses on three elements. These elements are project time, costs, and desired outcomes. By balancing these three aspects, the evaluation plan will help evaluators monitor the personnel and tasks previously designed and negotiate schedule changes given by internal or external circumstances that might affect the evaluation process accomplishment.

The training evaluation results inform enhancements to shape existing and future training programs, and it allows defining best practices and opportunities for optimizing scarce resources to determine the return on training investments (Marshall & Rossett, 2011). The evaluation will also allow tracking the evaluation costs and budget adjustments and keeps stakeholders informed of the evaluation progress and underlying problems (Preskill & Russ-Eft, 2016).

There are some challenges that evaluation processes must prevent and overcome to carry out the evaluation plans. For instance, the evaluation cannot be completed on time, overruns costs, and members of the evaluation teams leaving the evaluation process. Also, restructure changes of the organization for which the training program is under evaluation, and political pressures that might skew the evaluation outcomes to refrain from overcoming potential problems (Preskill & Russ-Eft, 2016). Other barriers to the evaluation process and results are related to inadequate data capture tools, lack of transparent methodology, and lack of management support in prioritizing the causes of the barriers or offering actionable suggestions (Berk, 2011).

This objective of this paper is to provide a Training Evaluation Plan to evaluate the impact of the training program designed to increase the use of the Learning Management System (LMS) by teachers at Concord High School (CHS) to support student learning. The upcoming sections of this paper refer to the following topics: a summary of the problem identified at CHS related to the LMS usability by teachers, with the proposed implementation plan for improvements. Also, a proposed plan to evaluate the training program based on the four levels of training evaluation offered by Kirkpatrick and Kirkpatrick (2016) New World Kirkpatrick Model (NWKM) -which allows evaluating the program context, the purpose and impact of the evaluation, and the needs of stakeholders (Moreau, 2017).

This paper will also include a discussion about the expected return of investment by the institution in which the training program will be conducted. Further, the document contains two more sections relating to a training program with stakeholder involvement and impact on supporting training success. This work includes a summary of how the evaluation plan satisfies political, social, cultural, psychological, and technological factors that helped cause the issue of technology use at CHS.

## Technology Use Issues at Concord High School

Because the LMS and other resources provided by the district were not used appropriately to maximize learning efficacy, the CHS administration decided to train all teachers to help them use the LMS for teaching and learning enhancement. The issue of lack of LMS usability by teachers at CHS is compressed as follows. The district provided schools under its domain with the LMS and additional resources for teacher usability and student course completion and learning. Teachers at CHS do not use as expected by the district the support provided for that purpose. The current situation about using technology at CHS shows that some teachers use the LMS system, unfortunately, at flow capacity. However, other teachers lack familiarity with the LMS and its future implementation for student learning effectiveness.

A performance improvement plan to improve the LMS usage by teachers at CHS was designed for student work completion. It contemplated both types of teachers, novices (less skilled) and expert teachers from June 2 to December 15, 2020. There are two main performance objectives defined for the training program, which hold both entry and subordinate skills, and it was based on the ADDIE and ARCS models of instructional design. These objectives are related to teachers' ability to list all the benefits of the LMS for teaching and learning purposes and describe the LMS features to design and support the online components of their courses.

The second performance objective is related to teacher actual ableness to set up their course content in the LMS to support student work completion and motivation for learning. The performance implementation plan also included the role of stakeholders in developing and implementing the program and how the technology will be used to support the training to achieve its performance goals and performance objectives.

## Training Program Evaluation NWKP Reaction (Level 1)

Level 1 Reaction intends to measure the reactions from learners to the training content relevance, methods used throughout the training, instructor/trainers, learning qualifications, and assessment methods (Kirkpatrick, 1996). The perception captured from learners about the training content allows describing the standpoints of learners about the content of the training and the efficiency and effectiveness of the training delivery method. Moreover, judgments help determine some gaps in learning needs, training strengths and weaknesses, and barriers to learning. Some of the core items used to measure learners' reactions are as follows (Kirkpatrick & Kirkpatrick, 2016; Moreau, 2017; PERLC, n.d.).

## Core Training Reaction Evaluation Items

- Overall satisfaction with the course
- The extent to which the training program enhanced the knowledge of the subject matter (technology use/LMS usability)
- The extent to which the course was relevant compared to expectations from learners of what they might be expected to do to apply technology to support student learning.
- The extent to which each objective of the course used productive learning activities, supplemental material, motivational tools to participate and learn from the events, the quality of the content presentation, learner participation, assessment, and feedback provided to them after finishing practice sessions). This item intends to find information to evaluate performance objectives defined in the performance implementation plan.
- The extent to which the content of the training was relevant to participants' daily jobs.
- The extent to which the training content keeps learner captive which makes them be involved with the content and practice throughout the course duration (engagement).
- The extent to which the training course contributes to the learning experience.

## The extent to which learners are willing to recommend the training program to others.

Defined in the performance implementation plan, as the training program progresses, the outcomes of the objectives will offer data about the course learning outcomes achievement, and relevance. This will allow getting up to date information about the training program's significance, and correct deviations proactively. Thus, the permanent data generated from the feedback will be useful for the final evaluation of the training program (written comments, post-training questionnaires). The post-fact relevance evaluation level will be performed by a team conformed by the trainer/instructor, school administrator, and district representative from January 12 to February 13, 2021. A sample of both novices (less skilled) and expert learners will provide with perceptions and attitudes toward a long-term successful technology use by teachers at CHS.

## Training Program Evaluation NWKP Learning (Level 2)

Learning Level 2 measures how much learners improve their knowledge and skills by taking the training program. This level allows for determining the quality and relevance of the training content and the appropriateness of the assessment tools used as part of the program to evaluate learner's learning progress. The evaluation process participants are expected to use the following items to assess learning for the training program. They should determine how best to measure the two performance objectives defined in the performance implementation plan. Evaluators will focus on assessment tools items, training format, and training modes of delivery to tailor assessments to most effectively and efficiently measure learning across knowledge, skills, and attitudes domain levels.

### Core Learning Evaluation items

- The extent to which each objective of the course used productive learning activities, supplemental material, motivational tools to participate and learn from the activities, the quality of the content presentation, learner participation, assessment, and feedback provided to them after finishing practice sessions). This item intends to find information to evaluate performance objectives defined in the performance implementation plan.

- The extent to which learners believe that the training content and experience will be worthwhile to do on the job (attitude).
- The extent to which learners think that they can apply all the knowledge learned throughout the training program on the teaching journey (confidence).
- The extent to which learners are willing to apply the knowledge and skills gained throughout the course on the daily job (commitment).
- Assessment tools such as quizzes, performance-based activities such as oral presentations, exercises, case studies, case scenarios, and practice outcomes (course set on the LMS) are broken down by novices and expert learners.

The post-fact learning evaluation level will be performed by a team conformed by the trainer/instructor, school administrator, and district representative from January 12 to February 13, 2021. A sample of both novices (less skilled) and expert learners will provide perceptions and attitudes toward a long-term successful technology use through interviews and on-the-job observations as a triangulation method.

## Training Program Evaluation NWKP Behavior (Level 3)

Evaluating behaviors (level three) verifies whether learners apply their knowledge and skills obtained from the training program to their daily job (teaching). It intends to evaluate how learners transfer knowledge and skills to design and use the course online component through an LMS. It allows strengthening the chain of evidence between learning and changes to the performance of the learner (teacher) and identifying factors that limit the effectiveness of the training. The results of evaluating level three are complemented by the findings from level one and two evaluation results. Evaluators should consider the following when preparing an evaluation strategy (PERLC, n.d.).

## Core Behavior Evaluation items

- The extent to which the duration of the training allows producing changes of behavior in learners given by actual LMS usability.
- Because in this Training program, learners will participate in multiple sessions over time where the same performance objectives (lessons and practice sessions) are repeatedly targeted to lead to behavior change. Then, it is possible to evaluate the extent to which each of the learning gained in each lesson is materialized via practice sessions.
- The extent to which the training content matches the practice session content.
- The extent to which each teacher is followed to the field setting (LMS installed in the institution).
- The extent to which learners are followed up from the training sessions to the practice sessions.
- The extent to which the learner behaviors are measured by using specific and reliable measures or competencies.

Behavior evaluation level will be performed by a team composed of the trainer/instructor, school administrator, and district representative from January 12 to February 13, 2021. The evaluation team will look at course material, practice session plan, learners' perceptions and attitudes to verify whether the behavior has been transferred effectively.

## Training Program Evaluation NWKP Results (Level 4)

The level four results aim to identify the degree by which training outcomes and change in teacher performance are given by the application of the knowledge and skills developed as a result of the training program. The changes experienced by teachers after taking the training should yield measurable results that directly contribute to the school administration and the district (USOPM, 2011). Evaluators should design evaluation tools to assess the effectiveness and impact of the training program process and effect (PERLC, n.d.).

## Core Results Evaluation items

### *Training Program Process*

- What aspects of the training program development were effective, and which need improvements?
- What impact did the training program's learning activities have on the teacher's knowledge and skills in using LMS at CHS?

### *Training Program Impact*

- The extent to which the training program services were successful in helping achieve the training performance goal and objectives.
- The extent to which the training content is considered by the learners beneficial to CHS.
- The extent to which the following capabilities contributed to the most in CHS (teacher preparedness to using LMS, school organization in supporting training development, trainer/instructor skills to encourage teachers to learn, practice sessions organization, and district involvement to support the training program).
- The extent to which specific training learning and practice activities are considered highly auspicious.
- The extent to which the training program added value to teachers and their skills gained for long-term usability.
- The extent to which CHS benefits if this level of training support is sustained.

Results evaluation level will be performed by a team composed of the trainer/instructor, school administrator, and a district representative from January 12 to February 13, 2021. The evaluation team will look at overall training performance satisfaction from the teacher, school, and district levels.

## Training Program Return on Investment and Return on Expectations

Return on Investment (ROI) is a performance measure to evaluate the efficiency of an investment made at any level. It tries to measure the amount of return of an investment relative to the costs incurred in the investment (Chen & Mansa, 2020). Because any training programs imply resource allocation and expenditures, administrators are called to offer results based on the value-added by the training program and the costs incurred in delivering it. It is in terms of money invested. However, in an educational setting, there are other added value measures to consider when evaluating the impact of a student educational program or teacher training program. The outcomes of education are measured by using intangible indicators related to individuals within a social context. The money invested in teacher training programs will produce teacher attitudes, behavior, and benefit society in other ways (Diem, n.d.). For instance, a trained teacher will be able to transfer their knowledge to students resulting in a better educated and prepared individually for the job market and the society.

Educational training program results should come up with solutions, and the better the time and effort spent will cost-effectively accomplish that end (Kirkpatrick & Kirkpatrick, 2016). Teacher training in technology use must be related to the highest level of CHS educational goals. It is important to find the proper resources allocated to that purpose and compare that expenditure to the results in terms of educational achievement to find the added value. Following this reasoning, it is better to identify the return on expectations (ROE) as an added-value measure of the training program contribution. Stakeholders evaluate the effectiveness of the training program based on the benefits expected through educational goals and objectives definition. Thus, the ROE should be based on what is expected by stakeholders in each of the four levels of the Kirkpatrick Model. If the evaluation outcomes satisfy the training program's performance goal and objectives, it pays off.

## Issues with Stakeholders

There might be some potential issues with stakeholders during and after the training program. Because teachers, school administration, and the district are expecting an effective training program, what if their expectations cannot be fully covered? Some prevention should be taken before the training program starts implementation. Let us say that teachers might perceive the frustration of wasting time in training sessions and practice sessions content (CogBooks, n.d.). The training designer can avoid defrauding in teachers by carefully examining the performance and defining with precision what to cover with the training program.

Other stakeholders are CHS administrators. CHS administrators founded high expectations on the training program, so they were motivated to provide knowledge and skills to teachers to contribute to student learning and to satisfy district expectations for the resources allocated for technology use purposes. CHS administrators expected to have all teachers pass the training and see them using the technology effectively to enhance student learning. The training program must provide teachers with the knowledge, skills, and tools required to succeed after the training. Consequently, CHS administrators will satisfy their expectations.

Moreover, the education district is also part of the stakeholders. The district desires to see how the schools' resources bring positive outcomes to district education and reputation. The use of resources adequately by the district will contribute to a stable position in front of politics, department of education, state government, and help support budget increases request for the upcoming years to benefit district schools. The training program designer can satisfy the district by assuring the quality of the training from the very beginning by considering district expectations and training program evaluation checklist.

## Conclusions

This training evaluation plan will satisfy the political expectations given by the education district. As mentioned in the previous section, the district will receive a satisfactory accomplishment if the training program is successful. The school administration's political image will be positive and reinforced since teachers and students will recognize the effort made in supporting knowledge and skills acquisition, curriculum integration to benefit education, and setting a precedent for consequent funding opportunities. Moreover, the training program will reverse teachers' negative feelings given by some self-perceived isolation, the sensation of being behind from a technological standpoint, and fear of being replaced by advantageous peers and losing their jobs. The training program will also contribute to fortifying a technology-and-innovation-based culture at CHS. In assuming that technology advances, teachers will be more open and receptive to embrace technological changes and incorporate them into teaching for student learning benefits.

# Exisiting Online Program: A Need for Improvement

Improving degree programs and student experiences in higher education is a global trend. In the past two decades, the interest in increasing the quality of teaching and student experience is visible (Dyjur & Lock, 2016). The need to improve a degree program comes for actions and recommendations that emerged from an institutional mandate and a faculty-led curriculum review. Moreover, the need arises from observing current job market demands requiring higher education institutions to review the program's content to ensure that graduates satisfy these new demands (Jacobsen et al., 2018).

The 2021 trends impacting business education are an essential platform to make considerations for business degree program improvements. Business education must go on par with the way businesses, the economy, and society evolve to prepare future professionals capable of facing the real world. Business education will have to prepare individuals as responsible leaders for conducting dynamics changes. Based on an exponential change driven by technology, business education will be an ongoing lifelong learning process. Higher education institutions will play the role of knowledge and experienced hubs professionals can visit for updates and careers. Moreover, the need for managing fast, frequent, and fiercely competitive changes, will demand from business degree programs adaptive agility of students' engagement, program development, critical and analytical thinking learning strategies, and entrepreneurial mindset development (Nugent, 2021).

The role of the assessments for program improvements is paramount. Using assessment results inform educational stakeholders (students, faculty, staff, and community) about new programs or changes to existing programs to satisfy learners and society demands. The assessments' results allow modifying the frequency and schedule of course offerings, removing or adding courses from the program content, implementing pedagogical models to share among learners and faculty, and revising course content or learning activities to satisfy new demands (Suskie, 2009).

Nevertheless, the assessment results yield new opportunities for increasing classroom space, adding lab resources for practical skills development and critical thinking, and re-assigning or hiring faculty or staff within the institution. From an academic standpoint, the assessment results permit revising course prerequisites for upper-level courses, revising criteria for admission to the program, and advising protocols. Finally, the assessment results will provide information for communication of the student performance, perceptions, student work, and success to stakeholders (Suskie, 2009).

First, this paper offers a general perspective of current trends in business education and the role of assessment for program improvements. Second, it briefly describes the bachelor's in marketing (BM) content and explains the reasons for making improvements to this specific program based on the program's needs assessment, identifies the market demand and characteristics of the students in the program, and describes the processes of evaluating teaching effectiveness and learning outcomes. It also identifies current marketing strategies to drive enrollments and the learning platform or technologies used to deliver the program.

Moreover, this paper elaborates on two other specific elements that are key for academic programs' success. These elements are the ethical issues and risks associated with the program and the cost of funding it. Finally, it presents recommendations to improve the existing BM program to satisfy learners and business context demands.

## Bachelor's in Marketing Content

After ten years of offering a generic bachelor's in business administration at the university, the academic unit decided to offer the BM back in 2017. The decision came from three main reasons—first, the institutional need to offer new bachelor's degree programs in the business administration knowledge area. Second, the latest trends in marketing and sales practices supported by the advances of the information technology applications to marketing and sales contexts, demand from business schools well-prepared marketing and sales students to satisfy that new business context. Third, the increasing demands of jobs in the marketing and sales-specific fields. Based on these three conditions, the academic unit opened this bachelor program to form professionals equipped with the novel marketing and sales techniques to succeed in the real business world.

The BM provides business students with an understanding of marketing processes and the skills necessary to analyze and solve marketing and sales problems and opportunities. This program is a 120-credit degree program; it holds 45 general education requirement credits, lower-level courses (55 credits), upper-level courses (36-credits), and elective courses (20 credits). It also prepares students to pursue advanced professional certifications in marketing, such as the Certified Professional Marketer (American Marketing Association).

## Need for Improvement

Some deficiencies are identified from applying permanent formative and summative assessments conducted within the academic unit analyzed during the Planning and Assessment Process in May. The 2018-2019 institutional assessment results showed that some students rated the program's satisfaction as "good," indicating some opportunities for the program's improvements.

Also, the class observation results achieved to instructors during the year, the learning outcomes report submitted by the instructors when each term (8-weeks) finishes, the Online Student Engagement Survey, and the student-Faculty Evaluation applied to students revealed that the instructors use a predominant teaching approach. The teaching and learning approach implemented in this program is an instructor-centered approach. In the instructor-centered approach, the knowledge is transmitted by the instructor. Even though students participate in some activities, the student's participation is still passive; the instructor is the leader. There are few assessments designed mainly for grading with an emphasis on learning correct answers. In other words, the academic culture is primordial individualistic and competitive (Northern Arizona University, n.d.).

The Academic unit also uses the National Standards for Quality Online Programs (NSQOP) Methodology (Pape & Wicks, 2009) to assess its academic programs. The NSQOP methodology covers four sets of standards (institutional, teaching and learning, support, and evaluation criteria). The methodology's application also yielded some deficiencies that motivated academic unit to design an improvement plan for the BM aligned with the Quality Assurance standards for online programs.

## Recommendations for Improvement

As evidence, the assessment conducted to the BM suggested the following improvement goals that will endow the program with a higher-quality strength:

1.  Change the learning approach centered on the instructor/ teaching approach to a student/learner approach.

2. nclude a mission statement as a quality online program demands.

3. Add the requirement for resources that effectively and efficiently serve their students, including curriculum, technology, support, and professional development.

4. Incorporate sufficient administrative and support staff to carry out the mission and annual organizational goals.

5. Implement quality instructional materials and appropriate technology that enable and enrich student learning.

6. Offer a wide variety of professional development opportunities.

7. Provide students with an orientation about online learning technologies and academic and administrative services to address students' intellectual and developmental needs.

8. Provide tools and information to help students determine the appropriateness of specific courses for their educational needs.

## Market Demand for the Existing Bachelor's in Marketing Program

Based on the modern marketing concept, marketing satisfies customer needs by engaging them, managing solid and profitable customer relationships, and creating value to capture it from customers in return. By creating value for customers, marketers capture value through the sales process (AMA, 2016); thus, sales are part of the marketing process. It functions along with market research, promotions, advertising, distribution, and product and pricing strategy design. It is critical to know the market demand for marketing and sales careers from a degree offerings standpoint to serve those individuals who aspire to occupy present and future market occupations.

The market demand is described in terms of employment and occupations 2019-2029 projections. Identifying the market demand in terms of the points mentioned previously will help make suggestions for improvement purposes to the current BM at the university.

## Careers in Marketing

There are several roles that marketers and salespersons perform in the marketing and sales job market. Professionals in marketing and sales can perform functions such as market researcher and analyst, advertisers, public relations representative, salesperson, marketing and sales managers, who work for marketing firms, advertising agencies, and public relations agencies. There are managerial positions under different titles within these positions, such as advertising account executive, brand manager, digital marketing officer, eCommerce manager, email marketing manager, media buyer, social media manager, among others.

Marketing and sales professionals not only work for marketing-based companies; they also perform functions in a diverse number of companies from various industries that implement marketing functions. The occupational outlook handbook shows diverse occupations related to marketing and sales as indicators of actual demand for jobs in these fields (U.S. Bureau of Labor Statistics, n.d.). This indicator is a valuable source for higher education institutions that plan for designing and offering degree programs in the marketing and sales field.

More information about the jobs in this field is also gathered for program design purposes. Information about the job duties, earning potential, and projected job growth rates are relevant variables to consider attracting freshmen students to pursue opportunities in this profession as marketing event planners, marketing project managers, media planners, and digital marketing professionals.

As a response to the job market demands and potential professional development in this field, many higher education institutions currently offer degrees in marketing and sales (Carlton, 2021). Suppose a degree program aligns with market demands and professional job descriptions in the field. In that case, it makes the program more competitive, and graduates will have a higher probability of satisfying job demands offered by the job market.

## Employment and Salaries for Marketing Job Positions

The outlook for marketing and sales job market positions, the employment expectations continue to grow. See Table 1. The job market indicates that marketing and sales job positions are expected to attract individuals interested in pursuing their careers in the marketing field (U.S. Bureau of Labor Statistics, n.d.1a).

Salaries become a pivotal motivator to apply for job positions. According to labor market data, the median salary for a marketing manager with a bachelor's degree, for instance, is $101,391 - $109,762. It is also higher for graduates from a master or doctorate degrees in the marketing subject (Salary.com, n.d.). See Figure 1.

**Table 1**

*Employment by detailed marketing and sales occupation, 2019 and projected 2029 (Numbers in thousands)*

| 2019 National Employment Matrix title and code | Employment | | | | Change, 2019-29 | | Occupational openings, 2019-29 annual average |
| | Number | | Percent distribution | | | | |
| | 2019 | 2029 | 2019 | 2029 | Number | Percent | |
| Advertising, marketing, promotions, public relations, and sales managers | 836.7 | 879 | 0.5 | 0.5 | 42.3 | 5.1 | 70 |
| Advertising and promotions managers | 28.6 | 28.3 | 0 | 0 | -0.3 | -1.1 | 2.5 |

| | | | | | | | |
|---|---|---|---|---|---|---|---|
| Marketing and sales managers | 720.1 | 754.6 | 0.4 | 0.4 | 34.5 | 4.8 | 59.9 |
| Marketing managers | 286.3 | 305.4 | 0.2 | 0.2 | 19.1 | 6.7 | 24.6 |
| Sales managers | 433.8 | 449.2 | 0.3 | 0.3 | 15.4 | 3.5 | 35.3 |
| Public relations and fundraising managers | 88 | 96.1 | 0.1 | 0.1 | 8.1 | 9.2 | 7.6 |

**Figure 1**

*Marketing Manager Salaries by Degree Level*

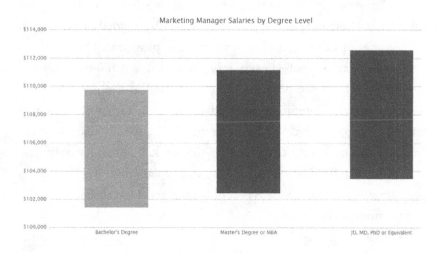

## Student Demographics and Characteristics

Understanding learner characteristics and determining what they can do is a crucial element of any instructional plan. From analyzing learners' characteristics, instructional designers can identify the level of knowledge, expectations, motivations, and satisfaction with the learning experience. To modify a program, lesson, or instruction requires consideration of the learner's current learning experience, knowledge, abilities, perceived needs, and future expectations. It also requires some information about the learner's lifestyle to plan the appropriate instructional material to adapt to their personal and professional conditions (Green & Brown, 2016).

The BM started in 2017. It is a brand-new bachelor's degree, and the enrollment is still low. As of today, the program has 18 active students. Both genders are equally represented; most are US Non-citizens, predominantly Hispanics, single, and US High School as previous education. They are working professionals with family responsibilities; some of them have more than one job. Thus, they require specific, yet high-quality instruction, to succeed in the job market because of the work schedule and time constraints. See Table 2.

The program assessment performed to the BM in the last institutional effectiveness cycle (2018-2019) yielded information to consider making some changes to the program. The Students Faculty Evaluation applied every term (8 weeks) also showed students' perceptions about the program. As commented in the previous week 2 paper, students' opinions triggered the need to review the teaching approach implemented in the program. Students said that there are too many materials to cover during the week; instructors only post instructions on Blackboard without enough explanation; and instructors post some instructional videos that only offer general information about the assignment content.

Students' perceptions corroborated the need to introduce some changes in the teaching approach from an instructor-centered to a learner-centered approach (Bransford et al., 2000). It will require modifying instruction and including learning activities that allow students to digest factual knowledge. It will also require switching courses from the upper-level requirements to electives and vice versa, as well as, changing some content-based electives courses to internship-based delivery to satisfy learners who need a more efficient way of consuming knowledge to learn because of their time, personal, and professional constraints.

**Table 2**

*BM Student Demographics*

| Demographic Variable | Count | Percentage |
|---|---|---|
| Male | 9 | 50.00% |
| Female | 9 | 50.00% |
| Merried | 1 | 0.05% |
| Single | 17 | 94.40% |
| American | 5 | 28.00% |
| Latin America | 11 | 61.00% |
| Europe | 1 | 0.05% |
| Unknown | 1 | 0.05% |
| US Citizen | 6 | 33.30% |
| US Non-citizen | 12 | 66.70% |
| Black | 2 | 11.10% |
| Hispanic | 15 | 83.30% |
| White | 1 | 0.05% |
| US High School | 10 | 55.50% |
| Foreign High School | 8 | 44.40% |
| **Total** | **18** | **100.00%** |

## Evaluating Teaching Effectiveness and Learning Outcomes

Effectiveness in teaching is defined as observable behaviors seen during class observation of a typical lesson (Ko, 2010). An instructor is effective if he or she shows the ability to produce gains on student achievement scores, considering a baseline measure of student's prior attainment. It is identified concerning students' progress measured by later attainment (Little et al., 2009).

The impact on learners' performance of various factors, such as teaching methods, teacher expectations, classroom organization, and classroom resources to help acquire knowledge, shows the relationship between instructors' behaviors and classroom practices and student outcomes. Thus, effectiveness changes from one instructor to another because the impact of an instructor on student achievement varies upon the consistency of instructor effects in terms of time stability and differentiation in stakeholders' requirements (i.e., colleagues, students, parents). Also, it varies because of the working environments given by the institution type, community, and the subject consistency (Campbell et al., 2004). Hence, teaching effectiveness depends on both teacher effectiveness and how the context of teaching ensures that teaching is delivered effectively.

The nucleon of teaching effectiveness is instructor effectiveness. The following sections describe instructor/teacher effectiveness, methods of measuring instructor effectiveness, and evaluating learning outcomes to measure learning effectiveness. In this case, assessing learning outcomes will refer to the evaluation approach used to evaluate degree programs, particularly the BM at the university.

## Instructor Effectiveness

The role of instructors involves much more than simply providing subject-matter instruction. Effective instructors have high expectations for all students and support students for learning measured by value-added. They contribute to positive academic, social, and attitudinal outcomes for students, such as on-time promotion to the following degree program level, on-time graduation, regular attendance, self-efficacy, and cooperative behavior. Effective instructors are also characterized by using alternative resources to plan and structure engaging learning momentum, follow up student progress, adapt instruction when needed, and evaluate learning using varied sources of evidence.

Moreover, instructors are considered adequate when they contribute to the development of classrooms and institutions that value diversity and civic mindsets. Instructors collaborate with other stakeholders such as administrators, parents, other instructors, and education professionals to ensure student success (Goe et al., 2008).

Besides, Porter & Brophy (1988) offered a general profile of effective teachers. An effective teacher is clear about instructional goals and shows a deep knowledge about the curriculum content and strategies for teaching it and their students, adapting instruction to their needs, and anticipating misconceptions in their current knowledge. Effective teachers communicate to the students what is expected of them, use existing instructional materials, use metacognitive strategies for teaching and address higher and lower cognitive objectives, monitor students' progress, and provide feedback for improvement purposes. Besides, effective teachers integrate instruction with that in other subject areas and accept responsibility for student outcomes.

## Methods of Measuring Instructor Effectiveness

The most widely implemented measure of instructor effectiveness is classroom observations. However, there are other instruments also used to evaluate instructor performance when teaching a subject. These other instruments are supervisor evaluations -program director, division heads, department chair, vice president of academic affairs, instructor portfolios, analysis of classroom artifacts -rating of instructor assignments or other instructional materials, and learner work. Other instruments are instructor self-reports -learning outcomes reports, surveys, teaching logs, interviews, and student-faculty evaluations. Other measures that assess instructor competency are instructor demonstration of knowledge, instructor responses to theoretical teaching situations, or stakeholders -other than instructors, and added-value model, which is used to determine instructors' contributions to students' test score gains (Goe et al., 2008).

## Instructor Effectiveness Evaluation
## in the BM at the University

Instructor evaluation in the BM at the university is an ongoing process. There are different methods to evaluate instructors. The academic unit uses face-to-face and online class observations, student faculty evaluations, and faculty self-assessment. Class observation is conducted three times a year. Department chairs discuss the results of the class observations with instructors to identify areas for improvement. The discussions also include the student-faculty evaluation about the courses taught during the term (8-weeks) to share with instructors the students' perceptions about their learning experience. The department chair also contributes to the evaluation from their perception of the instructor's performance.

Another instrument used to evaluate instructor effectiveness is the grade book each instructor turns into the department chairs when finishing their courses. The tool is an excel-based spreadsheet which keeps the student grades and learning objectives/outcomes (LOs/LOs) achievements. Specifically, the LOs/LOs tab provides information on how students achieve each result. It allows identifying both students who performed excellent or poor and those LOs/LOs that did not reach the cutoff established to measure achievement. For instance, Los/LOs that reach 75 (100-point-based scale) or above are considered accepted-high performance achievements. Alternatively, below 75, it is considered low and instructors review, analyze, and design specific actions to improve these LOs/LOs next time they teach the course. When the class period finishes and instructors submit the grade book to department chairs, the latter review them and contact the instructor for clarification if they find inconsistencies in the grade book content.

Once a year, the university holds the Planning and Assessment Process in May. All the evaluations conducted to the instructors throughout the year are discussed individually as part of the Annual Instructor Evaluation. From debating the evaluations, each instructor will design the next-year Faculty Development Plan. The academic unit prepares the academic report supported by the LOs/LOs results and present them with actions for divisions and departments' short and long-term development. As mentioned, LOs/LOs of each course are analyzed; however, each academic program also has program goals and program learning outcomes. Both goals and learning outcomes for the BM program are presented as follows.

## Marketing Strategies for the Bachelor's in Marketing Enrollment

Higher education institutions and businesses have been considered distinct contexts or worlds, with little or nothing in common. However, higher education institutions have learned much from business. Educational institutions have included budgeting systems, endowment investing, human resources functions, financial management procedures, and marketing practices. Terms such as market segmentation, marketing research, and strategic planning are part of the marketing function and have become widely applied by educational institutions (Kotler & Fox, 1995).

Even though the marketing activities of educational offerings were considered taboo, it is now done openly. The student-centered model most higher education institutions are implementing is not much different from the client-based marketing strategy. When marketing strategies are used in education, the course programs and materials are observed to be shaped per students' needs and desires. Thus, the implementation of marketing strategies in the context of the educational setting is justified.

The adoption of a market orientation approach by educational institutions allows these institutions to use various strategies to attract students to attend their institutions. Indeed, marketing has a vital role in educational institutions because marketing is an essential function of the organization to distribute educational products (degree and non-degree programs) to learners' hands (Nur Rohim, 2019). From the management standpoint, the design and implementation of marketing strategies are seen to increase institutional efficiency as an organizational response to industry (education) factors and competence to survive (Cherkunova, 2016).

This part is organized as follows. The first section describes the role of marketing strategies in the context of educational institutions. Second, it describes the elements of the marketing strategy. The following section is dedicated to explaining the marketing mix elements in service organizations (as educational institutions belong to). Finally, the last section is dedicated to describing the marketing strategy and mix used to market the BMS and recommendations for implementation purposes.

## Marketing Strategies for Educational Services

Marketing applied by educational institutions presents significant similarities with service marketing and social marketing, and it requires marketing objectives to promote academic programs to the market. Educational marketing objectives are set as acquiring fundamental knowledge, developing practical skills and competencies needed by learners to satisfy their educational needs. Learners are not the ones waiting to satisfy their educational expectations, but other educational stakeholders also expect academic institutions to meet learners' expectations.

According to Kotler & Fox (1995), the educational stakeholders are grouped into various primary publics such as current and prospective students, faculty, administration and staff, alumni, parents of students, competitors, suppliers, government agencies, mass media, the business community, foundations, trustees, accreditation organizations, local community, and the general public. Thus, educational marketing's role is to ensure harmonization between individuals' interests in training and learning with a collective need for a good social integration and adaptation to the labor market (Filip, 2012).

Services offered by educational institutions can be analyzed from a services marketing perspective; thus, service characteristics such as intangibility, heterogeneity, inseparability, and perishability determine specific marketing strategies, which will impact student satisfaction.

Educational service intangibility means that educational services cannot be seen, felt, taste, smelled, or heard. Heterogeneity means that educational services cannot be uniformed or standardized. Perishability means that educational services cannot be stored for sale or use. Inseparability means that educational services are produced and consumed at the same time. For instance, if professors' professionalism is the primary determinant of higher education satisfaction, then there are two service characteristics -heterogeneity and inseparability- that relate to that professionalism. Professionalism manifests through students' skills and how professors interact with the audience (Filip, 2012); thus, marketing strategies must highlight the inseparable interaction between professors and students to be perceived by students as a generator of satisfaction. Once the educational institution selects the marketing objectives through the strategic marketing process, the institution designs each academic program's marketing strategies.

## Marketing Mix for Educational Services

Since educational institutions are service organizations, several marketing variables characterize the educational offerings. These variables are academic product (product), price (in terms of cost for students), distribution, and promotions. However, in the educational context, the 4p's model was adapted by Kotler & Fox (1995) by including additional elements known as seven marketing tools: program, price, place, promotion, processes, physical facilities, and people. Moreover, within promotions, there are specific tools to combine for communication purposes according to the academic program's target market. The combination of these promotional tools is called "promotional mix" (Kotler & Armstrong, 2017).

First, educational institutions offer educational programs (products) such as undergraduate and graduate degree programs, certificate programs, diplomas, training, among others, and these products should satisfy an educational/learning demand. Second, price is frequently associated with tuition fees. Tuition fees are the primary revenue source for many educational institutions (i.e., universities and colleges). Price policies regularly consider the specific target profile and the impact on the overall university image. Some educational consumers perceive more expensive services as adding substantial value. As part of the price policy, institutions also offer discounts and scholarships to attract potential students and sponsorships and funding from the private sector.

Third, place, known as an educational delivery system, creates service availability and accessibility in terms of time and geographical distribution of teaching and learning (Kotler & Fox, 1995). However, technological developments have supported educational institutions to increase service accessibility by using electronic platforms such as learning management systems. So, eLearning programs are distributed to satisfy those learners who perceive geographic and time constraints in physically attending courses. The fourth mix component is promotion. Promotion is used to keep an ongoing dialogue with employers, students, professors, and other stakeholders by using advertising, sales promotions, public relations, personal selling as communication techniques, and specific tools as part of these categories such as direct-mail, webpages, and social networks.

In addition to the mix components described so far, there are other elements to consider as part of the mix. These elements are processes, physical facilities, and people. Processes indicate how things happen in the educational institution. Examples of the processes are management, enrollment, admissions, student services, payments, teaching, learning, sports, and social activities. Physical facilities represent the tangible component of a service organization. It refers to the aspects related to build-environment, technical infrastructure, equipment, textbooks, and laboratories, which students perceive when comparing their institution with competitor institutions. Finally, people refer to individuals, part of the educational system. It includes teaching and administrative staff and current and former students. The interaction among all these individuals helps deliver the service, builds customer relations, and the teaching skills perceptions by students, communication, and dialogue become a decisive influence on students' satisfaction (Kother & Fox, 1995).

## Marketing Strategy and Mix to Drive Enrollments in the BM at the University

The BM program as a product (P) strives to graduate well-prepared students academically and socially. The program's cost (Price) is based on tuition per credit. The university has a strategic location (Place), surrounded by high school institutions and a population of predominantly working professionals. The program is offered online, so it is ubiquitous. People from different areas -local, regional, national, and international-can enroll in the program. The promotion carried out by the university is diverse. The BM is promoted through program brochures, the institution's Website, social media platforms (Facebook), radio, television, billboards, and referrals -the first source of enrollment.

The physical evidence (PE) is given by the institution facilities and infrastructure that support the learning process. As mentioned above, Blackboard is the learning management system used to deliver the program entirely online. People (P) is another marketing variables part of the marketing mix. Institutional stakeholders are considered the BM-University people. From top management to bottom-line employees, considering students and board of governors, all contribute to its marketing promotions. Their behaviors manifest the university culture, and it is transmitted to potential candidates for the BM program.

Finally, process (P) encompasses a series of activities experienced by students during the education, such as a learning process conducive to expected outputs. Different procedures are performed simultaneously, such as enrollment, teaching, graduation, community services, and marketing communication processes that contribute to producing quality graduates. The output of these processes is an essential element to attract new students into the BM program.

However, the marketing mix elements described before and used in the university's communications to attract and enroll students in the BM program do not seem effective enough. So far, there are 16 students since the program started in 2017. It is necessary to redesign the marketing strategies to increase the number of enrollments. As an educational consultant, it is recommended the following strategies to improve the program figures.

1.  Change the teaching approach from instructor-centered to student-centered approach.
2.  Reinforce digital media to reach out to young prospect students through text messaging, a mobile responsive website, an in-person meeting.
3.  Increase Online display advertising, social media advertising (Instagram, Facebook, and YouTube, and re-targeted ads.
4.  Work closely with the admission department to gather deeper data from analytics, CRM, and search engine optimization sources.
5.  Increase Email message use with link to a personalized URL, self-mailer brochure or postcard, outbound phone call. Also, send videos with program content and student-centered teaching strategies currently used to reinforce learning quality to stimulate student learning satisfaction.
6.  Promote virtual or on-campus events, promote application and enrollment deadlines, major, program, or department-specific messaging, brand messaging, and showcase student/alumni stories and outcomes.
7.  Text high-school counselors and coordinate one-on-one meetings with them through email and call counselors after visits.
8.  Outsource parents/family engagement of admitted and enrolled students, contact systematically admitted students to code their level of interest in enrolling at the university.

Moreover, use statistical, analytical approaches to determine financial aid award levels by predicting enrollment rates based on awards.

9.  Include the following information on prospective families, such as phone number to the admissions team, cost, academic (major and minors), email links to connect with admissions, campus calendar, admission requirements, employment outcomes, financial aid scholarships, information request form, and career services.

## Learning Platform to Deliver the Bachelor's in Marketing

Learning Management Systems (LMS) is a software application to support (implementing and administering) online learning programs that can be completed remotely, great for modern technological educational environments. The LMS role is to centralize the learning platform, and allows organizing learning content, delivering it to the audience, and evaluating how learners perform. It also consolidates learning initiatives on a scalable web-based platform to benefit learners involved in the learning process (Inquisiq, n.d.). Moreover, LMS offers students complex analytics and reporting compared to in-person delivery format, and instructors can track course completion, engagement, knowledge retention, and gaps (Aston, 2021).

## Benefits of a Learning Management Systems

LMSs are gold standards for creating outstanding eLearning experiences for learners. This system offers several impactful benefits such as ease of use, support for multiple learning methods, improved efficiency, and game-changing insights. By using an LMS, learners can focus on studying rather than navigating through the web. An LMS allows eLearning to be easier because it allows searching course catalogs to configurable pages and dashboards, integrating with human resources systems and third-party services to create a seamless experience on the front back-end. Also, they feature multilingual support for global organizations to meet the international educational needs in their languages (Inquisiq, n.d.).

LMSs offer powerful learning automation features that reduce the overhead of implementing eLearning initiatives. It permits setting up rules to automatically enroll learners, define permissions, control access to courses, and avoid administrators handling these tasks manually. Thus, it offers improved efficiency. Moreover, there are other advantages that LMSs offer. Since learners learn differently, LMS can accommodate everything from traditional instructor-led instruction to defined learning paths with related courses. For instance, group projects with discussions included can be added for learners who do better in social environments, facilitating hands-on work and performance evaluation.

LMSs also give administrators access to essential data, such as incomplete assigned training, assignments, average evaluation scores, and see key performance indicators for regular delivery of the capability to generate them. Some other features that LMS offers are customizable user interface, social learning, eCommerce, mobile compatibility, learning automation, pre-built and custom courseware, and blended learning (Inquisiq, n.d.).

## Learning Management Systems Comparison

There are several LMSs available for both educational institutions and organizations (profit and non-profit). Aston (2021) enumerates the ten best learning management systems for 2021, along with their pros and cons. It is useful for those looking for an LMS to offer and support learning and those who evaluate their current LMS and replace it for improvement purposes. The best learning management systems Aston ranks are *Google classroom, Chamilo LMS, Moodle, D2L Brightspace, NEO LMS, Schoology, Blackboard Learn, SAP Litmos, Canvas, and Docebo.* Some of them are more used by educational institutions and others for the enterprise. Other options are *Edmodo, sThink LMS, Learnupon LMS, Joomla LMS, Talent LMS, ProProfs Training Maker, Rise, Firefly, Teachable, Thinkific, Absorb LMS, and Coassemble.* However, since the purpose of this paper is to describe the LMS used to support the BM and compared it with other LMS, this section only compares the most common LMS used in the educational environment, such as Moodle, D2L Brightspace, Blackboard, and Canvas. See Table 3.

**Table 3**

*LMS Comparison: Pros and Cons*

| LMS | Pros | Cons |
|---|---|---|
| Moodle | • Plenty of training/ tutorial materials<br>• Solid multilingual capabilities<br>• Good for bulk course creation | • No native video conferencing feature<br>• UI a bit outdated<br>• Steep learning curve |
| D2L Brightspace | • Great mobile/tablet app<br>• Can pin/unpin classes & tools<br>• Good, clear announcements system | • No native video chat feature<br>• Software outages for updates<br>• No way to delete batches of courses |
| Blackboard Learn | • Native messaging/ email functionality<br>• High impact reporting for learner progress<br>• Platform inclusive (MacOS/ iOS, PC, Android) | • Excessive clicks & Menuing<br>• Plain interface |
| Canvas | • Great mobile app<br>• Centralized course Q&A in a wiki/FAQ<br>• Well-structured To Do listings | • Weak search functionality means a lot of manual scrolling<br>• Discussion flow can get busy<br>• No built-in gamification tools |

## Learning Management System Evaluation Criteria

LMS yields excellent results. Both hardware and software must be considered for the architecture design to provide efficiency and effectiveness. The server must have a capacity greater than 20 GB and a minimum internet speed of 4 MB. The search for information in LMS resources should be higher than 40% (Juarez et al., 2020). The key LMS features relevant to the educational environment are gamification and social learning features, personalized learning paths, mobile learning support, skills, certification tracking, and test-out options for advanced learners. However, the decision to acquire an LMS is based on the following criteria (Aston, 2021):

1.  User interface: It provides cleanliness and attractiveness, quick adaptation to designated interfaces, ease of finding analytics, and interpretation from the platform.
2.  Usability: How easy it is to build and consume course content. Does the vendor offer customer support, user support, tutorials, training, ready-to-go courses to sprint? Does the LMS system work on all mobile devices?
3.  Integrations: Does it connect easily with other media creation tools, video conferencing, CMS, and other relevant learning content creation tools?
4.  Value for money: Does the tool pay for itself by the amount of virtual training material learners have access to? Does the cost include pre-made courses and the tools needed to support your online course design from scratch?

The next section is dedicated to describing the current LMS used at the university to support the BM degree program, Blackboard Learn. It also provides the results of the Blackboard system assessment and some recommendations for improvements.

## Blackboard Learn as the LMS to Support
## the BM Degree Program

Blackboard Learn is an LMS designed with an intuitive and personalized interface that engages learners and eases instructors' burden. Using Blackboard as the LMS to support academic programs, the learning process gains the flexibility to support the pedagogical approach designed for the program and surface the data that inform student success. Blackboard allows learners and instructors to learn quickly and teach anytime, anywhere with a fully responsive design for all devices, ensure equity and access to improve the online learning experience.

Blackboard is also a powerful and straightforward tool, and workflows help learners and instructors stay organized, engage with content, and efficiently act, connect students with the resources available for them receive personalized support from the institutional resources, when and where they need it, deliver permanent teaching and learning experiences, eliminates downtime, and take advantages of the latest enhancements when they become available. Moreover, it is open to integrating, extending, and getting the data and offers comprehensive services to expedite success because it ensures a smooth transition, develops digital capabilities, and offers up-level student support services (Blackboard, n.d.).

Recently, the university uses to Blackboard Ultra. Blackboard Ultra is Blackboard Learn with the Ultra experience. It delivers a more straightforward and powerful teaching and learning experience with a modern, intuitive, fully responsive interface, and allows the engaging student more (Blackboard Learn Ultra, n.d.). However, since implementation started, the version in use is not as friendly as expected. Both instructors and students have expressed discomfort using it and some perceived disadvantages compared to Blackboard Learn (traditional version).

To respond to stakeholders' concerns, the academic unit and the Distance Learning Division at the university assessed the LMS's functionality to identify areas for improvements. The tool used to evaluate the LMS was *LMS Evaluation Tool* (NCAT, n.d.). This assessment tool holds 27 rubrics measured through points as follows: Fair (5 points), Good (8 points), and Excellent (10 points). The total amount of points to earn are 270 points. The assessment yielded 221 points, so there are some LMS rubrics demanding attention and worth improving for both students and instructors and the quality of the BM program delivery. 17 out of 27 rubrics did not cover the expectations of the institution. Five of them were classified as critical and detailed as follows. (See Appendix 1).

The functional areas of the LMS Blackboard Learn Ultra identified as critical are:

1. Archives courses are not available to be viewed by the instructor. On occasions, instructors need to review course content already taught for grading review given by student complaints, and they cannot access it. Then, they must request course availability to the Department chair and Distance Learning, causing delays in responding to students' requests and, as a result, uncomfortable experience to instructors and students.

2. Learning analytics. This feature allows gathering grades and basic statistics for each learner to evaluate the course design/content's impact on students' learning and experience; however, this feature generates basic reports.

3. Integration with campus portal. LMS is accessible through the campus portal but only by linking that requires a separate authentication by the user. It bothers instructors when they are required to enter information about the student's progress.

4. Support. The LMS administrators offer support only by email. It brings some vendor-institution conflicts. When having

issues with the LMS functionality, there is only one way to report them. It causes delays from the vendor to respond to institution requests.

5. Online help resources. Only a users' manual is accessible online; however, there are no help files at each step for students on high-speed connections and adequate for dial-up users.

Based on the issues found after assessing the LMS, both divisions agreed on crafting the following actions:

1. Request a meeting with the LMS administrators to provide them with our expectations and perceptions about the Blackboard Learn Ultra functionality and explain the consequences for the quality of the BMS program's online delivery of keeping some of the features without improvement.

2. Design informative sessions and support materials for instructors to explain how to deal with some of the LMS and potential solutions' weaknesses to minimize the negative impact of the LMS drawbacks.

3. Evaluate other LMSs using the same evaluation tool and the Aston (2021) criteria, compare them, and find an alternative LMS that brings better experience to the institution for programs delivery when the current license period expires before renewing it.

## Ethical Issues and Risks Associated with the Bachelor's in Marketing

The nature of an academic program delivered through distance education or online brings different ethical issues given by stakeholders' behaviors. Learners and society expect individuals are participating in the academic program to provide appropriate behaviors according to ethical and moral standards prevalent in an educational context. As actors and decision-makers, both faculty and students play an essential role in keeping ethical standards. Together with academic institutions, engage in online teaching and learning practices that directly or indirectly reflect ethical behaviors and issues in educational relationships (Thompson, 2019).

Students' ethical responsibilities focus on academic honesty and commitment to learning, and it continues to be areas of concern (Thompson & Wrigglesworth, 2013). Students taking online education feel the pressure to achieve their educational goals. They show a lack of preparation compared to traditional students and a perception that "everybody does it"; therefore, they might fall into unethical behaviors when they perceive a lower probability of not achieving their goals and succeeding. Attached to this, technology, particularly the internet, has become a feature of daily social, academic, and professional life, and a leading factor in discussions of why and how learners engage in academic dishonesty in online education (Strader, 2014).

On the other hand, instructors decide on instructional goals, objectives, course materials, technology, and assessments when designing and teaching distance education, and all these instructional components carry ethical implications. For instance, setting educational goals and objectives for adult learners implies considering what they need and want to learn; however, it has been found that this rule is not universal. The inherent nature of different instructional approaches suggests several ethical issues based on differing ideas about the goals of education and the rights and responsibilities of participants (Thompson & Kuhne, 2014). Therefore, the challenge is finding a balance among institutional priorities, faculty expertise, what students express, what they want, or what they might choose.

The decision about goals and objectives has become more challenging from an ethical standpoint in globalized distance education because some goals may disadvantage students from different geographical cultures. However, some of these practices may be perceived ultimately attractive, which shows how a practice with inarguably ethical dimensions may be observed as either ethical or unethical. It will depend on the value principles on which the ethical approach is based (Bates, 2001).

Other ethical implications for an academic program delivered online are about to course, design, copyright, and assessment. Course design should specify the technology determined primarily by learning objectives and other factors central to the teaching setting; however, decisions about course design are often influenced by factors such as costs, convenience, availability, instructor willingness, and institutional policies. For example, the learning management system (LMS) selection to support the instruction is decided at the institutional level, yet how the LMS is selected might be given by an established relationship with corporate vendors, which brings ethical questions.

Another example of a questionable ethical practice is given by how course design elements are done to serve student learning. Toprak et al. (2010) found significant differences between students' and instructors' ideas on technology choices. While students stated that only essential technical elements should be built into courses because of students' bandwidth challenges, just a few instructors agreed, highlighting the advantages of multimedia elements. Also, decisions about course materials showed a similar likelihood to limit access by learners. Some materials are unsuited or inaccessible to specific learning styles or cultural experiences, and these limitations present ethical issues (Thompson, 2019). Other challenges are related to cheating (academic dishonesty), copyright violations (Thompson & Wrigglesworth, 2013), and students' right to privacy (Ehrich et al., 2012).

The BM program abides by the university institutional policies. The institution establishes clear procedures related to ethical behaviors. Despite some modifications to the current program, this new set of changes will not violate the institutional policies. Ethical policies for both students and faculty will keep as established. The BM program within the university's academic unit will enforce them to align with institutional mandates as part of the educational context.

There are different policies designed to protect students and faculty in the BM program's rights and ethical responsibilities, such as students' code of ethics, accommodations for students with disabilities, confidentiality, grievance procedures, student's rights and responsibilities, regulation of behaviors, controlled substances, alcohol beverages and drug, anti-hazing, and sexual harassment. Others are the acceptable use policy regarding information technology, copyright infringement compliance plan, and copyright protection, student grievance and complaint, and accessibility to student records and privacy act.

The program will also enforce policies established by the LMS (Blackboard) and specific technology-based tools for teaching and learning within the program, i.e., regulations set by video content usage and graphic materials, audiovisuals, among others. Also, the BS program will continue educating students against plagiarism and cheating, which are categorized as unethical behaviors, and continue using plagiarism checkers in the courses taught to help students identify similarities with external sources, correct errors, and learn from the mistakes. It prepares students to be better professionals and citizens with a more robust ethical foundation.

## Cost of Funding the Bachelor's in Marketing

A holistic academic program planning is presented as the best practice at future-facing educational institutions. Higher education institutions face financial pressures and focus on developing a deeper understanding of their economy, growing revenues, and strategically approaching budgeting. In conjunction with this situation, student characteristics and interests in degrees are evolving rapidly; thus, institutions integrate an evidence-based understanding of the impact of all factors in devising a long-term academic strategy (Huron, n.d).

Financial margins or financial contribution of an academic program is an essential topic in higher education. Usually, 70 % to 80% of the total costs of an institution are related to faculty and staff or personnel costs. Thus, managing efficiently and effectively the costs is critical to sustaining a program because it provides the basis for decision-making on where to invest and how to efficiently staff.

The key cost components of an academic program are part of the costs of the educational institution. For example, program directors and administrators are required to keep an eye on the contribution margin -the one that allows investments and growth. A contribution margin is defined in terms of tuition amount (per student) plus course fees (paid per student), minus institutional aid (given per student), instructor cost (salary + fringe per instructor, from payroll entry by pay period), and other direct costs related to instruction (i.e., expenses coded to academic programs such as supplies) (Berg et al., 2016). The contribution margin sets the basis for future investment and growth.

There is an increasing recognition and expectations in higher education contexts that both teaching and learning technology should be used to promote the quality of teaching, student learning, and student experience. Since the use of technology to support teaching and learning has become a norm, technology incorporated into academic programs requires being measured to know their impact on the efficiency and effectiveness of the learning experience. In other words, it becomes another element of cost within the academic program.

The technology incorporated into academic settings is broadly classified as Web2.0 tools (blogs, podcasts, wikis, social networks, learning management systems, digital simulations), and its use requires changes in teaching practice. It will need the conditions necessary to support transitions, including faculty champions, faculty development, and adequate resources to guide technology adoption (Harrison et al., 2019). Therefore, it is also necessary to keep technology-related costs under control for investments and growth purposes.

In a practical sense, terms such as price, costs, and value are crucial to understanding the programs' cost structure and visualize ways of funding via self-revenue generation (tuition-driven) and external funding. Price is the monetary amount paid by the student. Cost is the total amount incurred to have the academic program available, and value is the utility or perceived worth of the educational programs by graduates. The value of an investment in academic programs, including the use of technology, is given by improvements in the quality of teaching - by incorporating different teaching approaches, student learning strategies-, and achievement of educational outcomes and competencies by students associated with the academic program teaching strategies implemented (Harrison et al., 2019). Also, the value is reflected in graduates and employers who perceive the benefits and quality of the educational products.

In brief, the value of an academic program becomes an essential component for funding opportunities. Suppose the educational program keeps the costs under control and the value increases. In that case, there will be a higher probability of experiencing growth because enrollment increases and the financial resources with it. So, there is potential for new investments.

## Conclusions

After assessing the BMS academic program, there are some thoughts worth highlighting and developed as conclusions.

- The need for improving an academic program comes from the internal and external analysis. The formative and summative institutional assessment results reveal perceptions from internal stakeholders (students, staff, administrators, and faculty. Moreover, the external analysis offers information about the industry and alternative offerings from other higher education institutions. The program in question described in this paper requires improvements. The need for its progress is derived from students' perceptions about the BM program content and implementation, surveys conducted by the academic unit, and the National Standards for Quality

Online Programs (NSQOP) Methodology, identifying areas or opportunities from a holistic standpoint.

- Since it is a fast-growing profession, the program content and the marketing strategies being implemented to market require a revision to identify areas for improvement. It will be needed to look at what other higher education institutions with similar student demographics offer to find similarities and differences and suggest changes.

- After implementing teaching effectiveness and evaluations and evaluating program goals and learning outcomes achievements for 2019-1020, the academic unit identified some opportunities for improvements. These opportunities relate to both instructors' teaching approaches and program content.

- Current practices for enrollment in the BM program at the university need a redesign and new ones. It will be essential to reinforce the image of the program based on a student-centered approach. Besides, the relationship with the admission department should be much closer. By working together with admission, new ideas and marketing strategies will increase enrollment into the BM program.

- LMS evaluation is paramount because it defines at a high level the quality of the online learning delivery. As part of the BM program evaluation, the delivery system for the program requires analysis and assessment. Online learning demands a robust delivery system. If instructors and students perceive deficiencies in the way the courses are taught via an LMS, it will negatively impact the learning experience's quality. It will then cause potential drops from the programs and damage the academic program's reputation and the educational institution.

# Appendix 1

*LMS Assessment Tool Results*

**INSTRUCTIONS:** Use the following evaluation to review each learning management system. Evaluate the set of criteria by scoring each item: 0 (Feature Not Present), 5 (Fair), 8 (Good), or 10 (Excellent) based on the information and demonstration provided by the vendor.

| Evaluation Rubric | Fair = 5 Points | Good = 8 Points | Excellent = 10 Points | Points |
|---|---|---|---|---|
| **Design and layout** | Functional interface with decent layout but somewhat complex and counterintuitive. Aesthetics are bland or distracting. | Good functional interface that can be navigated with minimal training. Good look and feel. | Simple, intuitive interface with minimal clicks to access materials, little or no training needed to get started, and the look and feel is inviting. | 10 |
| **Migration of existing courses** | Some migration tools exist but the tools and documentation are either inadequate or difficult to use. | Good tools are provided and well documented, but the migrated material will need additional formatting. | Excellent migration tools with great documentation. All migrated course materials are ready to use. | 8 |
| **Content authoring** | Provides a basic means for uploading and storing content in a hierarchical manner to support teaching and learning. | Allows basic content to be uploaded or created within an authoring system that is part of the LMS. | Provides a suite of tools for authoring media-rich content, importing content, drag-and-drop interfaces, as well as uploading rich content types such as podcasts, video clips, etc. | 10 |

| | | | Allows metadata creation for easier/better management. | |
|---|---|---|---|---|
| **Content organization** | LMS provides a basic repository for course content. | LMS provides a repository for content and basic tools for content organization. | LMS provides a framework for diverse storage and use strategies, from public, private and shared workspaces, to subscription-based content (e.g., podcasts and feeds) to archival content. | 8 |
| **Course export** | Permits course content to be exported and reimported into the LMS itself but may have limited ability to export to another LMS. | Allows course structure and content to be exported but in formats that constrain how the exported content may be imported elsewhere. | Exports course structure and content, as well as selected sub-elements of a course, using an industry-standard such as IMS Content Packaging so that courses can be imported into another LMS. | 8 |
| **Archives** | Some archival tools but much of the process is manual. Archived courses are not available to be viewed by the instructor. | Good archival tools that support backup of completed courses with student submissions and discussions intact. The LMS administrator must set up instructor access to the completed course. | Powerful archive tools that support automatic backup of completed courses with student submissions and discussions intact. Instructors have full access and control of completed courses. | 5 |

| Communication | | | | 8 |
|---|---|---|---|---|
| | LMS provides secure access to the email addresses that comprise the class roster, but individuals may not be selectable for private email. | Both asynchronous (email) and synchronous communication tools are present. | LMS provides a high level of flexibility for the use of email (asynchronous by roster, individual or group) as well as instant messaging, chat and threaded discussions. | |
| File exchange | | | | 10 |
| | LMS provides secure drop-box functionality so that students can exchange materials with instructors. | LMS provides drop-box and ability for students and faculty to upload resources to a central course repository. | LMS provides secure drop-boxes and shared folders for file exchange among students as well as instructors and allows for bulk downloads of attached files. | |
| E-portfolio | | | | 8 |
| | Basic tools allow students and instructors to gather student work products for assessment and presentation. | Tools allow students and instructors to create ad-hoc or structured presentations of resources. | A full-featured e-portfolio tool is integrated into the LMS and makes possible the gathering, review and presentation of work products to support any portfolio strategy (resumé, learning, tenure, etc). Reporting tools allow for individual, departmental or institutional assessments. | |
| Discussion tools | | | | 10 |
| | Adequate speed and functionality with the ability to attach files | Quick and functional with user profiles or pictures, file attachments and html interface. | Extremely fast and highly functional with user profiles and pictures, files attachments and easy html interface. | |

| Testing and assessment tools | A simple test generator with the ability to add multiple choice, true/false, short answer and essay questions. | More than a simple test generator, this system provides tools for creating assessments with images or other attached files. | More than a simple test generator, this system provides tools for creating assessments with multimedia, learning games, and other interactive tools such as polls. Tests can provide immediate feedback with tips for remediation. | 10 |
|---|---|---|---|---|
| Course evaluations | Basic survey tools for capturing student reflections on course, instructor | Anonymous evaluations that can be gathered by the faculty including question pools and templates. | Hierarchical and flexible system for anonymous evaluations at course, department and institutional level for either summative or formative purposes. Includes item pools, templating, announcements, reminders, and tools to easily target different audiences. | 8 |
| Gradebook and student tracking | Moderately functional grade book that is relatively easy to use. Minimal tools for student tracking. | Functional grade book that is easy to use. Grades can be exported to a spreadsheet. Student tracking tools give the instructor some information about student progress. | Highly functional grade book that is easy to use. Grades can be exported to a spreadsheet or student information system. Student tracking tools give the instructor information about what pages the student has viewed and what tasks have been completed. The student can be automatically emailed when their participation is substandard. | 8 |

| Calendar and selective release | Basic calendar. Selective release is possible but may be cumbersome to set up. | Basic calendar with pop-up announcements. Release of course content and assessments can be scheduled for student access with moderate effort. | Collaborative calendar with pop-up announcements. Release of course content and assessments can be easily scheduled for student access. | 8 |
|---|---|---|---|---|
| Collaboration | Allows shared access to files among users and some tools for asynchronous collaboration. | Provides access to shared files and some tools for asynchronous and synchronous collaboration and communication. Limited group functionality. | Provides a campus-wide framework that supports collaborative work such as wiki with version tracking, threaded discussion, instant messaging and chat, whiteboard, web conferencing (audio and video). Enables subgroups to be defined within courses for collaboration. Provides non-course sites to support special project work among small groups. | 8 |
| Learning analytics | Grades and basic statistics are gathered for each learner, and basic usage reports generated. | Grades, basic and fine-grained statistics are gathered for each learner, by course, by department and across the institution. Forensic reports are available for resolving controversies. | Provides in-depth data gathering and reporting on learning outcomes based on configurable rubrics, and allows for longitudinal analysis of cohorts as well as individuals, including eportfolios. | 5 |

| | | | | |
|---|---|---|---|---|
| **Integration with Student Information System** | Integration is possible but will require a high level of product customization. | Tools for integration are available but some tasks will need to be completed manually or in a batch process. | Seamless integration with automatic updating of student and faculty lists and all rosters. Students can be automatically emailed course access information. Student and faculty profiles with pictures and syllabi can be shared between the LMS and the SIS. | 10 |
| **Integration with Campus Authentication** | Ability to batch load users from a campus central identity system. | Ability to batch load users but also to integrate a campus single sign-on system such as CAS. | A real-time connection with a campus central identity system (LDAP, AD, Shibboleth) that avoids the need for batch processes. Integration with campus single sign-on. | 10 |
| **Integration with campus portal** | LMS is accessible through the campus portal but only by linking that requires a separate authentication by the user. | LMS is linked with the portal via single sign-on, but the only level of integration possible is the iFrame. | LMS and portal share single sign-on and select tools can be integrated with the portal via industry-standard integrations (JSR-168 or WSRP). | 5 |
| **Support** | Email support only. | Email support and limited phone support. | 24/7 phone and email support with tracking system to follow the progress of issue resolution. | 8 |

| | | | | |
|---|---|---|---|---|
| **Textbook publisher support** | Some textbook materials but difficult to find, request or install. | Several supported texts with good materials that can be installed with moderate efforts. | Many supported texts, excellent well-organized materials, easily installed and based on industry or community standards (*e.g.,* Common Cartridge) | 10 |
| **Training materials** | Fair printed materials, minimal online training or classroom training sessions available. | Good printed materials, some online training or classroom training sessions available. | Excellent printed materials and many opportunities for online and classroom training sessions. | 8 |
| **Online help resources** | A users' manual is accessible online. | Help files are accessible at each step of a process, and system documentation is accessible online. | Contextually-appropriate help files are accessible from all pages and provide assistance for students, faculty and system administrators as appropriate. Pop-ups or rollovers provide "just-in-time" information for specific actions. | 5 |
| **Speed of system** | Course material access times are adequate on high speed connections but frustrating for dial-up users. | Access times are very good for students on high speed connections and adequate for dial-up users. | The fastest system available with support for streaming media and/or offline companion materials to better serve dial-up users. | 10 |

| Server requirements | LMS only operates on one operating system and requires special configurations of hardware or supporting software. | LMS is available on multiple platforms but does not offer compatibility with an implementer's choice of application server or database. | Server software operates on a wide variety of operating systems (Windows, Linux/Unix, Mac) using commodity hardware and industry-standard web servers. | 8 |
|---|---|---|---|---|
| Scalability | LMS has no problem meeting demands of a small institution on a single server. | LMS supports clustering and the ability for multiple servers to act in unison, but there are few installations supporting over a thousand concurrent users. | LMS clusters well and has been known to support installations well over ten thousand concurrent users. | 10 |
| Browser setup and support | Supports the most popular browsers with end user set up and installation of necessary components. May have a "preferred" browser for proper operation. | Supports most browsers with minimal effort from the user. | Supports all browsers and platforms with no special setup requirements for the user. Is able to render the LMS experience in most browsers with consistency. | 8 |
| **TOTAL POINTS** | 221 out of 270 | | | |

## Plan for Interviewing Subject Matter Experts

The design and development of learning objects require a diverse range of knowledge to complete all the components of the learning object. The content of a learning object will be defined by instructional designers (IDs). They are the ones that are challenged by the uncertainty of lacking enough information about the learning object. Since instructional designers cannot be conversant in all content areas, they will require the support of the Subject Matter Experts (SMEs) to assist with defining the scope and accuracy of the unfamiliar content (Keppel, 2001).

Instructional designers can satisfy their lack of knowledge in a specific content area by interacting with SMEs to approach unfamiliar materials. The interaction with SMEs provides IDs with different options to close the existing knowledge gap. At the same time, the interaction with SME might be complicated because SMEs are busy individuals. Thus, IDs need to optimize the time spent with them when working together to obtain enough quantity and quality of information possible for the design of the learning objects (Keppel, 2001). The Content Production Process (CPP) offers a variety of theories, constructs, and methods that facilitate identifying information to be used by IDs when interacting with SMEs. Some of these theories are schema theory (Gordon & Rennie, 1987), script theory (Schank & Abelson, 1977), consultation practices (Rutt, 1985), knowledge acquisition strategies in constructing expert systems (Cohen, 1990), ethnographic and teach-back interviewing strategies (Pask, 1975), and knowledge mapping (Lambiotte et al., 1989).

Both IDs and SMEs play an essential role in the instructional design process. On one side, IDs apply instructional design principles to a full extent of content areas. The IDs job starts with analyzing goals, needs, and learner characteristics to understand the instructional problem. Despite having no content proficiency (Nelson et al., 1988), IDs role is to select, sequence, synthesize, and summarize the content for professional purposes. They should have the ability to extract and assimilate block of information to put it into a logical framework as defined by the SME. The latter have integrated content knowledge drawn from many years of experience. In other words, IDs help in the interaction with the SME to "formulate a working content structure which the information and skills to be taught can be formed into a sequence and hierarchy" (Wallington, 1981, p.30).

On the other side, SMEs, turn out to be authorities on a domain of knowledge from who the ID attempts to elicit structure, more highly organized, and well-integrated experience (Keppel, 2001). SMEs provide subject-related information and guidance that is required to finish the project. IDs may review a developmental subject matter or task analyses, suggested instructional strategy, or drafts of the actual instruction (Rodriguez et al., 1991) to assist the designers' conceptualization by clarifying and verifying the content (Keppel, 2001). The objective of this paper is to develop an interview content for SMEs to identify perceptions and expectations about technology updates and integration to their courses.

## Instructional Designers and Subject Matter Experts: Interview Process

The success of the outcome obtained from interviewing SMEs depends on the level of a relationship created between IDs and SMEs. A healthy and positive relationship with the SME should be marked by open and honest communication, which will help the ID in developing productive efforts in the design process. The relationship between an ID and SME should work as a parentship through which the process of interview flows smoothly. IDs should value the SMEs contribution and avoid treating them as a passive resource (Karaolis, 2019). Thus, when IDs get together through an interview process, they should define clear expectations and roles of both parties. They can also welcome SMEs' feedback, acknowledging their efforts, and setting realistic milestones and goals (Pappas, 2018) to make SMEs aware of how important they are for the design process. The interview process between IDs and SMEs calls for five stages (Rodriguez et al., 1991). These stages are (1) preparing for the interview, (2) starting the discussion, (3) conducting the interview, (4) concluding the interview, and (5) analyzing the results.

## Preparing for the Interview

Both IDs and SMEs should be prepared for the interview process. Both expect from each other to be ready for the information exchange about the topic they will dig in and share for the instructional design purposes. The IDs should review, previous the interview, the content terminology by reviewing materials related to the topic such as previous needs assessments, specialized glossaries, and training materials to be prepared for structuring preliminary interview questions. Also, IDs should hold a brief introductory meeting with the expert to explain the significance of the project (Zemke & Kramlinger, 1982).

The content of the interview should hold questions that help discover in-depth knowledge related to the topic discussed by IDs and SMEs. It is recommendable open-ended questions beginning with words such as "What," or "How," which elicit more information and impel more commitment from the SME to help create a conceptual scaffold and attach content extracted in the subsequent interactions with them by the IDs (Keppler, 2001). Open-ended questions allow good communications between the parties (Rodriguez et al., 1991). Questions allow conducting a content analysis to determine the most appropriate methods and media to deliver the content to learners by type (domain) and level (sequence) of the content (Chyung & Trenas, 2009). Moreover, the identification of content level identifies how learners will remember or use skills and knowledge acquired through the learning process.

Cognitive task analysis facilitates SMEs to describe the knowledge that experts use in designing and developing instructional materials and prevent experts from unintentionally misrepresenting the conceptual understanding on which they base their performance (Razak & Palanisamy, 2013). Thus, the questions of the interview should help identify levels of cognition that will define learning objectives to be achieved by subjects when learning how to integrate technology. Merril (1992) and Bloom's Taxonomy (n.d.) proposed a method of classifying cognitive levels. The model offered by Merril has two levels of cognition:

Remember and Use. On the other hand, Bloom Taxonomy (n.d.) identified six degrees, ranging from knowledge to evaluation.

Questions for the interview should follow a sequence from general to specific areas of concern. In that way, questions can be clustered topically. In other words, questions grouped around an aspect of the subject will deepen into the knowledge from different angles and interpretations. Cram (1981) suggested to IDs to question SMEs by addressing situations where individuals are doing a task and ask SMEs "put in the learners' shoes" to stimulate SMEs to tell what they think about doing the tasks.

## Interview Content

To determine SME knowledge level about technology applied to education (innovative technologies, instructional strategies, and methods of support they need most), and perceptions about technology adoption, I will interview SMEs for an innovative technology plan. The content of the interview is shown in the next section. The questionnaire content has been adapted from the SoC Questionnaire (Hall et al. 1977), and Survey of Technology Use in the College of Education (Jacobsen, 1998).

## SEMs Interview Questionnaire for innovative technology integration

### Learning about Technology

This section intents to identify the reasons for learning about technology.

- Why do you consider that learning about technology is important?
- Tell me, why is it essential to update innovative technology tools and applications for learning?

- Explain what the reasons for not applying technology as requested by the institutional leaders are?
- What are you thinking about student technology acceptance attitudes?

## Attitudes toward innovative technology adoption and implementation

This section intents to know what are the concerns that SEMs have about adopting technology use.

- What are the activities performed during a typical day in the institution? What are the activities that require the use of technology?
- What do you think about technology in education?
- What are the resources available at the institution to adopt innovative technologies?
- What is your self-perception about developing skills in technology use for learning purposes?
- What would be your concerns about not having enough time to teach and learn about technology innovations?
- What is your take on working with other teachers and external individuals in integrating technology in education?
- What is your opinion about financial resources available to develop technology integration here at Modern Valley School?
- Have you envisioned how your teaching and student evaluation can change by implementing technology in your courses?

## Patterns of Technology use

In this section intents to gather information about individual technology use patterns

*Indicate the extent to which you used the listed learning approaches in teaching.*

1 = Not used, 2 = rarely used, 3 = Sometimes used, 4 = Frequently used, 5 = Heavily used

| Learning approaches | 1 | 2 | 3 | 4 | 5 |
|---|---|---|---|---|---|
| Learning by experts | | | | | |
| Learning with others | | | | | |
| Learning through making | | | | | |
| Learning through exploring | | | | | |
| Learning through inquiry | | | | | |
| Learning by experts | | | | | |
| Learning with others | | | | | |

*Indicate the extent to which you used the listed tools, strategies/methods in teaching.*

1 = Not used, 2 = rarely used, 3 = Sometimes used, 4 = Frequently used, 5 = Heavily used

| | 1 | 2 | 3 | 4 | 5 |
|---|---|---|---|---|---|
| Rich Media Capture Technology, | | | | | |
| Interactive whiteboard | | | | | |
| Virtual learning environment | | | | | |
| E-Assessment to support assessing learning interactions | | | | | |
| Online social tools to support collaborative learning interactions | | | | | |
| Ludic interactions: Massive multiplayer online gaming | | | | | |
| Mobile technologies: smartphones, tablets | | | | | |
| Satellite-transmitted instruction | | | | | |

*Ernesto Gonzalez*

| | | | | | |
|---|---|---|---|---|---|
| Constructivist learning tools: Instant messaging, blogs, wikis, and podcasts | | | | | |
| Narrative in multimedia learning | | | | | |
| Infographic | | | | | |
| Virtual filed trips | | | | | |
| Videos for mini-lessons | | | | | |

*Indicate the extent to which you used the listed tools, strategies/methods in teaching.*

1 = Not used, 2 = rarely used, 3 = Sometimes used, 4 = Frequently used, 5 = Heavily used

| | 1 | 2 | 3 | 4 | 5 |
|---|---|---|---|---|---|
| Active learning | | | | | |
| Student response systems | | | | | |
| Formative assessments | | | | | |
| Summative assessments | | | | | |
| E-portfolio | | | | | |
| Feedback/Self check | | | | | |
| Brainstorming | | | | | |
| Collaborative learning | | | | | |
| Discussions | | | | | |
| Peer learning | | | | | |
| Social media/learning communities | | | | | |
| Case studies | | | | | |
| Online Concept mapping | | | | | |
| Multimedia instruction | | | | | |
| Digital storytelling | | | | | |
| Experiential learning | | | | | |
| Independent study | | | | | |
| Online sign-ups | | | | | |
| Simulation games | | | | | |

## Participant Information

This section intents to obtain information about teachers who participate in the interview.

- In which academic department do you hold your appointment?
- How many years have you been a teacher?
- Have you received formal training concerning innovation technology?
- How do you consider yourself?

Non-user ____ Novice____ Intermediate____ Old hand____ Past user____

## Conclusions

Institutional educations are being challenged by new technologies that can enhance student learning. Since the internet has changed notions of place, time, and space, new methods of teaching and learning, based on an understanding of cognition and virtual environment, can enable student learning. Several emerging technologies will have a significant impact on learning, teaching, and creative inquiry in education, particularly in the development of continuing pedagogies and learning strategies (Briggs, 2017).

Adaptive learning technologies use machine-driven data to measure student progress, adapting level, and type, of course, content to student's ability to accelerate student performance with the instructor and automated interventions. For instance, the University of Wollongong, Australia, uses Social Networks Adapting Pedagogical Practice Initiative software to track the dynamics of group discussions. Mobile learning allows for deeper and more connected student learning by facilitating the exploration of a new subject at the student's pace. Kent State University, USA, is implementing SpedApps that aims to develop a catalog of existing apps for special education. Moreover, the Internet of Things that consists of objects endowed through processors or hidden sensors capable of transmitting information across networks. It can inform the direction of the content delivery to provide students with hands-on experiences designing and building IoT devices by creating partnerships with industry. The University of Wisconsin-Madison, USA, has the Internet of Things System Research Center as a hub for industry-university collaboration centered on learning and research.

The other three educational technologies currently used by educational institutions are the Next Generation LMS, Artificial Intelligence, and Natural User Interfaces. Next Generation Digital Learning Environment (NGDLE). The University of Mary Washington, USA, and its Division of Teaching and Learning Technologies has developed "Domain of One's Own, which enables faculty, staff, and students to register their domain name and associate it with a university webspace and course activities. The other two institutions, Salt Lake City Community College and Johns Hopkins University, USA, are implementing MyOpenMath and Osmosis to make more affordable course materials to the students.

Artificial intelligence allows studying data from student learning through machine learning software to help interpret data for student retention purposes. This is the case of the University of Michigan, USA, that is implementing an Artificial Intelligence ab. Finally, the Natural User Interfaces technology which enables users to engage in virtual activities with movements similar to the ones we use in real-world and understand gestures and facial expressions to interpret interactive behaviors (Briggs, 2017).

Some of these technologies mentioned above can support the plan considered for Modern Valley School. The needs assessment performed in this case study yielded an imminent need for an upgrade in technology along with other aspects related to school organizational structure and policies about technology diffusion and integration. Teachers need to know what is emerging in technology applications for student learning. These upcoming trends will update teachers and allow them to think about how to use some of them in their subject matter, for instance, in math classes and human development courses.

# Section IV

Instructional design:
Importance, professional
outlook, and value

# IDT Jobs Today:
# What is Important to the Field?

The field of instructional design and technology (IDT) is continually changing. The ever-changing economic environment and the emergence of job opportunities make instructional design content dynamic and challenging (Reiser & Dempsey, 2018). Many instructional design jobs are looking for professionals in the field to satisfy the need for learning and development (Indeed, n.d.). This paper discusses the IDT field's challenges to cover the gaps between current IDT skills and what is being requested for employment. The paper presents different current job postings related to IDT in the business field and the companies demanding IDT professionals. Moreover, it mentions various types of position titles, the skills necessary to perform these jobs, and the types of work performed by IDTs in the business field. Finally, there is a reflection about the challenges the IDT field must face to satisfy the increasing demand for employee training in businesses.

## IDT Job Postings, Position Titles,
## Skills, and Types of IDT Work

Current job postings related to IDT in the business field in 2021. These job postings refer to companies belonging to the following subjects:

- Cable services (Comcast),
- Computer (Apple),
- Information technology services industry (Atrium Solutions, LLC.; General Dynamics Information Technology, LLC., NSW Nokia Software, Inc.).

- Human resources consulting services (Expert Technical Solutions, LLC.),
- Technical solution for logistic services (Premier Solutions Hi, LLC.),
- Analytical development skills services (Intrepid Minds, LLC.),
- Virtual, mixed, augmented, and desktop virtual products, and content development tools (Mass Virtual, Inc.),
- Cybersecurity technology services (CrowdStrike Holdings, Inc.),
- Business value creation services (Coupa, Inc.),
- Delivering quality professionals and technical services (Edgesource Corporation, Inc.),
- Investment services (Booz Allen Hamilton, Inc.).

There are different types of position titles and the skills required to perform these jobs. Some position titles are:

- Director of design and development.
- Mentor in instructional design.
- IT training specialist
- Marketing technology trainer/instructional designer (combine-role)
- Instructional designer/LMS administrator
- eLearning content development
- Training instructional designer
- eLearning developer
- Associate curriculum developer
- Instructional designer (Lever designer)
- Curriculum developer
- Instructional designer/content developer
- Instructional designer/technical specialist for programming courses
- Instructional system designer and developer

The skills required by these job positions are described as follows:

- Experience as an instructional designer: Knowledge of LMS, design courses, instructional strategies. Current adult learning theory and its application in corporate learning. Also, planning, designing, developing, testing, and implementing self-directed interactive training.
- Ability to create content for multicultural adult audiences
- Working knowledge of multiple learning creation tools, Google Suits, PowerPoint, project management applications.
- Analytical skills to conduct needs analysis.
- Three or more years of classroom teaching experience.
- Knowledge of current research in teaching and learning.
- Excellent verbal and written communications, editing, critical reasoning, interpersonal, communicate complex technical information, and capable of converting information into easily understandable learning content.
- Leading virtual teams.
- Ability to work independently.
- Ability to translate technical information to non-technical users.
- Training in specific training methodologies such as Prosci, and Sprinklr for training programs.
- Ability to adapt to a continually changing business and work environment and manage multiple priorities.
- Ability in agile software development processes.
- Strong special and layout skills.
- Show exciting, passionate, proactive, and self-motivated attitudes
- Experience in some domains depend on the field, e.g., incident response, computer forensic analysis, network forensic analysis.

- Capable of completing tasks on time without supervision and foster positive work environment and attitude. Also, prioritization and organizational skills.

In the business field, instructional designers perform different types of work. The following examples of tasks, duties, and responsibilities show varied job content instructional designers perform based on the skills required for these tasks.

- Develop multimedia and modality strategies.
- Ensure a quality user experience establishing standards to increase productivity and quality.
- Collaborate across the learning organization to build the best products for learners.
- Use a data-driven approach to analyze employee learning needs and collaborate with business subject matter experts and learners to assess, design, and develop standard learning solutions to support successful training execution.
- Active participation in teams.
- Organizing, promoting, courses, and delivering programs of learning activities.
- Preparing teaching materials based on instructional design principles and quality standards.
- Checking and assessing students' work and giving feedback.
- Make use of new technology, and spending contact time with learners or an individual or group basis.
- Assist in the management, maintenance, and troubleshooting of the training learning technology, data, and associated devices.
- Accountable for training delivery logistics, including planning, scheduling, coordinating resources, and maintaining training records.

- Develops, builds, and maintain all elements related to LMS functionality.
- Create templates as design architecture.

## Instructional Design and Technology. Challenges and Gaps

IDT in the business field must focus on current challenges identified by learning and development leaders of corporations to design instructional strategies capable of overcoming these challenges to satisfy the business community's learning needs. The business field is forced to continue attracting and retaining top talent, keeping employees engaged in their work and community, and providing learning opportunities to improve, reskill, and advance careers (DGHC, 2019). Also, modern employees are creative, entrepreneurial, and aspirational, and they are looking for an organization to help them build the skills needed to elevate their careers. Moreover, there is an increased emphasis on the organizational culture development toward enriching aspirational values. Based on these facts, instructional designers in the business field must design training programs to match employees' mental mindset with what they need to adapt to succeed in a modern workplace (Hart, 2020), and should emphasize how to understand employees' career development aspirations better to groom as potential managers (Dunn, 2019).

Instructional designers are also challenged by the current learning and development trends that emerge from businesses and organizations' practices. Thus, higher skills in developing effective LMS to fit employees' motivation and dedication to connect and learn quickly as the adaptive approach suggests, are highly needed (Dickens, 2018).

Based on the qualifications, skills, and type of work of instructional designers required by businesses and organizations found on the web search conducted in this study, it was identified some gaps between what is needed for employment and the challenges and trends in the future of corporate training. Most of the job postings content will require an update to stay synchrony with the future corporate training formats. IDT professionals in the business field must show high skills in designing training programs capable of occurs seamlessly in the flow of work to make sense of how employees live out in the world. For example, compartmentalized training sessions (microlearning) that combine morning learning sessions with afternoon current job functions as a flexible learning format. Employees received instruction with easily-digested pieces of information to be applied to a task or project being performed (Bleich, 2019).

## Conclusions

IDT professionals must develop skills in moving design courses to designing authentic experiences because real-time-3D technologies are already being used by people to learn in real-time (Dickens, 2018). IDT professionals will also need to know emerging design approaches to facilitate design instruction aligned with the way people live and work. For example, IDT professionals must know how to use the agile design thinking approach to use test-driven design methods. Agile design thinking is an approach to content development focused on speed, flexibility, and collaboration (Allego, 2013). Its consideration for designing training allows facilitating knowledge acquisition in business and organizations where employees must learn and work fast to satisfy market demands.

# Valued IDT Skills for Employers

Future instructional designers must always upgrade a basic understanding of learning theories and apply learning best practices to technology tools to create meaningful content for the end-user. The permanent effort for being up to date in designing instruction will make a robust professional profile that will facilitate obtaining a stable career in this field (Taylor, 2017). This paper discusses four instructional design and technology skills valuable for employers. This work posits some requirements that employers are requesting from instructional designers, the importance of the skills to the field, the current level of experience or proficiency the author shows with each skill, and some actions to increase the instructional design [capabilities].

The central instructional design and technology skills required by different IDT job positions demand experience as an instructional designer, current adult learning theory, and corporate learning application from analyzing various job postings from other job market offerings. Moreover, instructional designers must show planning and the implementation of self-directed interactive training and experience working knowledge with technology-based learning creation tools. Also, candidates must display analytical skills, excellent verbal and written communications, critical reasoning, and communicate complex technical information.

Additionally, interested candidates must have experience leading teams, working independently, adapting to changing business environments, completing tasks on time without supervision, and showing organizational skills (Gonzalez, 2020). From the vast number of instructional design and technology skills currently required by employers, there are four that deserve special attention without minimizing the rest of the skills. These skills are knowledge about current adult learning theory and its application in corporate learning, analytical skills, technology usage skills, and managerial skills.

## Current Adult Learning Theory. Application in Corporate Learning Skills

Adult learning theory offers knowledge about how adults learn through relevant material, the need to connect with experience, and the motivation to improve themselves. Instructional designers and technology candidates need to know about transformative, self-directed, experiential, and andragogy learning approaches because adults learn in different ways (Irish, 2019). Employers require this skill because they employ adult individuals with varied educational, demographics, and attitudinal backgrounds. Thus, instructional designers must know how to blend these approaches to develop a robust learning strategy to benefit learners and reinforce employees' knowledge acquisition and skills development to be more proactive, productive, and better social individuals.

In this regard, the instructional designer (author) of this paper has learned about learning theories that support the foundation as an instructional designer. Learning theories (behaviorism, cognitivism, and constructivism) offer different perspectives on how individuals learn (Stevens-Fulbrook, 2019). A great deal of knowledge and applications to corporate and classroom settings have yet to learn. Transformative learning implies changing individuals somehow through experiences, which requires spending time with adults and focusing on activities that challenge their assumptions and explore other points of view (Irish, 2019). Based on it, the paper's author has designed some lesson plans using a constructivist perspective supported by specific adult learning theories such as experiential learning, andragogy, and self-directed learning. Even though he has used some of the approaches mentioned above, he is aware that it has yet to improve. He must pay special attention to the transformative learning theory to use for adults.

## Instructional Design and Technology Analytical Skills

Analytical skills are the ones required to solve problems. These skills allow detecting patterns, observing, brainstorming, interpreting data, integrating new information with theory, and making decisions based on multiple factors and options. Instructional designers must describe goals and objectives, conduct formative evaluations, and revise instruction based upon data collected for improvement purposes. Also, analytical skills are necessary for assessing needs (performance), job tasks analysis, and instructional analysis (Reiser & Dempsey, 2018).

Employers look for instructional designers to investigate different problems and find the solution in a timely, efficient, and effective way to those problems that may not provide apparent solutions because these problems imply handling several variables. Employers are looking for analytical communication skills, analytical information processing for creativity purposes, critical thinking to evaluate information, and then deciding on designing based on findings (Doyle, 2020).

As an instructional design and technology professional, the instructional designer that this paper refers has developed analytical skills throughout his career. His engineering, teaching, and researching experience have equipped him with the analytical skills to solve problems. Besides, his studies in instructional design and experience have enriched these skills. Still, it is not enough. The fact of facing new learning theory application in the workplace environment, and the never-ending technological challenges, put him on the edge of solving problems skills. Therefore, he considers that his current analytical skills demand more profound development because of the highly complex world he lives in.

*Ernesto Gonzalez*

## Instructional Design and Technology (Media) Usage Skills

Media production skills are essential for instructional designers. Media is incorporated every day to deliver instruction even in the workplace environment. Instructional designers must know about audiovisual material for instructional purposes. They must learn to harness various media technologies, including cameras, digital movie cameras, audio recording equipment, learn how to create images, sounds, artifacts, and various computational aspects is crucial to support instruction based on these elements.

Since the growth of the internet over the last decade has brought an increment of jobs available for writers, illustrators, and video producers within the industry, employers are looking for instructional designers with a strong set of media production skills, especially in areas of e-learning and multimedia production (Sugar et al., 2012). Candidates for instructional design and technology positions to work for organizations must know how to integrate technology into training employees' learning theories. Thus, applying media production skills and learning theory is essential.

His current level of knowledge about media usage for instruction purposes is still incipient. Even though he has learned many different media tools to incorporate into his instruction; his skills in producing quality videos, putting voice into presentations, and using animations to facilitate instruction flow will require effort and dedication.

## Instructional Design and Technology Managerial Skills

As an instructional designer with experience and graduate from an instructional design degree program (undergraduate or graduate), the probabilities of performing managerial skills in management positions is highly probable and possible. Many graduates from instructional design programs express the desire to engage in administrative roles. The ability to influence employees within an organizational unit (Instructional

226

design department) comes with specific traits that facilitate managing people. So, instructional designers should have a shared vision, good communication, integrity, enthusiasm, empathy, competence, the ability to delegate, composure under pressure, team building, problem-solving skills, e-learning initiatives, and learning solutions skills (Zippia, n.d.). These skills are needed to perform as assistant project managers, working with subject matter experts, clients, and onsite-virtual-productive project teams (Reiser & Dempsey, 2018).

The instructional designer this paper refers currently holds a leadership position as department chair at a university and ten years of performing in this job position. This experience has allowed him to combine management functions as administrator for academic programs and as an instructional designer. When engaging in new program design or current program upgrades, both academic administrator and instructional designer manager roles go handy. Still, some managerial skills when working with faculty (subject matter experts) deserve more attention. For instance, he must improve his planning and reviewer coordination skills to design and implement design and technology projects, and time management skills for knowledge acquisition in multimedia applications to set achievable goals based on the designing demands.

## Conclusions

Based on the current instructional design and technology job market analysis, it is conclusive that jobs in the field require vast individual, technical, and managerial skills to succeed as an instructional design professional. Instructional design is getting more complicated because it requires more in-depth knowledge and experience in using technology-based instruction tools. The fact that the instructional design and technology field demands highly prepared professionals to work for organizations. The disparity between instructional design in education and the role of instructional design in organizations (businesses) is shortened in the extent to which technology is more and more available for all (educational institutions and companies). Thus, job opportunities in business and industry are increasing over time.

# What is Current in the Instructional Design Field?

The impact of uncertainty, climate change, political struggles, and the shaky-economic situation we are amid make learners feel the need of acquiring and practicing new knowledge. Thus, instructional designers recognize the need to attract, retain, motivate, engage, and upskill learners in educational settings and a tight labor market. Instructional design professionals desire to achieve a high level of success in designing instructional aids capable of satisfying flexible and open ideas required by different contexts. To satisfy learners, instructional designers seek the best tools possible for the job by reading and studying scientific materials and attending association conferences to update current technology usage advances for designing instruction (Hart, 2020).

This paper has two purposes. First, it discusses my philosophy about current best practices in instructional design after reviewing and analyzing recent reports and articles presented at association conferences and published in scientific journals. It is possible to find material dedicated to advances in instructional design in different fields. Second, this paper also discusses some trends and popular topics in technology implemented in instructional design, as well as the author's thoughts about the instructional design field's future.

## Conferences and Scientific Resources as a Pipeline for Instructional Design and Practices

Instructional design and its application to different fields (Business & Industry, Military organizations, Health Care, K-12, and Higher Education) respond to growing needs for producing knowledge to improve learning quality and employee on-the-job performance to solve organizational problems. As a result, instructional designers focus more than merely creating instruction and designing thinking approaches (Reiser & Dempsey, 2018). There are different avenues through which instructional designers can update their knowledge about the field. Let us say, visiting an eLearning conference is a must for instructional designers today, which provides the opportunity to obtain professional development, network with other eLearning professionals, and get the latest insights from industry leaders.

Instructional designers can attend conferences around the world that provide insightful knowledge about current learning practices through technology, for example, Learning futures and technologies, CIPD Festival of Work (London, England), ATD International Conference and Expo (Denver, U.S.), Pulse 2020 (California, U.S.). Moreover, Training Industry Conference and Expo (North Carolina, U.S.), The Higher Education Technology Agenda Conference (Wollongong, Australia), and World of Learning (Nevada, U.S.) (Lawless, 2019). Moreover, there are other professional associations through which instructional designers can be updated. These associations are the Association for Educational Communications and Technology (AECT), Association for Talent Development (ATD), Association for the Advancement of Computing in Education (AACE), and E-Learning Network (ELN) (Reiser & Dempsey, 2018).

The topics presented at these conferences feed us about latest trends, best practices, and new solutions for developing talent in employees (ATD International Conference, 2019); new experiences related to blended learning (Blended Learning in the Liberal Arts Conference, 2019); pedagogically effective ways to harness new technologies in the courses (Teaching Professor Technology Conference, 2019); engaging e-learning in the workplace through demonstrations, mini-seminars, case studies, interviews, debates and panel discussions (ICELW, 2019).

There are also other sources of knowledge available for instructional designers. For instance, papers from scientific journals, which allow learning from research results, applications to different contexts, and current trends. Some of these journals are not limited to American Educational Research Journal, Educational Researcher, and Review of Educational Research (Reiser & Dempsey, 2018), or recent papers published in scientific journals about Adaptive learning.

## Trends in Technology Supporting Instructional Design Trends

Technology has come to stay forever in the field of education and professional development. The advancements of technology to support learning make teaching and learning easier, digestible, fun, and useful. A review of the topics covered in conferences and scientific journals show considerable interest in the future of the Web, the standardization of its associated technologies, and the impact of technology not only on learners but on society and culture as well (The Web Conference, 2018). Some other topics focus on how to create and implement micro-learning videos for learning (CIPD, 2019); and applications of multimedia, hypermedia and telecommunications/distance education -human-computer interaction and infrastructure (EduLearn, 2020). It also offers information about e-Learning accessibility (EA), innovative learning software, and computer supported collaborative learning. Moreover, there are other technology-supported topics such as artificial intelligence in education, intelligent tutoring system, and adaptive learning, mobile technologies enhanced learning (Sambiran & Soenato, 2019), data mining, text mining, web mining in education, game and toy enhanced learning, and social computing in e-learning (LTLE, 2018).

## A Reflection on Instructional Design Best Practices

The topics mentioned in the previous section show an ample view of how online learning is becoming more accessible by implementing new pedagogical practices supported by information technology. After reading conferences abstracts and current journal papers, and the author reflects on how learning pedagogy can fit learners' learning needs supported by ever-never-ending technology breakthroughs. One of the current trends instructional designers must pay attention to is the adaptive learning approach that allows personalizing learning experience. Instructional designers must understand what individual students already know and what they need to learn, then modifying instruction to meet those diverse needs efficiently is a mandate. Adaptive learning customizes objective-driven content and assessment to create a personalized learning path for each learner according to their knowledge, skills, and learning needs (Cavanagh et al., 2020). Indeed, adapting learning is an emerging and promising technology to promote access and quality in higher education and business field. It must include dynamic and creative embedded assessments to scaffold and prove learner's mastery on content in specific course contexts (Association of Public & Land-grant Universities, n.d.).

The author also found that flipped learning is very used nowadays. Flipped learning with an emphasis on interaction generates improvements in the teaching and learning processes of learners. This innovative methodological tool improves learners' motivation within the learning process, develops a significant interrelation between a group of learners, learners autonomy in solving problems, and creating a strong relationship with instructors under a collaborative learning environment (Lopez Nunez et al., 2020). By the way, the importance of instructor-learner and learner-learner communication and collaboration, active learning techniques to engage learners are paramount. The online instruction must be energetic, organized, and communicative with learners and have a consistent presence in the online classroom to provide an active and quality learning experience (Tanis, 2020).

## Conclusions

Based on the review and analysis of recent conference abstracts and papers from scientific journals, some current trends are worth highlighting. First, adaptive learning is getting more and more attention and implementation. The advancement of information technology and its application to education allows personalizing knowledge acquisition and skills development. Second, the author observed that the terminology used for technology applications uses technical terms, such as intelligent tutoring, text mining, and web mining in education. Third, every year, we can find more information technology applications in education, which he would name as "penetrating information technology effect" in teaching and learning. Fourth, it is noticeable how technology applications are tailored to diverse learners, which is positive as an adaptation to specific learning needs. Finally, he also observed a short-time-learning-pace trend by learners. It means that technology's accessibility and usage supported by stimulating tools such as video and audio allow learners to acquire knowledge faster because it is more stimulating and engaging. In summary, the applications of technology to learning and its pedagogy impact tremendously on student engagement. Thus, learners' engagement for learners' success is critical.

# Section V

## Professional development in instructional design field

# Analysis of Professional Development Policies

The presence of internal and external educational forces impacts professional development (PD). Forces such as problems in educational system, political development, cultural development, institutional resource shortage and allocation, and institutional culture always influences the efficiency and effectiveness of the PD in educational institutions. It is necessary for educational institutions and students to keep evaluating PD policies and modify them when required. Updating policies demands from educational stakeholders knowing how to analyze, develop, implement, evaluate, and disseminate strategies to support policies creation and review processes.

Given the critical role of PD in all educational institutions, this paper aims to provide a policy review framework based on previous research results and theory about PD definition, types, measurement, policy analysis, development, implementation, and evaluation and review. It will help create and modify educational policies in general, more precisely PD policy at university level, by defining PD policy analysis and goal, developing PD policy, rules, and procedures with all stakeholders, and implementing the policy throughout the institution. First, the paper offers a policy review framework and provides in-depth content related to different approaches for analyzing educational policies, as well as policy development, implementation, and evaluation and review. Second, it describes the current situation about performing the PD policy at the university, which will help university stakeholders count with a deeper understanding of policy creation, analysis, and modification for Faculty development improvements.

## Regulatory context of PD in the State of Florida, U.S.

Section 1012.98, Florida Statute, School Community Professional Development Act, states that all educational entities as part of the Florida state educational system are called to contribute to educators' professional development (FLDOE, 2019). These institutions have the capability of maintaining professional learning systems (FLDOE, 2019) and gathering enough information from different informational sources and research institutions to provide educators, at all educational levels, with in-depth, up-to-date knowledge. The updated knowledge acquired by educators will impact positively on the ultimate member of the educational chain, which are students.

However, approximately $3.0 billion in federal funding under Title II, Part A, goes to the professional development of educators in different educational institutions. There is little evidence that these expenditures have raised the educator teaching effectiveness (USDOE, 2019). Therefore, the professional development funding from federal and state levels continues, but the actual impact and implementation of the policy on educators continue being uncertain.

## Professional Development, Definition, Types, and Measurement

PD is the learning activities through which faculty develop their teaching and pedagogic abilities to ensure efficient and effective competences of continuing instruction (Jaiswal, 2017). In an educational setting, students learn more when faculty have a high preparation level provided by any PD format.

PD also prepares educators through local, national, or international conferences, institution courses, community practices (Little, 1987, 1993), as well as embedded PD practices such as co-teaching, mentoring, reflections on specific lessons (Schifter and Fosnot, 1993), educator study group (Greenleaf, et, al., 2001), curriculum materials (Remillard,

2005), and designing or choosing new curricula or textbooks, including assisting instructors with opportunities (Guskey, 2000). In the way knowledge and educational practices evolve, varied PD activities will emerge to satisfy faculty which reveal the dynamic nature of the PD (Desimone, 2009).

PD permits achieving positive impacts on instructors, students, and institutions when (1) it is seen by instructors to be relevant to their needs; (2) it allows fostering collaboration and the sharing experience among instructors; (3) Inquiry, reflection, and discussions are the nucleon of professional learning process; also, (4) student learning triggers motivation for professional learning, among others (Borg, 2015). Commonly, each educational institution establishes its PD policies, rules, and procedures to support high-quality teaching and learning processes. Thus, PD must be one of the top activities at any educational institution.

Some research supports that the central point on measuring PD is to focus measurement on critical factors of the activities and make it more useful for instructor learning and developing practice than focusing on the type of activity (Desimone, et al., 2002).

## Variety of Educational Policies

An acceptable policy allows interpretation from unambiguous assortment of indicators. It uses a particular terminology and should continue to be reliable with other institutional policies (Clemmer, 1991), to provide real direction to the institution. There are different kinds of educational policies. They are consequential policies, de-facto policies, delegated policies, and formal policies. Consequential policies are defined at any specific educational entity. They are defined due to external factors like state, district, federal legislative actions, which impose control and requirements affecting the institutional policies. De Facto policies are actions perceived by the employees as about them and assumed by them as a policy. These policies are not usually written and seem like informal or unofficial policies, but over time, these policies become legitimate ones (Clemmer, 1991).

The following type of policy is delegated policies. Delegated policies emerge when the staff of administrative do not know how to perform delegated tasks, and the responsibility is relegated to a superior. Finally, formal policies are legitimate and consciously developed by the institution. These policies follow the policy formulation stage, public involvement, request administrative recommendations, and are analyzed by all stakeholders before approval and adoption (Clemmer, 1991).

Reviewing educational policies implies an effort fraught with different systemic elements. These elements are policy values and principles, policy analysis, policy development, policy implementation, policy evaluation, and policy dissemination. But the assessment is the critical element. Policy evaluation is a process of defining how effective and efficient the policy is to determine if it has achieved its goal. Therefore, the evaluation process reveals whether the analysis, development, implementation, dissemination, goal achievement, and effectiveness of the policy (in terms of pertinent, timely, functionality, and practicability) have been adequately managed (Downey, 1988).

All educational policy should have one or more goals to achieve. Stakeholders should participate in setting policy goals, allocating resources to meet them, and structuring internal operations to support the goal achievement and policy implementation. Likewise, parties involved in the policy examine why certain things are happening, how policy components fit together, and how other educational actors perceive the policy implementation. In other words, they check how the policy performance is developed rather than the policy itself (Delaney, 2015). Pertinent and timely refer to that only policy on relevant topics deserve development and should respond to actual needs. A policy is functional when it makes possible what needs to be done. Also, it is practicable when the policy is adopted only when it can be implemented; otherwise, the policy should not be defined.

The policy evaluation is especially critical with already established policies or new ones, or in cases where enforcement is visibly difficult (Clemmer, 1991). The results obtained from the evaluation will show us whether the policy needs modifications or a total redefinition. The following section addresses different approaches to policy analysis, development, implementation, and evaluation.

## PD Policy Analysis Framework Approaches

*Policy analysis* definitions are available in the literature; however, it can be defined as the study of what government and institutions do, why and with what effects, by recognizing that educational institutions at all levels of the educational system are part of the public and private system. There are several educational policy analysis approaches.

1. The *Heuristic approach* is a highly simplified approach to a complex set of interrelationships. It helps a stakeholder think systematically about all the factors that affect the policy. It acknowledges the importance of looking at the content of the policy (structural, situational, international, and cultural factors), the processes of policy making (problem identification and issue recognition, policy formulation, evaluation, and implementation), and the content of the policy (system level policy, resource allocation policy, and Teaching and Learning policies) (Din Jie, 2016). PD policy fits into the policy content component, specifically in the teaching and learning factor.

2. *The policy-making theory* refers to the use of an existing theory body formulated by various federal, state, local, and organizational policies to provide, for example, professional development services across the continuum of teaching and the advance of several policy agendas in the profession. The legislative body creates professional development policies

in terms of laws, acts, and status. It makes governmental administrative agencies to develop policies in terms of regulations, rules, or codes holding law enforcement (Sheldon, 2016). These agencies may generate rules based on the interpretation of the statue and lead to conform, e.g., professional development rules. There are competitive, regulatory policies related to ensuring the proper functioning of markets. And, social regulatory policies, which lead to address transparency and any adverse consequences of producing professional development service delivery (Sabatier & Weible, 2014).

3.  *Pluralistic-incrementally perspective and rational-democratic perspective.* These two perspectives (Carley, 1980), mostly focused on policy analysis at a macro level and in conceptual terms, are the foundation for the Four frames perspective (Cheong a& Ming, 1995). It states that policy analysis can be made through four frames. They are (1) an analysis of the background, and it underlines principles of the studied subject, (2) analysis of the policy formulation process, (3) analysis of educational policy implementation and (4) analysis of educational policy effect.

4.  *Munger Policy analysis approach.* This framework establishes a sequence of five steps to analyze policy: (1) analysis, (2) selection of criteria to evaluate alternatives ranked by importance, (3) comparison of other options using criteria and ranking, (4) consideration of political and organizational constraints to define and implement policies, and finally, (5) implementation and evaluation of the policy (Munger, 2000).

Once the policy analysis finishes, and the stakeholders have a clear definition of the policy subject context, in this case, professional development, the next step is to define the policy goal. After having a measurable, realistic, and achievable goal, then the participants formulate the policy content, which is part of the policy development (Delaney, 2015).

## PD Policy Development

There are several areas to consider when formulating policy. They are the characteristics of the policymakers (legitimacy, representation of groups of interest, personal traits, experience, and the composition of the policy body), aspects of the processes (which considers the process of consultation to define the policy content, level of participation and the consensus reached among groups of interests), and the technology approach to use for setting the policy (systemic, economic, management analysis, information procuring, processing, dissemination, decision tools, and others (Cheong & Ming, 1995).

Also, there are additional elements considered to policy development. Making political decisions about the values will be allocated, in addition to problem identification, clarification of values, goals and objectives, and identification of options to achieve goals, cost/benefits analysis of alternatives, selection of a course of action, evaluation of the course of action and modification to the program (Taylor et al., 1997), and the need to recognize that the bureaucratic structure will also impact upon the actual policy achieved. Once the policy is developed, it is disseminated to anticipate and evaluate several factors prior to the appropriate course of action (Delaney, 2015).

## Policy Implementation

Policy implementation is considered the execution of the policy. There are two approaches to implement educational policies, vertical perspective, and horizontal perspective (Colebath, 1998). In the first one, vertical view, the authorized decisions at the top (top-level of the institution) match the outcomes at the bottom (results of the policy implementation). On the other hand, in the horizontal perspective, the focus is on the desired outcome to the process and the individuals through which the result should be accomplished.

Two exciting conclusions are learned from research about policy implementation. First, that policy success depends on local capacity (Viennet & Pont, 2017) and will. Both are difficult to handle. Capacity can be developed through training, but will, or motivation underlining an implementer's response is less amenable to policy intervention (McLaughlin, 1991). Also, the success of the policy implementation requires a combination of pressure and support from policy (Fullan, 1986).

## PD Policy Evaluation

The policy evaluation process is required while the policy is in the implementation stage. The evaluation process measures how efficient and effective rules and procedures are. The institutional stakeholders monitor the policy goal (Downey, 1988) and the resources allocated to carry out the policy. It allows determining how timely, pertinent, functional, and practical the policy has been defined and implemented. The evaluation process will dictate further modifications based on whether the content is in tune with other institutional policies (Clemmer, 1991). The following section describes briefly the PD currently implemented at the university.

## University Professional Development Policy Context

Since the university values faculty for the contribution made to student learning, the institution does perform some actions to develop faculty. Examples of these actions are in-service activities held throughout the academic year. The institution invites all faculty to discuss educational issues and speakers to share academic and professional experiences. Also, it prepares different workshops, and updates faculty in technology-based advances to apply in teaching. The institution also posts educational materials related to class management, academic rigor, multiculturalism in education, and student engagement teaching strategies at the website for faculty review.

Additionally, the institution does require additional PD from faculty, which can be acquired by accessing external PD providers. These providers are edX, Coursera, Higher Education institutions, among others; the institution evaluates faculty performance once a year for improvement purposes. But how is the PD Policy development at the university? The next section describes what the university does in terms of PD Policy development.

## Policy Review at the University

The university PD Policy review is based on two elements of the policy review, policy goal achievement and policy impact or performance. Additionally, the evaluation also includes four criteria, such as pertinent, timely, functional, and practicable (Clemmer, 1991).

PD actions currently implemented have never evaluated their performance and impact on Faculty teaching effectiveness. Only the knowledge acquired by them is taken into consideration when the institution conducts the annual faculty evaluation as part of the Human Resources requirements. However, the policy is somewhat pertinent and complies with the condition of being timely because there is an effort for providing PD to all faculty. But it lacks functionality and practicability. Due to PD actions are precarious, they cannot make possible what a PD policy needs to do. It means that it is not functional nor practicable because the policy cannot be implemented as should be.

## Conclusions

Policy evaluation process offers a window for policy improvements and redefinitions. It suggests going back to analysis, goal definition, policy development, and implementation stages to tailor the policy content to current institutional internal and external conditions. Policy review or evaluation process will offer prudent paths for both faculty and institution development.

PD policy at university can be implemented somewhat and might be formally stated or not. If an institution is concerned about the faculty, it is necessary for a formal and structured PD policy based on faculty teaching needs to better contribute to their development. An institution must meet all institution leaders, discuss and analyze the current situation regarding Faculty PD. Then they should ask them to meet with faculty to discuss professional development needs and implement actions for improvements. The departmental units will elevate the proposed activities to the academic division, which will present the suggested activities to the university's top authorities. Once the policy is defined correctly, including policy goals, the institution will start implementing it, and it will allow providing higher quality instruction for student learning purposes.

# Personal Professional Development Plan

The instructional design and technology field (IDT) is evolving rapidly (Reiser & Dempsey, 2018). IDT trends are constantly changing because advances in technology drive them. Thinking on how to be aligned with the IDT trends, it is necessary to follow up on the ongoing progress in learning and performance that props the instruction design and delivery. Thus, personal, professional development is the way to be up to date in the art and techniques of IDT. IDT professionals have different avenues to be current in the IDT field. For instance, IDT professionals can attend conferences, join IDT professional organizations, and read publications, contributing to their knowledge base. Since the resultant knowledge from technology applications emerge and become old very frequently, it will require IDT professionals to keep abreast of current instructional design models, e-learning evolution, learners and industry learning expectations, media, and technology (Reiser & Dempsey, 2018).

Professionals in the IDT field must apply this knowledge to themselves and design and implement their strategies for effectively using these channels. Being actively involved in the IDT field will make a considerable contribution to their professional development. As an IDT professional, one needs to plan professional growth and design their professional development plan (PDP) to progress. By creating and implementing a PDP, an IDT professional will help others develop individual growth plans and, even more, it can be part of the services offered as consultants.

This section aims to create a PDP that will allow me to renew and develop expertise in IDT continually. After conducting extensive research to identify elements to support a PDP, the author identified some determinants of a successful PDP. Specifically, he mentioned some theoretical aspects that support the content of a PDP, IDT competencies needed by professionals to maintain up to date in the industry, and the standards associated with the essential competencies for exercising the profession as sources for a PDP. He also commented about modalities of PDP, the role of technology as a pivotal factor to keep current in the field, and the skills demanded by the IDT industry. All these factors will be the foundation to design IDT professional goals.

## Sources of Personal Professional Development Plan

IDT professionals serve others (faculty, staff, administrators) in designing instruction based on current and future trends of instruction design, including technology-based learning models. As commented previously, there is a just-in-time term that refers to engaging in information gathering when needed via different electronic devices and the internet. It is a trendy topic; thus, as an ID professional, he must be familiar with both new terminology in the field and what the latest trends are all about to be able to provide instructional design solutions.

For instance, he also needs to know about the relevant impact of tracking learner behaviors and their level of engagement with faculty-generated materials. In other words, the performance analytics trend based on data analytics systems is applied to the educational sector (Yilmaz et al., 2020). It provides educational setting access to information about selecting those courses to be discontinued (prescription), suggestions for future support needed by learners (prediction), and reflections on past actions such as correlations of learning outcomes with page view for online courses (description) (Daniel, 2015). Moreover, he must know about virtual communities and interactivity with streaming videos to incorporate these tools as part of the supportive, dialogic, and exploratory instructional strategies for effective design as part of the meaningful online learning approach (Dabbagh et al., 2019).

There are other areas in which he must be knowledgeable to contribute to instruction design. For instance, he will demand current knowledge about the impact of active learning, how to develop technology-based skills for implementation in teaching, and how to design collaborative tools to be used by faculty (GoGuardian Team, 2019). One of the topics to follow up for updates in the IDT field is the best practices in an online environment. IDs need to know about research-based practices to suggest faculty, help them design their instruction, and play the role of facilitators, instead of lecturers (Alexiou-Ray & Bentley, 2015) to enrich online teaching quality level. In addition, he will be motivated to inquire about practices such as visibility, intentionality, and active and reciprocal engagement (Jaggars et al., 2013), to be able to guide faculty on how to apply them into instruction.

By reading different sources of information about IDT and learning (e.g., scientific journals in the IDT field), there are many topics to be followed by me as an ID, for example, how mobile learning (emerging technology) and digital pedagogies are changing and evolving. Educational institutions do not face the challenge of PD just for faculty; institutional leaders need to embrace digital transformation from a holistic standpoint and the context in which it operates. Then he must learn how to use a systems approach when involving institutional stakeholders to ensure equity of access to technical support, sustainable funding and resourcing, and learning spaces for both students and instructors to optimize collaboration and learning (McCarthy et al., 2019).

The subject of research involvement is essential for IDs. As an ID, he should research methods to suggest experimentation when testing a specific instructional strategy or learning activities. For instance, Melton et al. (2019) conducted a study to know how a hybrid PD program impacted the cooperating teachers' ability to facilitate effective mentoring conversations with preservice teachers. The study results supported the PD model (hybrid) for mentoring and created the potential for studying online sequences to promote effective mentoring. The results enrich IDs by giving them in-depth knowledge about alternative ways of introducing collaboration and peer interaction as part of meaningful online learning strategies (Dabbagh et al., 2019).

The findings offered by Cassada & Kassner (2018) can complement the findings provided by Melton et al. (2019). The latter authors carried out a study to observe the impact of peer video coaching on professional development. Using a video-recorded classroom at two intervals in a semester-long course, they formed groups and shared their videos for feedback purposes and professional growth. This technique is called autoscopy. Autoscopy implies the video recording of practical activity as a source of analysis and self-evaluation to obtain feedback from the practice (Sadalla & Larocca, 2004).

Consequently, the subjects can learn from themselves and incorporate that learning into their daily teaching or working performance. When IDT professionals learn about autoscopy and how to use it, they will be able to include it as part of their portfolio of instruction design and suggest using it as part of faculty's instruction. It is, indeed, a potential topic to be included in an IDT-PDP.

## ID Competencies and Standards

Instructional designer competencies and standards offer a frame for professional development. Competencies are the knowledge and skills that entitles one to effectively perform a given function, task, or occupation to the standards expected in the employment context (Richey et al., 2001). Then, competencies are specific to a body attempt in which professionals define the competencies valuable to the profession (Martin & Ritzhaupt, 2020). Therefore, satisfying ID competencies, IDs can communicate the value-add of their proficiency in the field to stakeholders outside of the community and in various professional contexts. He must attend, for example, webinars as an alternative format to renew competencies or acquire new ones. By holding the field competencies, he will be able to guide academic programs to align with the expectations of the needs in the academic field (Martin & Ritzhaupt, 2020), so that it will demand from me to be on the top of competencies enhancement through PD constantly.

IDs will have the opportunity to find PD activities to engage with related to different competencies and standards. Hence, competencies and standards become an excellent referent for them to enrich their knowledge and skills through PD activities. Therefore, PD about keeping effective communication in visual, oral, and written form, research, and theory to the ID discipline improves knowledge, skills, and attitudes of the ID process and related fields. In addition, data collection and analysis skills in ID projects, ethical, legal, and political implications of design in the work environment, which needs assessment to recommend adequate design solutions, will be part of his PDP (ibstpi, 2012).

Other potential topics to consider as an instructional designer to keep updated in the field through PD, are the selection and use of analysis techniques for defining ID content and the analysis of existing emerging technologies and their potential use. In addition, he should know about the organization of instructional programs and interventions, non-instructional interventions, and learning assessments. Moreover, he should understand the application of business skills to manage instructional design functions, collaborative relationships, and ID projects (ibstpi, 2012). It will help improve his management competencies contemplated as part of the professional standards.

A PDP holds career goals and strategies to achieve the goals. This plan helps identify and develop the IDT professional skills needed to achieve his goals. Consequently, it will keep him on the way to success. A PPDP is a process to help instructional designer achieve his potential and guide his PD. A PPDP is one's responsibility, and its implementation will help achieve long-term goals. Also, it will assist him in identifying those skills that need renewal, acquisition, and improvement (Martinelli, 2017). A PPDP needs to follow a process by assessing his current IDT knowledge and abilities, identifying IDT career goals, defining career development strategies to achieve goals, and defining the assessment system to measure the career progress. The following section outlines the IDT professional goals.

## IDT Personal Professional Development Plan (PPDP)

### Current Status of Career Progress

There are generic areas in the IDT professional content in which knowledge acquisition, knowledge renewal, and skill development are a must. The IDT expertise needs to be updated in ID theory, ethical, reflective decision making, ID management, instructional design systems, cutting edge technology, and evaluation and assessment.

The author has learned about different learning theories such as behaviorism, cognitivism, and constructivism (Steven-Fulbrook, 2019). In addition, instructional design theories and perspectives give him a solid foundation for future application in the IDT field. Some of these theories are Attribution theory, Cognitive Dissonance Theory, Cognitive Load Theory, Conditions of Learning, Connectivism, Constructivist Theory, and Experiential Learning Theory (InstructionalDesign.org). In addition, he also learned about instructional design models such as ARCS, ADDIE, Dick and Carey, Instructional Systems Design, Cognitive Apprenticeship Models (InstructionalDesign.org).

Current Adult Learning Theory is an area of my interest since he is working with adult learners. he learned that adults learn through relevant and concrete materials; they need to connect with experiential learning and show a high motivation for learning. He may need to know more about andragogy, transformative, experiential, and self-directed approaches (Irish, 2019). During his career as an ID, he has designed different lesson units based on a constructivist perspective. However, he is aware that he must improve his skills in transferring his expertise to new instruction designs, mainly with the inclusion of technology applied to learning.

Analytical skills are nowadays necessary across industries. They are essential to assess needs and identify performance gaps, instructional analysis, and job tasks analysis (Reiser & Dempsey, 2018). In addition, other areas in which analytical skills apply are analytical communication skills, analytical information processing, and critical thinking. These areas are required to be high in industry contexts (Doyle, 2020). Since information technology advances are evolving very fast, he would have to deepen down into the analytical world to update my current knowledge and apply it to instruction design.

Another area of interest is the application of emerging technologies to instruction. He needs to acquire more knowledge, improve his skills in identifying, and using audiovisual material for teaching, find out about media technologies, audio recording equipment, movie cameras, image creation, artifacts, and sounds to apply principles of e-Learning theory. Also, he needs to learn more about multimedia production management (Sugar et al., 2012). Even though he started implementing these technologies in his instruction design, he will have to improve his skills in producing video-based materials, voice-on, and animations to provide instruction design flow for students' learning.

Regarding ID management, he would say that he has extensive managerial skills since he is holding a leadership position at a university since 2010. However, his management skills in managing instructional design teams require improvement. His ID team management skills have just been essential when dealing with faculty in their instruction improvement efforts.

In ID, IDs decide the instructional design theory and model to use for the instructional design, instructional and learning activities, the appropriate technology to support learning, and management decisions. However, there is an area that deserves special attention. Ethical behaviors in the ID field are paramount. As actors and decision-makers in the instructional process, they are equally responsible for keeping ethical standards. When engaging in online teaching and learning practices, there are different unethical behaviors that we must avoid (Thompson, 2019).

IDs must develop skills in identifying and responding to ethical, legal, and political implications of instruction design as mandated by the professional standards. Concretely, they must be committed to identifying unethical behaviors, recognizing, and respecting intellectual property rights, adhering to regulatory guidelines and institutional policies, and complying with organizational and professional codes of ethics (ibstpi, 2012). I would need to update my knowledge about current ethical behavior issues in the ID profession and ethical issues involved with the technology used in learning processes.

As mentioned earlier, there are many instructional design models for instruction development. He has used two of them, the ADDIE model and the Dick and Cary Systematic design of instruction model. He may need to study other instructional design models as alternative tools for specific instructional problems.

He also learned that instructional design requires evaluation and assessment. The evaluation process is conducted to both learner achievement and instructional design as a product. He is more familiar with learner evaluation since it is part of the teaching process. He is also familiar with programs and course evaluation when the university performs its Annual Planning and Evaluation institutional effectiveness once a year. The university's academic unit the author leads started implementing the Quality Matters tool in 2021 for online course evaluation. It yielded interesting results by identifying areas for improvement at the instructor level. However, he needs to learn more about assessment for improvement purposes since higher education institutions use advanced technology-based tools.

## 2021 Career Goals

My priorities for 2021 regarding my IDT career development are defined as follows:

1. Increase collaboration with stakeholders to identify instructional improvements from a holistic standpoint.
2. Apply instructional theories and models when designing instructional projects and solving instructional problems and needs assessment.
3. Create multimedia objects for online course development.
4. Market instructional design services.
5. Conduct project reviews with other instructors as a team to promote collaboration.
6. Research emerging technologies, collaborating with other professionals by attending professional conferences, workshops, Webinars, and networking events.

## Conclusions

For IDT professionals, it is imperative to assess and develop professional status to find areas for improvement. IDs need a plan for professional development. The field of ID is constantly changing because human beings, the economy, and society evolve with technological advances. Since information technology is impacting educational contexts, IDs must be updated in the art of instructional design. There are always opportunities for improvement; therefore, IDs need knowledge acquisition and skills development for the field in different ID areas. Staying alert about new instructional theories, models, and emerging technologies is necessary for teaching and learning.

# Technology-Based Learning Through Professional Development Training

Professional development (PD) in the educational context now demands an alignment with the current rapid, self-regulated, and on-demand faculty needs in using technology for teaching and learning (Yilmaz et al., 2020). Technology-based teaching and learning experiences are enhancing the traditional PD education based on seminars, longitudinal programs, and workshops with various devices with content via instant feedback options. Some specific examples of technology support for PD education are interactive video and online quizzes, learning management systems, eLearning authoring tools, search engines, social media, and productivity platforms (Border, 2019). Thus, attending the faculty's needs to satisfy their motivations and expectations from using these technologies will influence their perceptions, acceptance, and adoption of these innovations.

Current literature about technology and PD shows five internet-based education strategies that can be used for faculty PD. These strategies are Just-in-time faculty development, performance analytics, and virtual communities of practice (CoPs), which allows going from streaming to interactivity and building capacity for teaching and presenting with technology. *Just-in-time faculty development strategy* focuses on delivering a small amount of content in various formats such as perceived, on-demand or push, micro-content, or chunks of learning, making possible asynchronous and fast-forwarded knowledge acquisition and skills development. *Performance analysis strategy* facilitates analyzing data to frame appropriate, effective, and relevant insights and respond to these insights to interpret the relationship between learner behaviors and outcomes (Yilmaz et al., 2020).

*Virtual communities of practice strategy* allows faculty members to face challenges in participating in synchronous activities with other geographically dispersed faculty e.g., through a blog-based online resource (Steinert et al., 2016). *Going from streaming to interactivity strategy* facilitates faculty to overcome barriers given by lack of time and logistics for learning. Using streamed videos affords opportunities such as delivering bite-size content, engaging a targeted audience, and reaching geographically dispersed individuals (Eva & Regehr, 2008). Finally, *building capacity for teaching and presenting with technology strategy* accumulates digital experience that positively affects teaching skills and develops positive attitudes toward embracing innovation for teaching delivery purposes. Implementing the mentioned strategies in faculty PD training programs will allow faculty to visualize the advantages of technology for effective teaching and enable faculty to include these strategies in their future teaching design to contribute to meaningful online learning.

After commenting about the relevance of moving faculty PD needs for technology-based learning and current strategies for PD, it is also necessary to evaluate those instructional design theories and models that help create a more effective eLearning-based PD experience.

This section aims to develop a training program that teachers and professional development specialists can use to satisfy training in technology-based learning. The training program is based on essential instructional design theories and models to design the training content. It is also designed based on the instruction design system, which contemplates the program's goals, objectives, outcomes, learning environment, emerging technologies, instructional activities, and the evaluation system to assess learners and the training. In addition, this design will contemplate the ethical considerations for designing instruction.

## Theoretical Foundation for Designing
## PD Training Programs

Before defining the elements of instructional design for a PD training program, instructional designers should know how people think and learn. By knowing so, instructional designers can design and develop efficient, effective, and meaningful instructional interventions. Instructional designers must understand cognition and the essential cognitive functions such as memory, mental power, specific cognitive abilities, executive abilities, and metacognition. These elements explain how individuals think, which is fundamental to finding the appropriate strategies for learning (Brown & Green, 2016).

As in the case of thinking, learning is the second concept instructional designers must understand. Learning is defined as the relatively permanent change in behaviors and mental representations, or associations brought about by experience (Ormrod, 2011). Experiences are events that occur in a learners' life in interaction with the environment. Therefore, the analysis of the environment within the learning experience should happen, which is essential to gain actual learning. As there are two different types of changes when learning occurs, two different psychological perspectives have emerged: behaviorism and cognitivism. Both views are the foundation for varied instructional design learning theories and models. The following section will describe some of these learning theories, which are considered the pillars of instructional design.

As mentioned above, both behaviorism and cognitivism offer the major psychological concepts and principles of learning foundational for the instructional design field. The behavioral learning process contributed to concepts such as feedback, reinforcement, behavioral objectives, and practice to design instruction (Reiser & Dempsey, 2018). Those concepts are present in the instruction design. On the other hand, cognitive approaches show images such as information processing and schema theory that shifted the focus on instructional design, highlighting learners' role and prior knowledge in learning new ones and skills. Concretely, there are instructional design theories built upon the two main paradigms (behaviorism and cognitivism). These theories are Behavioral Learning Theory, Cognitive Information Processing Theory, Schema Theory, and Cognitive Load, Situated Learning Theory, Gagne's Theory of Instruction, Constructivism, and Connectivism (Reiser & Dempsey, 2018). There are other theories and models that instructional designers consider when designing instruction; they are Sociocultural Learning Theory, the ADDIE Model, Merril's Principles of Instruction, and Individualized Instruction, as well as Bloom's Taxonomy of Learning Outcomes, the SAM Model (eLearning Industry, 2019), and the E-learning Instructional Theory (Clark & Mayer, 2003).

## Technology-Based PD Training Program

Instruction design is the process of defining what should be done and how to achieve learning goals and outcomes (Schweitzer, 2019). The process is performed by identifying learning needs in learners, defining content by units, creating instructional maps, and creating assessment tools to evaluate the instruction design (Glatthorn et al., 2016). Recently, the academic division at the university developed the Institutional assessment Week. For seven days, key stakeholders (faculty, staff, and institutional leaders) met to assess the 2019-2020 institutional effectiveness cycle.

The Academic Division requested faculty to evaluate their online course design by using the Quality Matter rubric tool. This tool allows assessing the design of the online or hybrid (blended) courses to ensure it meets the Quality Matter standards (Course overview and introduction, learning objectives, assessment and measurement, instructional materials, as well as course activities and learner interaction, the technology used in the course, student and instructor support, and accessibility and usability) (QM, 2015).

259

After discussing online course design results individually and in the group, one common problem emerged among faculty related to one standard: course activities and learner interaction. The discussion yielded the conclusion that instructors have difficulties in making online learning meaningful for students. They do not know how to integrate strategies, activities, and technology in their instruction design to make it meaningful for students.

Meaningful learning derives from implementing active engagement between students and instructors. Moreover, it derives from a high-quality learning experience by using varied instructional strategies supporting technologies (Dabbagh et al., 2019). Meaningful learning is based on different learning theories such as constructivism, and situated cognition theory, two of the approaches mentioned in the previous section. Tasks that include active, constructive, intentional, cooperative, and authentic elements led to meaningful learning (Howland et al., 2012). The following section aims to develop the PD training content, following the instruction design systems developed by Dick et al. (2015).

## Meaningful Online Learning PD Training Program

As mentioned earlier, this section shows the content of the PD Training program with the elements of essential instructional design theories, models, and the instruction structure by implementing the Dick et al. (2015) systematic design of instruction. The title of the PD training will be *Meaningful Online Learning Training Program* (MOLTP). The instruction design systems created by Dick et al. consist of several sequential steps to identify instructional goals, conduct instructional analysis, analyze learners and context. It also defines performance objectives, develops assessment instruments, develops instructional strategies, develops and selects instructional materials, and designs and conducts the formative and summative evaluation. However, the process should start by defining the faculty's needs to be addressed.

## Needs

The present MOLTP is intended to cover the performance gap in faculty. First, it is necessary to identify the performance gap to address the instruction design. Faculty recognize that they have challenging symptoms related to determining the appropriate strategies, activities, and learning technologies to make their online teaching meaningful for students (actual status). Faculty must know different strategies, activities, and technology-based learning tools to use them in their instruction (desired status). The performance gap identified yielded from the needs assessment conducted through the Quality Matter Rubric tool compared to the desired status of knowledge application in this particular subject (Kauffman & Guerra-Lopez, 2013).

## Audience

The intended audience for this training program is the business faculty who have teaching experience in using technology tools to conduct online learning. Although faculty show some technology-based tools used in their teaching, there is still a gap to provide a higher quality learning experience. The program's content will be delivered in a three-module professional development format. Faculty should be able to complete the training autonomously to focus on their strengths and areas for improvement. An assessment will follow each program's section (lesson) to gauge faculty progress.

In addition, the instruction will provide learners with in-depth and practical educational resources, such as reading materials, videotaped oral presentations, and interactive media to show knowledge application. Finally, the instructor will support faculty and add the appropriate level of social interactivity to the experience, as suggested by the Individualized Instruction Theory from the Personalized System of Instruction (PSI) (Keller, 1968). The E-learning Instructional Theory is the instruction delivered via computer or mobile devices for learning (Clark & Mayer, 2003).

## Instructional Goals

An instructional goal describes the main objectives of the MOLTP (Glatthorn et al., 2016) and the skill, knowledge, or attitude expected to acquire (Dick et al., 2015). The goals defined for the MOLTP are described as follows:

- Faculty will know different strategies, activities, and learning technologies for effective instructional design.
- Faculty will demonstrate skills in integrating strategies, activities, and learning technologies in their online instruction designs.

## Instructional Analysis

An instructional analysis conducted by the instructional designer allows identifying what the learner must recall and determine what he/she must be able to do to perform the tasks. This MOLTP faculty must reflect the content of exploratory, supportive, and dialogic strategies for meaningful online learning. They must recall the categorization of technologies for supporting meaningful online learning.

These categories are (1) Collaboration and communication (verbal, audio, text support, among others). (2) Content creation tools (LMS-based tools -e.g., course document to display, shared content areas such as wikis or digital dropbox, and mashups to insert web-based videos). (3) Information search and resource management. (4) Knowledge representation (email, discussion forums, blogs, wikis, social communities such as Facebook and document storage). (5) Immersive tools (simulation games, virtual-reality environments). Finally, (6) Assessment and analytics (e-library resources, internet search engines, e.g., Google, and content collection, aggregation, and annotation tools) (Dabbagh et al., 2019). In addition, faculty must know how to integrate these categories into different strategies mentioned before.

## Performance Objectives

Performance objectives describe what the faculty will be able to do when they complete the three-module-based MOLTP (Dick et al., 2015). A performance objective is structured in three parts: condition, behavior, and criteria (Dick et al., 2015).

### Objective 1

At the end of the MOLTP taken by the faculty at the university or elsewhere (CN), faculty will be able to mention the strategies, activities, and learning technologies for meaningful online learning (B) to include in their instruction design (CR).

### Objective 2

During the instruction planning (CN), faculty will be able to integrate meaningful strategies, activities, and learning technologies for specific instructional goals (B). Faculty should identify the appropriate strategy, activities, and learning technologies to achieve the instructional goal in their instruction design (CR).

## Learning Outcomes

- Faculty demonstrate comprehension in identifying the strategies, activities, and learning technologies for meaningful online learning.
- Faculty demonstrate understanding in integrating strategies, activities, and learning technologies for meaningful online learning to achieve instructional goals.

## Instructional Strategies

Instructional strategies are the components of the instruction that enable students to achieve learning objectives and outcomes. Instructional strategies define content sequencing, clustering, what faculty will teach, and how to transfer the content to a performance environment (Dick et al., 2015).

## Learning Environment, Technologies, and Instructional Activities

The learning environment alludes to physical locations, contexts, and culture in which faculty learn (Glossary of Education Reform, 2013). For this PD training program, faculty will have the opportunity to take it from where they find it appropriate. It is built on learning technologies such as audio, visual, and digital support via regular desktop computers, laptops, or mobile devices, from home or university. Emerging technologies such as artificial intelligence, virtual reality, and augmented reality into instruction aim to enable more innovative and engaging instructional methods and learning. It will have a tremendous impact on the faculty learning experience. For instance, 84% of US teachers think using technology better prepares students for the future (Google Education, n.d.), which indicates a high level of receptiveness of teachers for accepting technology-based learning.

As instructional activities, faculty will achieve performance objectives and cover the performance gap by:

- Receiving learning content guidance via multimedia-based sequential content through three content modules.
- Knowing training program instructional goal, objectives, and outcomes within the course content.
- Obtaining attention via multimedia module content element.

- Being exposed to stimulus material through videos and visual material.
- Receiving feedback from the instructor via oral presentation rubric as well as formative and summative assessments.

The training content will align the ethical mandates for online instructional training relative to course, design, copyright, and learner evaluation. The training will be delivered through Blackboard Ultra (LMS); therefore, there are clear policies and regulations for using the information in an online environment. The learning technologies for training faculty comply with ethical standards defined by the LMS provided and the university, and faculty are advised about following the code of conduct as established in the university faculty handbook.

## Scope and Sequence

As mentioned previously, this training program is planned to be delivered in three modules. Faculty will take it at their own pace for 1 month. Faculty will access the training through Blackboard Ultra LMS, they will learn from video-based lessons with multimedia tools, interactive quizzes, and they will have the opportunity to post videotaped oral presentations. The scope and sequence of the training program and the curriculum map are shown in Tables 1 and 2.

## Assessment Tools

The purpose of the evaluation is to determine the success level of the instruction and learning. There are two levels of evaluation, learner evaluation, and instructional design product. Learner evaluation helps determine the performance effectiveness because of the instruction. Even though formative and summative assessments tend to be more focused on the instructional design process, they also apply to leaner evaluation (Brown & Green, 2016).

Ernesto Gonzalez

On the other hand, instructional design product evaluation consists in assessing the instructional design process and structure through different criteria. The elements of the instructional design product subject to evaluation (summative evaluation) are instructional design product purpose, use, audience, significant characteristics, design constraints, the purpose of data collection, measures, frequency of data collection, and the sample size used, as well as questions asked about what worked and what triangular information did not work (Fitzpatrick & Worthen, 2004).

**Table 1**

*Technology-based Learning PD Training Program. Scope and Sequence*

| Module | Access to the Training | Learning Outcomes covered | Activities |
|---|---|---|---|
| 1 | Faculty time availability | 1 | Video lecture, exercises, post-module quiz |
| 2 | Faculty time availability | 1 | Video lecture, exercises, post-module quiz |
| 3 | Faculty time availability | 2 | Knowledge application. Faculty will design an online instruction supported by any emerging technologies. |

# Table 2.

*Technology-based Learning PD Training Program Curriculum Map*

| Module | Essential questions | Content | Skills | Assessment |
|---|---|---|---|---|
| 1 | What are the learning theories? What are the instructional design theories and models? What is technology-based learning? | -Learning theories (behaviorism, cognitivism, constructivism). -Instructional design theories and models. | -Faculty will understand the role of learning theories, and instructional design theory and models within and online environment. | -Module 1 Quiz |
| 2 | How to include emerging technologies into instruction design from instructional design theory standpoint? What are the meaningful online learning strategies to integrate into an online course? How to assess students? How to evaluate the quality of the instruction? | -Applications of instructional design theories and models in technology-based learning (examples) -Meaningful online learning strategies (supportive, dialogic, exploratory) -Summative and formative assessment tools. -Rubrics to evaluate the quality of the technology-based design. | -Faculty will understand the applications of instructional design theories and models to online learning. Faculty will explain the content of supportive, dialogic, and exploratory learning strategies. -Faculty will describe different summative and formative assessment tools to evaluate student learning. -Faculty will familiarize with different rubrics to measure the quality of a technology-based instruction for improvement purposes. | -Module 2 Quiz |

| 3 | What technology-based learning and instructional design theory and model will support my instruction design? How to integrate learning strategies? | -Design a technology-based online instruction by using emerging technologies, and supportive, dialogic, and exploratory learning strategies. | -Faculty will demonstrate their skills in designing a technology-based online instruction. | Final project/ Videotaped oral presentation supported by technology. |
|---|---|---|---|---|

The MOLTP will use both formative and summative assessments for faculty (Eberly Center, n.d.). Formative assessment will be based on interactive quizzes at the end of each module. Summative assessment will be through designing an online lesson plan in which faculty will demonstrate comprehensive knowledge and skills in integrating strategies, activities, and learning technologies for meaningful online learning. The training will be evaluated through the Quality Matter Rubric tool to identify the impact of the online design and all the design elements on learners and instructors. It will provide perceptions from both parties and triangulate information for improvement purposes.

## Conclusions

Continued institutional support for providing professional development to faculty is paramount. Since instructional design covers different areas, educational institutions are called to provide ongoing support for faculty involvement by developing instructional knowledge and skills. All the areas of instructional design -instructional theory and models, instructional goals, learning objectives and outcomes, learning technologies for learning processes, assessment, instruction design systems all are equally important. As instructional designers, it is imperative to keep faculty up to date in teaching based on the theoretical framework supporting instruction design.

# References

Association for Educational Communications & Technology (AECT). (2020). *Educational technology*. www.aect.org.

Agozzino, A. (2014). Building and maintaining relationships through social media. In I. Management Association (Ed.), *Digital arts and entertainment: Concepts, methodologies, tools, and applications*, pp. 104-125. IGI Global. doi:10.4018/978-1-4666-6114-1.ch005.

Ahn Farzan, J. R., & Brusilovsky, P. (2006). Social Search in the Context of Social Navigation. *Journal of the Korean Society for Information Management, 23*(2), 147-165.

Alexander, K., & Alexander, M. D. (2019). *American public school law*. West Academy Publishing.

Allego. (2013, July 10). *Agile learning design*. https://trainingindustry.com/wiki/content-development/ agile-learning-design/

Allen, I. E., & Seaman, J. (2014). *Grade change: Tracking online education in the United States*. Babson Survey Research Group and Quahog Research Group LLC. http://www.onlinelearningsurvey.com/reports/gradechange.pdf

Alexiou-Ray, J., & Bentley, C. (2015). Faculty Professional Development for Quality Online Teaching. *Online Journal of Distance Learning Administration, 18*. https://www.westga.edu/~distance/ojdla/winter184/ray_ bentley184.pdf

Alshammari, M., Anane, P., & Hendley, R. J. (2015). Design and usability evaluation of adaptive e-learning systems based on learner knowledge and learning style. In *Proceedings of the Conference* on Human-Computer Interaction--INTERACT 2015, 584–591. Springer.

American Marketing Association (AMA). (2016). *Marketing definition.* www.marketingpower.com/_layouts/Dictionary. aspx?dLetter=M, accessed September 2016.

American Psychological Association (APA). (2020). *Publication Manual of the American Psychological Association* (7th ed.). American Psychological Association, Washington, DC, United States.

Asimov, E. G., & Shchukin, A. N. (2009). *New dictionary of methodological terms and concepts (the theory and practice of language teaching).* Publishing House: ICAR.

Association of Public & Land-grant Universities. (n.d.). *Personalizing learning with adaptive courseware.* Personalizing Learning with Adaptive Courseware (aplu.org)

Aston, B. (2021, March 29). *Ten best learning management systems for 2021: Comparison.* https://thedigitalprojectmanager.com/best-learning-management-systems/.

Bada, S. O. (2015). Constructivism learning theory: A paradigm for teaching and learning. *IOSR Journal of Research & Method in Education, 5*(6), 66-70.

ATD International Conference. (2 019). https://atdconference.td.org/

Backhouse, J. (2013). What makes lecturers in higher education use emerging technologies in their teaching? *Knowledge Management & E-Learning, 5*(3), 345-358.

Baldwin, N. (2016). Instructional scaffolding. In Dabbagh (Ed.), *5 things you need to know about constructivist-based pedagogical models and instructional strategies.* https://www.slideshare.net/NadaDabbagh/5-things-you-should-know-about-cle-models-and-strategies.

Bamrara, A. (2018). Applying Addie model to evaluate faculty development program. *Issues and Ideas in Education, 6*(1), 11-28. doi:10.15415/iie.2018.61001.

Bates, T. (2001). International distance education: Cultural and ethical issues. *Distance Education, 22*(1), 122-136.

Bays, T., Carchidi, D., Carter-Galvan, S., Chambers, P., Fons, G., Gooding, I. (2009). *Code of best practices in fair use for Opencourseware.* Created for the OCW Consortium. http://www.centerforsocialmedia.org/files/pdf/10-305-OCW-Oct29.pdf

Beach, D. (2016, October 3). *The impact of technology on employee training.* LinkedIn. https://www.linkedin.com/pulse/ impact-technology-employee-training-david-beach

Berg, C., Chapman, C., & Alemany, O. (2016, December 7). *Understanding academic program costs and margins* [Webcast]. RSM International. https://rsmus.com/events/understanding_academic_program_ costs_margins.html.

Berk, J. (2011). *Measuring learning's impact on the business.* http://www.knowledgeadvisors.com/wp-content/ uploads/2010/06/ Approaches_to_Measurement_Business_ Impact.pdf

Blackboard. (n.d.). https://www.blackboard.com/teaching-learning/ learning-management/blackboard-learn.

Blackboard Learn Ultra. (n.d.). https://www.blackboard.com/learnultra

Bleich, C. (2019). *What should we expect for the future of corporate training in 2020?* EdgePoint Learning. https://www.edgepointlearning.com/blog/ future-of-corporate-training-2019/.

Blended Learning in the Liberal Arts Conference (2019).
https://www.brynmawr.edu/blendedlearning/conference

Bloom taxonomy action verbs (n.d.).
https://www.nbna.org/files/Blooms%20Taxonomy%20of%20
Learning.pdf

Bomboy, S. (2017). *Is high school student speech protected on social media?*
Constitution Daily.
https://constitutioncenter.org/blog/
is-high-school-student-speech-protected-online.

Border, S. (2019). Assessing the role of screencasting and video use in
anatomy education. *Advances Experimental Medicine and Biology,
1171*, 1-13.

Borg, S. (2015). Researching language teacher education, In Paltridge B,
and Phatiki, A (eds), *The continuum comparison to research methods
in applied linguistics* (2nd ed.) London: Bloomsbury, 541-560.

Bransford, J. D., Brown, E. R., & Cocking, R. R. (2000). *How people
learn: Brain, mind, experience, and school.* National Academy Press.

Briggs, S. (March 28, 2017). *Six emerging educational technologies and
how they are being used across the globe.* INFORMED.
https://www.opencolleges.edu.au/informed/
features/6-emerging-educational-technologies-used-across-globe/

Brown, A. H., & Green T. D. (2016). *The essentials of instructional
design. Connecting fundamental principles with process and practice.*
Routledge.

Bui, S. (2020, November 19). *Top educational technology trends in 2020-
2021.* eLearning Industry.
https://elearningindustry.com/
top-educational-technology-trends-2020-2021

Clark, R. C., & Mayer, R. E. (2003). *E-learning and the science of
instruction.* Jossey-Bass.

Campbell, J. Kyriakides, L., Muijs, D., & Robinson, W. (2004).
Assessing teacher effectiveness: Developing a differentiated model.
Routledge Falmer.

Campus Technology (2015). *baldwin and MIT face lawsuit for lack of online captioning.*
https://campustechnology.com/articles/2015/02/12/harvard-and-mit-face-lawsuit-for-lack-of-online-captioning.aspx

Carley, M. (1980). *Rational techniques in policy analysis.* Heinemann Educational Books London.

Carney, M., & Indrisano, R. (2013). Disciplinary literacy and pedagogical content knowledge. *The Journal of Education, 193*(3), 39-49. DOI: 10.2307/24636920
https://www.jstor.org/stable/24636920

Carpenter-Aeby, T., & Aeby, V. G. (2013). Application of andragogy to instruction in an MSW practice class. *Journal of Instructional Psychology, 40*(1), 3-13.

Cassada, K., & Kassner, L. (2018). Seeing is believing: Peer video coaching as professional development done with me and for me. *Contemporary Issues in Technology and Teacher Education, 18*(2).
http://www.citejournal.org/volume-18/issue-2-18/general/seeing-is-believing-peer-video-coaching-as-pd-done-with-me-and-for-me

Cavanagh, T., Chen, B., Maalem Lahcen, R. A., & Paradiso, J. R. (2020). Constructing a design framework and pedagogical approach for adaptive learning in higher education: A practitioner's perspective. *International Review of Research in Open and Distributed Learning, 21*(1).

Center of Innovative Teaching and Learning. (n.d.). *Gagne's nine events of instruction.* Gagne's Nine Events of Instruction - NIU - Center for Innovative Teaching and Learning

Centre for Teaching Excellence (2019). Lesson Planning. Singapore Management University.
https://cte.smu.edu.sg/approach-teaching/integrated-design/lesson-planning

Chalk. (2020, January 15). *Seven reasons why your curriculum matters more than you think.*
https://www.chalk.com/resources/7-reasons-why-your-curriculum-matters-more-than-you-think/

Chen, C. (2008). Intelligent web-based learning system with personalized learning path guidance. *Computer & Education, 51*(2), 787-814.

Chen, J., & Mansa, J. (2020, April 37). *Return on Investment (ROI)*. Investopedia. https://www.investopedia.com/terms/r/returnoninvestment.asp

Cheong, Y., and Ming, W. (1995). A framework for the analysis of educational policies. *The 2ⁿᵈ International Journal of Education Management, 9*(6).

Cherkunova, N. G. (2016). The formation of marketing strategy of the higher educational institutions to increase their efficiency. *International Journal of economics and Financial Issue, 6*(S2), 37-42.

Chyung, Y., & Trenas, A. S. (2009). Content analysis: Key to excellence in your blended learning. *Learning Solutions Magazine.* https://learningsolutionsmag.com/articles/150/content-analysis-key-to-excellencein-

CIPD. (2019). CIPD Learning and Development Show. https://www.cipd.co.uk/events/learning-development-show.

Clemmer, E. F. (1991). *The school policy handbook.* Needham heights, MA: Allyn and Bacon.

CogBooks. (n.d.). *Motivating stakeholders for a successful personalized leaning approach.* https://www.cogbooks.com/2016/08/24/motivating-stakeholders-successful-personalized-learning-approach/.

Cohen, M. S. S. (1990). Cognitive factors and their role in the enhancement of the knowledge elicitation process. *Unpublished doctoral dissertation.* State University of New York.

Colebath, H. K. (1998). *Policy.* MN: University of Minnesota.

Copyright Act, 17 U.S.C. § 101 et seq. (1976).

Cram, D. D. (1981). Designing instruction: Meeting the SME. *NPSI Journal, 20*(4), 5-7.

Croxson, P. L., Walton, M. E., O' Reilly, J. X., Behrens, T. E., & Rushworth, M. F. (2010). Effort-based cost-benefit valuation and the human brain. *The Journal of Neuroscience, 29*(14), 4531-4541. doi:10.1523/JNEUROSCI.4515-08.2009.

Dabbagh, N., Marra, R. M., & Howland, J. L. (2019). *Meaningful online learning*. Routledge.

Daniel, B. (2015). Big data and analytics in higher education: Opportunities and challenges. *British Journal of Educational Technology, 46*(5),899-1129.
https://doi.org/10.1111/bjet.12230

David, L. (2015). E-learning theory. In R. E. Mayer, J. Sweller, & R. Moreno (Eds), *Learning Theories*.
https://www.learning-theories.com/e-learning-theory-mayer-sweller-moreno.html.

Dean, C. B., Ross Hubbell, E., Pitler, H., & Stone, B. (2012). *Classroom instruction that works: Research-based strategies for increasing student achievement* (2$^{nd}$ Ed.), ASCD.

Delaney, J. G. (2015). *Educational policy studies*. A practical approach. Canada, Brush Education, Inc.

Demiray, U., Nagy, J, & Yilmaz. R. A. (2007). Strategies for the marketing of higher education with comparative contextual references between Australia and Turkey. *Turkish Online Journal of Distance education, 8*(2), 157-173.

Department of Justice (DOJ). (2013). Justice Department settles with Louisiana Tech University over inaccessible course materials.
https://www.justice.gov/opa/pr/justice-department-settles-louisiana-tech-university-over-inaccessible-course-materials

Desimone, L. M.; Garet, M.; Birman, B.; Porter, A.; and Yoon, K. S. (2002). How do district management and implementation strategies relate to the quality of the professional development that districts provide to teachers? *Teachers College Record, 104*(7), 1265-1312.

Desimone, L. M. (2009). Improving impact studies of teachers' professional development: Toward better conceptualizations and measures. *Educational Researcher, April, 38*(3).

Downey, L. W. (1988). *Policy analysis in education*. Detselig.

Din Jie, Ng. (2016). Towards a framework of educational policy analysis. The Head Foundation. Retrieved from http://www.headfoundation.org/papers/2016_-_5)_Towards_a_ Framework_of_Education_Policy_Analysis_.pdf

Diamond, R. M. (2008). *Designing and assessing courses and curricula. A practical Guide*. San

Francisco, CA., United States, Jossey-Bass.

Dick, W., Carey, L., & Carey, J. O. (2015). *The systematic design of instruction*, (8 Ed.). Pearson.

Dickens, B. (2018, June 27). *The future of instructional design: Experience design. Training Industry*. https://trainingindustry.com/articles/content-development/ the-future-of-instructional-design-experience-design/

Deloitte Global Human Capital (DGHC). (2019). *Leading the social enterprise: Reinvent with a human focus*. Deloitte. https://www2.deloitte.com/ro/en/pages/human-capital/ articles/2019-deloitte-global-human-capital-trends.html.

Diem, K. G. (n.d.). *Measuring impact of educational programs*. Fact Sheet. New Jersey Agricultural Experiment Station. http://florida4h.org/staff/evaluation/Resources/RUTGERS- mesuring%20impact.pdf

Doran, G. T. (1981). There's a S.M.A.R.T. way to write management's goals and objectives. *Management Review, 70*, 35-36.

Doyle, A. (2020, September 17). *What are analytical skills?* The Balance careers. https://www.thebalancecareers.com/analytical-skills-list-2063729

Dunn, J. (2019, January 6). *Maker mind vs manager mind. They are different. Here is how*. Tech People Leadership. https://medium.com/coaching-notes/ maker-mind-vs-manager-mind-f4e01d294d34.

Durak, G., & Ataizi, M. (2016). The ABC's of online course design according to Addie model. *Universal Journal of Education Research, 4*(9), 2084-2091. doi: 10.13189/ujer.2016.040920.

Dyjur, P., & Lock, J. (2016). Three strategies for moving curriculum mapping online. *Educational Developments, 17*(2), 15-19.

Eberly Center. Teaching Excellence & Educational Innovation (2019). *Creating and using rubrics.* https://www.cmu.edu/teaching/assessment/assesslearning/rubrics.html

Eberly Center. (n.d.). *What is the difference between formative and summative assessment?* Carnegie Mellon University. https://www.cmu.edu/teaching/assessment/basics/formative-summative.html.

Educational Technology. (n.d.). *ADDIE. Instructional Design.* https://educationaltechnoclogy.net/the-addie-model-instructional-design/

Educause. (2020, March 2). 2020 Educause horizon report. Teaching and Learning Edition. https://library.educause.edu/resources/2020/3/2020-educause-horizon-report-teaching-and-learning-edition

EduLEarn. (2020). *12th Annual international conference on education and new learning technologies.* https://iated.org/edulearn/

Edward, C. N., Asiryatham, D., & Johar, M. G., (2018). Effects of blended learning and learners' characteristics on students' competence: An empirical evidence in learning oriental music. *Educational Information Technology, 23,* 2587-2606. https://doi.org/10.1007/s10639-018-9732-4.

Ehrich, L. C., Cranston, N., Kimber, M., & Starr, K. (2012). (Un) Ethical practices and ethical dilemmas in universities: academic leaders' perspective. *ISEA, 40*(2), 99-114.

eLearning Industry (2019). *How to kick start and boost an amazing instructional design career.* https://elearningindustry.com/free-ebooks/how-to-kick-start-and-boost-an-amazing-instructional-design-career.

Engelbert, N. (2020, March 2). *2020 Educause horizon report. Teaching and learning edition.*
https://library.Engelbert.edu/resources/2020/3/2020-educause-horizon-report-teaching-and-learning-edition.

Eva, K. W., & Regehr, G. (2008). I'll never play professional football" and other fallacies of self-assessment. *The Journal of Continuing Education in the Health Professions, 28,* 14-19.

Explore Talent LMS. (n.d.). *Know your audience.*
https://www.talentlms.com/ebook/effective-courses/know-your-audience.

Ferriman, J. (2020, January 13). *Critical elements of instructional design.* LearnDash.
https://www.learndash.com/critical-elements-of-instructional-design/

Filip, A. (2012). Marketing theory applicability in higher education. *Procedia Social and Behavioral Sciences, 46*(2012), 912-916.

Flores, R., Ari, F., Inan, F. A., & Arslan-Ari, I. (2012). The impact of adapting content for learners with individual differences. *Educational Technology & Society, 15*(3), 251-261.

FLDOE (2019). *Coordinated system of professional development.*
http://www.fldoe.org/teaching/professional-dev/coordinated-system-of-professional-dev.stml)

Florida Center for Instructional Technology. (n.d.). *Multimedia in the classroom.*
https://fcit.usf.edu/multimedia/overview/overviewa.html.

Frances Payne Bolton School of Nursing. (n.d.). *Systems Thinking Scale.* Case Western Reserve University.
https://case.edu/nursing/research/research-studies-labs/systems-thinking/systems-thinking-scale-manual.

Fullan, M. (1986) Performance appraisal and curriculum implementation research, "Manuscript for the Conference on Performance Appraisal for Effective Schooling, Ontario Institute for Studies in Education, Toronto, February.

Gagne, R. M. (1985). *Conditions of learning* (4thr Ed.). Holt, Rinehart and Winston.

Gagné, R. M., Wager, W. W., Golas, K. C., & Keller, J. M. (2004). *Principles of instructional design* (5th ed.). Belmont, CA: Wadsworth/Thomson Learning.

Glatthorn, A. A., Boschee, F., Whitehead, B. M, & Boschee, B. F. (2016). *Curriculum Leadership. Strategies for development and implementation.* Thousand Oaks, CA, United States, SAGE Publications, Inc.

Glossary of Education Reform. (2013, August 29). *Learning environment.* https://www.edglossary.org/learning-environment/

Goe, L., Bell, C., & Little, O. (2008). *Approaches to evaluating teacher effectiveness: A research synthesis.* National Comprehensive Center for Teacher Quality. EvaluatingTeachEffectiveness.pdf.

GoGuardian. (2020). https://www.goguardian.com/.

Gonzalez, E. (2020). *IDT jobs today: What is it important to the field?* Unpublished working paper. Instructional Design and Technology Education Specialization. Keiser University.

Google Education. (n.d.). *Future of classroom.* https://services.google.com/fh/files/misc/future_of_the_ classroom_emerging_trends_in_k12_education.pdf?utm_ source=web&utm_campaign=FY19-Q2-global-demandgen- website-other-futureoftheclassroom

Gooler, D. (1980). Formative evaluation strategies for major instructional projects. *Journal of Instructional Development, 3*(3), 7-11. https://doi.org/10.1007/BF02909012

Gopalan, V., Abu, J., Zulkifli, A. N., Alwi, A., & Mat, R. C. (2017). *A review of the motivation theories in learning.* [Paper presentation}. The 2$^{nd}$ International Conference on Applied Science and Technology (ICAST'17). AIP Conf. Proc. 1891, 020043-1-020043-7. https://doi.org/10.1063/1.5005376.

Gordon, C. J., & Rennie, B. J. (1987). Restructuring content schemata: An intervention study. *Reading Research and Instruction, 26*(3), 162-188.

Greenleaf, C.L. Schoenbach, R., Cziko, C., and Mueller, F.L. (2001). Appreciating adolescent readers to academic literacy. *Harvard Educational Review, 71*(1), 79-129.

Guest Jr., C. L., & Guest J. M. (2011). Legal issues in the use of technology in higher education: Copyright and privacy in the academy. In D. W. Surry, R. M. Gray Jr., & J. R. Stefurak, *Technology Integration in Higher Education: Social and Organizational Aspects.* IGI Global.

Guskey, T.R. (2000). *Evaluating professional development.* Corwin Press.

Hall, G. E., George, A. A., & Rutheford, W. L. (1977). Measuring stages of concern about the innovation: A Manual for use of the SoC Questionnaire. *The Research Development Center for Teacher Education.*

Harnett v. The Fielding Graduate Institute, 198 F. App'x 89 (2d Cr. 2006).

Hart, D. (n.d.). *2020 instructional design trends and learning and development trends: From aspiration to activation.* https://insights.sweetrush.com/ instructional-design-trends-report-2020.

Hart, D. (2020, March 16). *Learning and instructional design trends 2020: Activating L&D aspirations.* eLearning Industry. https://elearningindustry.com/ learning-and-instructional-design-trends-2020.

Harrison, M., Quisias, J., Frew, E., & Albon, S. P. (2019). A cost-benefit analysis of teaching and learning technology in a faculty of pharmaceutical sciences. *American Journal of Pharmaceutical Education, 83*(6), 1310-1319.

Harvard Business Publishing Education (2019*). Marketing Simulation: Using conjoint analysis for business decisions.* https://hbsp.harvard.edu/

Harvard Business Review (2019). *Store24(A): Managing Employee Retention.*
https://store.hbr.org/product/store24-a-managing-employee-rete
ntion/602096?from=quickSearch

Henze, N., & Nejdl, W. (1999). Adaptivity in the KBS Hyperbook System. In: P. Brusilovsky, P.D. Bra and A. Kobsa (eds.) *Proceedings of Second Workshop on Adaptive Systems and User Modelling on the World Wide Web*, Toronto and Banff, Canada, May 11 and June 23-24, 1999. Published as Computer Science Report, No. 99-07, Eindhoven University of Technology, 67-74.

Herzberg, F., Mausner, B., & Syndernman, B. (1959). *The motivation to work.* Willey.

Higher education Law (2017). *Social media and students' freedom of expression.*
http://www.highereducationlaw.org/url/2017/6/17/social-media-and-students-freedom-of-expression.html

Howland, J., Jonassen, D., & Marra, R. (2012). *Meaningful learning with technology* (4th ed.) Pearson.

Hollingshead, B. (2009). The concerns-based adoption model: A framework for examining implementation of a character education program. *National Association of Secondary School Principals. NASSP Bulletin, 93*(3).

Huron. (n.d.). *Assessing the true costs of the academic portfolio.*
https://www.huronconsultinggroup.com/insights/
assessing-true-costs-academic-portfolio

ICELW. (2019). *The Learning Ideas Conference. Innovations in learning and technology for the workplace and higher education.*
https://www.learningideasconf.org/

ISTE (n.d.). *ISTE Standards.*
https://www.iste.org/standards.

Indeed. (n.d.). www.indeed.com.

Inquisiq. (n.d.). *What is a learning management system (LMS? Definition and features.*

https://inquisiq.com/resource/learning-management-system-lms/.

InstructionalDesign.org. (n.d.). *Instructional design models.*

International Board of Standards for Training, Performance and Instruction (ibstpi). (2012). *Instructional designer standards: Competencies and Performance Statements.*
http://ibstpi.org.

Irish, K. (2019, January 10). *What is adult learning theory and why is it important?* Ej4.
https://www.ej4.com/blog/
what-is-adult-learning-theory-and-why-is-it-important
https://www.instructionaldesign.org/models/

Jacobsen, M. (1998). *Individual computer use patterns survey.*
https://people.ucalgary.ca/~dmjacobs/phd/phd-survey.
html?USERNAME=dmjacobs&Permission+Form=

Jacobsen, M., Eaton, S. E., Brown, B., Simmons, M., & McDermott, M. (2018). Action research for graduate program improvements: A response to curriculum mapping and review. *Canadian Journal of Higher Education, 48*(1), 82-98.

Jaggars, S. S., Edgecombe, N., & Stacey, G. W. (2013, April). *Creating an effective online instructor presence.* Community College Research Center, Teachers College, Columbia University.
http://files.eric.ed.gov/fulltext/ED542146.pdf

Jaiswal, V. (2017). Continuing professional development: Inevitable for academic excellence. *Educational Quest: An international Journal of Education and Applied Social Science, 8*(3), 595-603.

Jankowska, M., & Atlay, M. (2008). Use of creative space in enhancing students' engagement. *Innovations in Education and Teaching International, 45*(3), 271-279.

Januszewski, A., & Persichitte, K. (2008). A history of the AECT's definitions of educational technology. In A. Januszewski, & M. Molenda, (Eds), *Educational Technology: A Definition with Commentary,* 259–282. Lawrence Erlbaum Associates.

Johnson, R. (2019). *Ten psychological principles to design with. 3.7 Designs.*
https://3.7designs.co/
blog/2012/08/10-psychological-principles-to-design-with/

Joshi, A. (2012). Multimedia: A technique in teaching process in the classrooms. *Current World Environment, 7*(1), 33-36.

Jonassen, D. H., Peck, K. L., & Wilson, B. G. (1999). *Learning with technology: A constructivist perspective.* Prentice Hall.

Juarez, B., Olivares, J. M., Rodriguez-Resendiz, J., Dector, A., Garcia, R., Eduardo, J. E., & Ferriol, F. (2020). Learning management system-based evaluation to determine academic efficiency performance. *Sustainability, 12*, 4256. doi:10.3390/su12104256.

Kaplin, W. A., & Lee, B. A. (2014). *Law of higher education.* Jossey-Bass.

Karaolis, S. (July 16, 2019). *How to work better with your subject matter experts.* ELUCIDAT.
https://www.elucidat.com/blog/subject-matter-experts-tips/

Karatas, I., Tunc, M. P., Yilmaz, N., & Karaci, G. (2017). An Investigation of Technological Pedagogical Content Knowledge, Self-Confidence, and Perception of Pre-Service Middle School Mathematics Teachers towards Instructional Technologies. *Educational Technology & Society, 20*(3), 122–132.

Kauffman, R., & Guerra-Lopez, I. (2013). *Needs assessment for organizational success.* ASTD Press.

Keller, F. S. (1968). "good-bye, teacher…" *Journal of Applied Behavior Analysis, 1*, 79-89.

Keller, J. M. (1983). *Motivational design of instruction. Instructional design theories and models: AN overview of their current status.* Erlbaum Associates.

Keller, J. M. (1987). Strategies for stimulating the motivation to learn. *Performance & Instruction, 26*(8), 1-7.

Keller, J. M. (2016). Motivation, learning, and technology: Applying the ARCS-V motivation model. *Participatory Educational Research, 3*(2), 1-13.

http://www.partedres.com.

Kentucky Department of Education. (n.d.). *Digital citizenship.* https://education.ky.gov/pages/search. aspx?terms=digital+citizenship&affiliateId=EDUCATION.

Keppel, M. (2001). Optimizing instructional designer-subject matter expert communication in the design and development of multimedia projects. *Journal of Interactive Learning Research, 12*(2/3), 209-227.

Kintu, M. J., Zhu, C., & Kagambe, E. (2017). Blended learning effectiveness: The relationship between student characteristics, design features and outcomes. *International Journal of Educational Technology in Higher Education, 14*(7).

Kirkpatrick, D. L. (1994). *Evaluating training programs: The four levels.* Berret-Koehler.

Kirkpatrick, D. (1996). *Evaluating training programs: The four levels.* Berret-Koehler Publishers, Inc.

Kirkpatrick, J. D., & Kirkpatrick, W. K. (2016). *Kirkpatrick's four levels of training evaluation.* ATD Press.

Koehler, M. J., & Mishra, P. (2005). What happens when teachers design educational technology? The Development of technological pedagogical content knowledge. *Journal of Educational Computing Research, 32*(2), 131-152.

Knowles, M. S. (1970). *The modern practice of adult education: Andragogy versus pedagogy.* Association Press.

Ko, J. (2010). Consistency and variation in classroom practice: A mixed-method investigation based on case studies of four EFL teachers of a disadvantaged secondary school in Hong Kong. Doctoral Thesis. Nottingham, UK: University of Nottingham. http://etheses.nottingham.ac.uk/1363/1/ CVCP_SUBMISSION_(FINAL)PB3.

Kotler, P., & Fox, K. (1995). *Strategic marketing for educational institutions.* (2ndEd.) Prentice-Hall.

Kotler, P., & Armstrong, G. (2017). *Principles of Marketing.* Pearson.

Kurt, S. (2018). Instructional design models and theories. *Educational Technology, 9.*
https://educationaltechnology.net/
instructional-design-models-and-theories/

Lambiotte, J. G., Dansereau, D. F., Cross, D. R., & Reynolds, S. B. (1989). Multirelational semantic maps. *Educational Psychology Review, 1*(4), 331-367.

Lattuca, L.R.; Bergom, I.; Knight, D.B. (2014). Professional development, departmental contexts, and use of instructional strategies. *Journal of Engineering Education, 103,* 4.

Lawless, C. (2019). *The top eLearning conferences to attend in 2020.* LearnUpon.
https://www.learnupon.com/blog/best-elearning-conferences/

Legal Information Institute (n.d.). *Individuals with Disabilities Education Act,* 20 U.S. Code § 1400.Short title; findings; purposes.
https://www.law.cornell.edu/uscode/text/20/1400

Legal Information Institute (n.d.). *Prohibition of discrimination by public accommodations,* 42 U.S.C. § 12182(B)(2)(A)(ii).
https://www.law.cornell.edu/uscode/text/42/12182

Leonard, K. (2012, March 12). *The roles of stakeholders in the planning process.* Chron.
https://smallbusiness.chron.com/roles-stakeholders-planning-process-32051.html

Liang, T.-H., Huang, Y.-M., & Tsai, C.-C. (2012). An Investigation of Teaching and Learning Interaction Factors for the Use of the Interactive Whiteboard Technology. *Educational Technology & Society, 15*(4), 356–367.

Lindsay, M & Krysik, J. (2012). Online harassment among college students.
*Information, Communication & Society, 15*(5), 703-719.

LITE. (2018). 7th International conference on learning technologies and learning environments.
http://www.iaiai.org/conference/aai2018/ltle-2018/

Little, J.W. (1987). Teachers as colleagues. In V. Richardson-Koehler (Ed.), *Educators' handbook: A research perspective*, 491-518. Longman.

Little, J.W. (1993). Teachers' professional development in a climate of educational reform. *Educational Evaluation and Policy Analysis*, *15*(2), 129-151.

Little, O., Goe, L., & Bell, C. (2009). *A practical guide to evaluating teacher effectiveness*. National Comprehensive Center of Teacher Quality.

Liu, S. H. (2012). A multivariate model of factors influencing technology use by preservice teachers during practice training. *Educational Technology & Society*, *15*(4), 137-149.

López, O. S. (2010). The Digital Learning Classroom: Improving English Language Learners' academic success in mathematics and reading using interactive whiteboard technology. *Computers & Education*, *54*(4), 901-915.

López Núñez, J. A., López Belmonte, J., Marrero Guerreo, A. J., & Poso Sánchez S. (2020). Effectiveness of innovative educational practices with flipped learning and remote sensing in earth and environmental sciences – An exploratory case study. *Remote Sensing*, *12*, 897; doi:10.3390/rs12050897.

Loyd, A. (2012-Spring). Facebook vs. the First Amendment: Student free speech in the digital age. *The Legal Issue*, *6*(1). https://www.cu.edu/sites/default/files/Vol%206%2C%20 Issue%201--Final.pdf

Lynch, W. (2015). The eight principles of ethical leadership in education. https://www.theedadvocate.org/ the-eight-principles-of-ethical-leadership-in-education/

Maddux, C., & Cummings, R. (2004). Fad, fashion, and the weak role of theory and research in information technology in education. *Journal of Technology and Teacher Education*, *12*(4), 511-533.

Mager, R. F. (1988). *Making instruction work*. Lake Publishing Company.

Mager, R. F. (1987). *Preparing instructional objectives* (3rd Ed.). Center for Effective Performance.

Mager, R. F., & Pipe, P. (1997). *Analyzing Performance Problems: Or, You Really Oughta Wanna* (3 ed.): Center for Effective Performance. https://hptmanualaaly.weebly.com/mager-and-pipes-model.html

Malamed, C. (n.d.). *Chunking information for instructional design.* The eLearning Coach. http://theelearningcoach.com/elearning_design/chunking-information/#:~:text=Chunking%20Defined,of%20information%20at%20one%20time.

Maloy, R. W., Verock, R., Edwaurds, S., & Trust, T. (2021). *Transforming learning with new technologies* (4th ed.). Pearson.

March, J. & Peters, K. (2008). *Designing instruction: Making best practices work in standards-based classrooms.* Corwin Press.

Marshall, J., & Rosset, A. (2011). Perceptions of barriers to the evaluation of workplace learning programs. *Performance Improvement Quarterly, 27*(3), 7-26.

Marzano, R., Pickering, D., & Pollock, J. (2001). *Classroom instruction that works: Research-based strategies for increasing student achievement.* Alexandra, VA, ASCD.

Martin, F., & Ritzhaupt, A. D. (2020). Standards and competencies for instructional design and technology professionals. In J. K. McDonald & R. E. West (Ed.), *Design for learning.* EdTech Books.

Martinelli, K. (2017, September 20). *Writing a professional development plan. Example and template.* Hub. https://www.highspeedtraining.co.uk/hub/professional-development-plan/#:~:text=A%20Professional%20Development%20Plan%20(PDP,PDP%20takes%20time%20and%20planning.

Marzano, R. J., Pickering, D. J., & Pollock, J. E. (2004). *Classroom instruction that works: Research-based strategies for increasing student achievement.* Prentice Hall.

Melton, J., Miller, M., & Brobst, J. (2019). Mentoring the mentors: Hybridizing professional development to support cooperating teachers' mentoring practice in science. *Contemporary Issues in Technology and Teacher Education, 19*(1). 23-44.

McCarthy, A., Maor, D., & McConney, A. (2019). Transforming mobile learning and digital pedagogies: An investigation of a customized professional development program for teachers in a hospital school. *Contemporary issues in Technology and Teacher Education, 19*(3), 498-528.

McLaughlin, M.W. (1991). The rand change agent study: Ten years later. In A.R. Odden (Ed.). *Education Policy Implementation,* 143-155.

Mclver, D., Fitzsimmons, S., & Flanagan, D. (2015). Instructional design as knowledge management. *Journal of Management Education, 40*(1), 47-75. doi:10.1177/1052562915587583.

McLeod, S. A. (2019, July 17). *Constructivism as a theory for teaching and learning.* Simply Psychology.
https://www.simplypsychology.org/constructivism.html.

McLoughlin, C., & Oliver, R. (2000). *Instructional design for cultural difference: A case study of the indigenous online learning in a tertiary context.*
https://www.ascilite.org/conferences/brisbane99/papers/
mcloughlinoliver.pdf

Merril, M. D. (1992). Constructivism and instructional design. In T. M. Duffy, & D. H. Jonassen (Eds.), *Constructivism and the technology of instruction: A conversation,* 99-115. Lawrence Erlbaum Associates.

Meyers, L. S., Gamst, G., & Guarino, A. J. (2016). *Applied multivariate research: Design and interpretation.* Thousand Oaks, CA, United States, SAGE Publications, Inc.

Moreau, K. (2017). Has the new Kirkpatrick generation built a better hammer for our evaluation toolbox? *Medical Teacher, 39*(9), 999-1001.

Morrison, G. R., Ross, S. M., &Kemp, J. E. (2006). *Designing effective instruction* (5 Ed.). John Wiley & Sons.

Morrison, G. R. (2010). *Designing effective instruction*, (6 Ed.). John Wiley & Sons.

Munger, M.C. (2000). *Analyzing policy: Choices, conflicts, and practices.* WW Norton and Co:1-286.

Murphy. D. M., Hanchett, M., Olmsted R. N., Farber M. R., Lee, T. B., Haas J. P., & Streed, S. A. (2012). Competency in infection prevention: A conceptual approach to guide current and future practice. *American Journal of Infection Control, 40.* https://doi.org/10.1016/j.ajic.2012.03.002

National Center for Educational Statistics. (2018). *Status and trends in the education of racial and ethnic groups.* https://nces.ed.gov/pubs2019/2019038.pdf

Nelson, W. A., Magliano, S., & Sherman, T. M. (1988). The intellectual content of instructional design. *Journal of Instructional Development, 11*(2), 29-35.

Nilsson, P., & Driel, J. (2010). Teaching together and learning together: Primary science student teachers' and their mentors' joint teaching and learning in the primary classroom. *Teaching and Teacher Education, 26*(6), 1309-1318.

Nkana, E. (2020). The conversionism theory of education; improving instructional practice in higher education through faculty development and cross-institutional learning communities. *Journal of Higher Education Theory and Practice, 20*(1), 136-140.

Nakic, J., Granic, A., & Glavinic, V. (2015). Anatomy of learner models in adaptive learning systems: A systematic literature review of individual differences from 2001 to 2013. *Journal of Educational Computing Research, 51*(4), 459-489.

Niekerk, M., & Blignaut, S. (2014). A framework for Information and Communication Technology integration in schools through teacher professional development. *Africa Education Review, 11*, 236-253. 10.1080/18146627.2014.927159.

Nielsen, J., & Loranger, H. (2006). *Prioritizing web usability.* Nielsen Norman Group.

North Carolina Agricultural and Technical State University (NCAT). (n.d.).
https://www.ncat.edu/_files/pdfs/provost/lms-evaluation-tool.pdf.

Northern Arizona University. (n.d.). *Learning-centered vs teaching centered.*
https://in.nau.edu/ocldaa/
learning-centered-vs-teaching-centered/.

Nugent, T. (2021). *Trends impacting business education in 2021, according to deans.* Business Because.
https://www.businessbecause.com/news/mba-degree/7366/business-education-trends-deans.

Nur Rohim, M. (2019). Marketing strategy for educational services. *Advances in Social Science, Education and Humanities Research, 387,* in 3rd International Conference on Educational Innovation (ICEI 2019).

Ohei, K. N., & Brink, R. (2019). A framework development for the adoption of information and communication technology web technologies in higher education systems. South African *Journal of Information Management, 21*(1), a1030.
https://doi.org/ 10.4102/sajim.v21i1.1030.

Oliveira, A. W., Wilcox, K. C., Angelis, Aj., Applebee, A. N., Amodeo, V., & Snyder, M. A. (2012). Best practice in middle-school science. *Journal of Science Teacher Education, 24,* 297-322. DOI 10.1007/s10972-012-9293-0

Olweus, D. (2001). Peer harassment: A critical analysis and some important issues. In J. Juvonen and S. Graham (Eds.), *Peer Harassment in school: The plight of the vulnerable and victimized* (pp. 3-20). The Guilford Press.

Ormrod, J. E. (2011). *Educational psychology: Developing learners.* Pearson.

Papadimitriou, A., & Gyftodimos, G. (2017). The role of learner characteristics in the adaptive educational hypermedia systems: The case of the Mathema. *International Journal of Modern Education and Computer Science, 10,* 55-68. DOI: 10.5815/ijmecs.2017.10.07

Pape, Liz, & Wicks, M. (2009). National Standards for Quality Online Programs.
http://www.aurora-institute.org/wp-content/uploads/national-standards-for-quality-online-programs.pdf.

Pappas, C. (2016, August 20). *Ten instructional design elements to include in every eLearning course.* eLearning Industry.
https://elearningindustry.com/instructional-design-elements-include-every-elearning-course

Pappas, C. (2018). *Eight top tips to work with a subject matter expert in eLearning.* eLearning INDUSTRY.
https://elearningindustry.com/top-tips-work-subject-matter-expert-elearning

Park, J., & Luo, H. (2017). Refining a competency model for instructional designers in the context of online higher education. *International Education Studies, 10*(9).

Pearson. (2018, August). *Beyond millennials: The next generation of learners.*
https://www.pearson.com/content/dam/one-dot-com/one-dot-com/global/Files/news/news-annoucements/2018/The-Next-Generation-of-Learners_final.pdf.

Porter, A., & Brophy, J. (1988). Synthesis of research on good teaching: Insights from the work of the Institute for Research on Teaching. *Educational Leadership, 46,* 74-85.

Pask, G. (1975). *Conversation theory: Applications in education and epistemology.* Elsevier.

PennSate (n.d.). Accessibility.
https://www.ed.gov/news/press-releases/civil-rights-agreement-reached-south-carolina-technical-college-system-accessibi.

Picciano, A. G., & Seaman, J. (2010). *Class connections. High school reform and the role of online learning.* Aurora Institute. https://aurora-institute.org/resource/class-connections-high-school-reform-and-the-role-of-online-learning/.

Phillips, J. (1991). *Return on investments programs in training and performance improvement programs* (2nd Ed.). Routledge.

Power, J., Kannara, V. (2016). Best-practice model for technology enhanced learning in the creative arts. *Research and Learning Technology, 24.*

Pratt, D. D. (1993). *Andragogy after Twenty-five years. New directions for adult and continuing education.* Jossey-Bass.

Preparedness and Emergency Response Learning Centers (PERLC). (n.d.). *Kirkpatrick level 1 (reaction).* PHF. http://www.phf.org/programs/preparednessresponse/evaluationrepository/Pages/PERLC_Evaluation_Working_Group.aspx

Preskill, H., & & Russ-Eft, D. (2016). *Building evaluation capacity.* SAGE.

Public Law Number 102-561 (1992).

Quality Matter (QM). (2015). *Course design rubric standards.* https://www.qualitymatters.org/qa-resources/rubric-standards/higher-ed-publisher-rubric

Ramorola, M. (2013). Challenge of effective technology integration into teaching and learning. *Africa Education Review, 10.* 654-670. 10.1080/18146627.2013.853559.

Razak, R. A., & Palanisamy, P. (2013). Cognitive task analysis of experts in designing multimedia learning object guideline (M-Log). *The Malaysian Online Journal of Educational Technology, 1*(1). https://www.researchgate.net/publication/257367449_Cognitive_Task_Analysis-Based_Training_A_Meta-Analysis_of_Studies

ReadWriteThink (2019). *Oral presentation rubric.*

http://www.readwritethink.org/classroom-resources/printouts/
oral-presentation-rubric-30700.html

Reeves, T. C., & Reeves, P. M. (1997). The effective dimensions of interactive learning on the WWW. In B. H. Khan, (Ed.), *Web-based instruction* (pp. 59-66). Englewood Cliffs, NJ: Educational Technology.

Reigeluth, C. M., & Keller, J. B. (2009). Understanding instruction. In C. M. Reigeluth & A. A. Carr-Chellman (Eds.), *Instructional-design theories and models: Building a common knowledge base* (pp. 27-39). Taylor & Francis.

Reis, R. (n.d.). *The constructivist approach and online learning. Tomorrow's teaching and learning.* Stanford University. https://tomprof.stanford.edu/posting/987.

Reiser, R. A., & Dempsey, J. V. (2018). *Trends and issues in instructional design and technology.* Pearson.

Remillard, J.T. (2005). Examining key concepts in research on teachers' use of mathematics curricula. Review of Educational Research, *75*(2), 211-246.

Richard, V. E., & Dempsey, J. (2002). The Effect of Competition and Contextualized Advisement on the Transfer of Mathematics Skills in a Computer-Based Instructional Simulation Game. *Educational Technology Research and Development, 50*(3), 23-41. https://www.learntechlib.org/p/95371/.

Richardson, W. (2011). Foreword. In N. Walser (Ed.), *Spotlight on technology in education* (pp. xi-xii). Harvard University PressRichey.

Richey, R. C., Dennis, C., & Foxon, M. (2001). *Instructional design competencies: The standards,* (3rd Ed.). Eric Publications.

Rhode, J. (June 15, 2004). *Critical factors to instructional design.* https://www.jasonrhode.com/ critical-factors-to-instructional-design

Ribble, M. (2011). *Digital citizenship in schools.* ISTE. https://id.iste.org/connected/resources/product?ID=2111

Richey, R. C., & Morrison, G. R. (2002). Instructional design in business and industry. In R. A. Reiser, & J. V. Dempseym (Eds.), *Trends and issues in instructional design and technology* (p.207). Merrill Prentice Hall.

R.L. v. Central York School District, 183 F. Supp. 3d 625 - Dist. Court, MD Pennsylvania, 2016.

RNL. (2020). *2020 Marketing and recruitment practices for undergraduate students*. www.RuffaloNL.com.

Robinson, D. G., & Robinson, J. C. (2008). *Performance consulting: Moving beyond training* (2nd ed.). Berrett-Koehler.

Rodriguez, S., Stephens, R., & Arena, S. (1991). Interviewing subject matter experts: Strategies for instructional design success. *Educational Technology, December,* 27-32. www.jstor.org/stable/44427558.

Rosset, A. (1995). Needs assessment. In: Angun, G. J. (ed) (1995). *Instructional technology: Past, present, and future.* Libraries Unlimited.

Rowland, G., & and DiVasto, T. (2001). Instructional design and powerful learning. *Performance Improvement Quality, 14*(2), 7-36. Doi:10.111/j.1937-8327.2001.tb00207.x

Rovai, A. P., Wighting, M. J., & Lucking, R. (2004). The classroom and school community inventory: Development, refinement, and validation of a self-report measure for educational research. *Internet and Higher Education, 7*(4), 263-280.

Rutt, D. P. (1985). *Consultation in instructional development: A first look.* In R. K. Bass & C. R. Dills (Eds). Instructional development: The state of the art, II, 294-309. Kendall/Hunt.

Sabatier, P.A., and Weible, C.M. (2014). *Theories of the policy process,* (3 Ed.). Press.

Sadalla, A. M., & Larocca, P. (2004). Autoscopia: um procedimiento de pesquisa e de formacao. *Educacao e Pesquisa, 30*(3). https://www.revistas.usp.br/ep/article/view/27948

Sharma, A. (2015). *Discovering learning management systems: Basic functions and benefits.* sLearning Industry. https://elearningindustry.com/discovering-learning-management-systems-basic-functions-benefits.

Schank, R. C., & Abelson, R. (1977). *Scripts, plans, goals and understanding.* Lawrence Erlbaum.

Schifter, D., and Fosnot, C. (1993). Reconstructing mathematics education: Stories of teachers meeting the challenge of reform. Teachers College Press.

Scheiter, K., Gerjets, P., Vollmann, B., & Catrambone, R. (2009). The impact of learners characteristics on information utilization strategies, cognitive load experienced, and performance in hypermedia learning. *Learning and Instruction, 19*(5), 387-401.

Scheel, N. P., & Branch, R. C. (1993). The role of conversation in the systematic design of instruction. *Educational Technology, 33*(8), 7-18.

Salary.com. (n.d.). *Salaries for marketing manager with a bachelor's degree.* https:// www1.salary.com/Salaries-for-Marketing-Manager-with-a-Bachelors-Degree#:~:text=According%20to%20our%20100%25%20employer,Bachelor's%20Degree%20is%20%24101%2C391%20-%20%24109%2C762.

Sambiran, A. M, & Soenarto, S. (2020). Using Mayer's principles of designing mobile-based learning module: Implementation in the subject of simulation and digital communication for vocational high schools. ICSTI. DOI 10.4108/eai.19-10-2018.2281718.

Sheldon, M.R. (2016). Policy-making theory as an analytical framework in policy analysis: Implications for research design and professional advocacy. *Physical Therapy, 96*(1), 101-110.

Schmidt, D. A., Baran, E., Thompson, A. D., Mishra, P., Koehler, M. J., & Shin, T. S. (2009). Technological pedagogical content knowledge (TPCK): the development and validation of an assessment instrument for preservice teachers. *Journal of Research on Technology in Education, 42*(2), 123-149.

Schweiter, K. (2019). *Curriculum design: Definition, purpose, and types.* https://www.thoughtco.com/ curriculum-design-definition-4154176

Seth Warner, N. C. (2015, March 3). *Importance of pre-assessment.* Naiku. https://www.naiku.net/naiku-coach/ importance-of-pre-assessment/

Shen v. Albany Unified School District, Case No. 17-cv-02478-JD (N.D. Cal. May. 26, 2017.

Smith, P. L., & Ragan, T. J. (2005). *Instructional design* (3rd Ed.), John Wiley & Sons.

Smith, F., Hardman, F., & Higgins, S. (2006). The impact of interactive whiteboards on teacher–pupil interaction in the National Literacy and Numeracy Strategies. *British Educational Research Journal, 32*(3), 443-457.

Stauffer, B. (2019, September 1). *What is a lesson plan and how do you make one?* Applied Educational Systems. https://www.aeseducation.com/blog/what-is-a-lesson-plan.

Steinert, Y., Mann, K., Anderson, B., Bernett, B. M., Centeno A., Naismith L. (2016). A systematic review of faculty development initiatives designed to enhance teaching effectiveness: A 10-yer update: BEME Guide 40. *Medical Teacher, 38*(8), 769-786.

Steven-Fulbrook, P. (2019, April 18). *15 learning theories in education (A complete summary).* Teacher of Sci. https://teacherofsci.com/learning-theories-in-education/

Stone, R. (2004). *Best teaching practices for reaching all learners: What award-winning classroom teachers do.* Corwin Press.

Strader, T. J. (2014). Offline and online content piracy activities: Characteristics and ethical perceptions. *International Journal of Technoethics, 5*(2), 22-36.

Sugar, W., Hoard, B., Brown, A., & Daniels, L. (2012). Identifying multimedia production competencies and skills of instructional design and technology professionals: An analysis of recent jobs postings. *Journal of Educational Technology Systems, 40,* 227-249.

Surjono, H. D., & Maltby, J. (2003). *Adaptive educational hypermedia based on multiple student characteristics.* In Proceedings of the 2nd international conference on web based learning, 442–449.

Surry, D. W., Stefurak, J., & Kowch, E. G. (2011). Technology in higher education: Asking the right questions. In D. W. Surry, R. M. Gray Jr., & J. R. Stefurak, *Technology Integration in Higher Education: Social and Organizational Aspects.* IGI Global.

Suskie, L. A. (2009). *Assessing student learning: A common sense guide.* Jossey-Bass.

Tam, M. (2000). Constructivism, instructional design, and technology: Implications for transforming distance learning. *Educational Technology and Society, 3*(2).

Tanis, C. J. (2020). The seven principles of online learning: Feedback from faculty and alumni on its importance for teaching and learning. *Research in Learning Technology, 28.*

Taylor, P. C., Fraser, B. J., & Fisher, D. I. (1997). Monitoring constructivist learning environments. *International Journal of educational Research, 27*(4), 293-302.

Taylor, T. (2017, July 22). *Top ten in demand instructional design skills.* eLearning Industry. https://elearningindustry.com/ instructional-designer-skills-top-10.

Teaching Professor Technology Conference. (2019). https://eventegg.com/teaching-professor-conference/.

Technology, Education, and Copyright Harmonization Act, Pub. L. No. 107-273, §13301 116 Stat. 1910 (2002).

Teo, T., Lee, C. B., Chai, C. S., & Wong, S. L. (2009). Assessing the intention to use technology among preservice teachers in Singapore and Malaysia: A multigroup invariance analysis of the Technology Acceptance Model (TAM). *Computers & Education, 53*(3), 1000-1009.

Texas Education Agency (2006). *Rubric for classroom discussion.* https://www.northwestern.edu/searle/docs/Discussion%20 Rubric%20Examples.pdf

The Web Conference. (2018). *Let us build the Web of tomorrow.* https://www2018.thewebconf.org/

Thompson, M. M., & Wrigglesworth, J. (2013). Students and teachers as ethical actors: Reflections on the literature. In M. Moore (Ed.), *Handbook of distance education* (3rd ed., pp. 403-418. Lawrence Erlbaum Associates.

Thompson M. M., & Kuhne, G. (2014). Ethics matters: Ensuring quality at the program level. In K. Shattuck (Ed.), *Assuring quality in online education: Practices and processes at teaching, resource, and program levels* (pp. 165-183). Stylus.

Thompson, M., M. (2019). The ethical character of distance education. Relationship and responsibility. In G. Moore (Ed.), *Handbook of distance education,* (pp. 189-206). Routledge.

Toprak, E., Ozkanal, B., Kaya, S., & Aydin, S. (2010). *What do learners and instructors of online learning environments think about ethics in e-Learning?* A case study from Anadolu University. https://asianvu.com/digital-library/elearning/ethics.pdf.

United States v. Angevine, 281 F.3d 1130 (10th Cir. 2002), cert. denied, 537 U.S. 845 (2002)

U.S. Bureau of Labor Statistics. (n.d.). *Occupational Outlook Handbook.* https://www.bls.gov/ooh/.

U.S. Bureau of Labor Statistics. (n.d.1a). *Occupational Outlook Handbook.* https://www.bls.gov/emp/tables/emp-by-detailed-occupation.htm

United States Copyright Office. (2009). *United States Copyright Office: A brief introduction and history,* Circular 1a. http://www.copyright.gov/circs/ circ1a.html

United States Office of Personnel Management (USOPM). (2011). *Training evaluation field guide: Demonstrating the value of training at every level.* https://www.opm.gov/policy-data-oversight/training-and-development/reference-materials/training_evaluation.pdf

United State Department of Labor (2019). *Bureau of Labor Statistics.* https://www.bls.gov/ooh/business-and-financial/market-research-analysts.htm#tab-6

University of Cincinnati (n.d.). *Resolution agreement.* OCR Compliance Review #15-13-6001. https://www2.ed.gov/documents/press-releases/university-cincinnati-agreement.pdf

University of Washington (n.d.). *Accessible technology.* https://www.washington.edu/accessibility/requirements/legal-cases-by-issue/

U.S. Constitution (1868), *14th Amendment.* https://www.law.cornell.edu/constitution/amendmentxiv

U.S. Department of Education (n.d.). *Office for Civil Rights.* https://www2.ed.gov/about/offices/list/ocr/index.html

U.S. Department of Education (2013). *Civil rights agreement reached with South Carolina Technical College System on accessibility of Websites to people with disabilities.* https://www.ed.gov/news/press-releases/civil-rights-agreement-reached-south-carolina-technical-college-system-accessibi.

U.S. Department of Education: Teacher professional and career development. https://www.ed.gov/oii-news/teacher-professional-and-career-development.

Vallerand, R. J., & Losier, G. (2001). The temporal relationship between perceived competence and self-determined motivation. *Journal of Social Psychology,* 793-801.

Vallor, S., & Green, B. (2018). *Tech ethics: Best practices. Markkula Center for Applied Ethics.* https://www.scu.edu/media/ethics-center/technology-ethics/BestPracticesinTechFinal.pdf

Van Zee, E. H., & Roberts, D. (2006). Making science teaching and learning visible through web-based "snapshots of practice. *Journal of Science Teacher Education, 17,* 367–388.

Vejvodova J. (2009). *The ADDIE model: Dead or alive?* http://virtuni.eas.sk/rocnik/2009/pdf/paper_127.pdf

Viennet, R., and Pont, B. (2017). Education policy implementation: A literature review a proposed framework. OECD Education Working Paper No. 162 (EDU/WKP (2017)11).

Wallington, C. J. (1987). Conceptualizing unfamiliar content. *Journal of Instructional Development, 10*(3), 16-21.

Wormeli, R., & Ground, M. (2011, August). Building Our Data Analysis Skills. *Westerville, 15*(1), 39-41.

Worthen, B.R., Sanders, J.R., & Fitzpatrick, J.L. (2004). *Educational evaluation: Alternative approaches and practical guidelines.* (3rd ed.). Boston: Allyn & Bacon.

Writing@CSU. (n.d.). *Planning introductions.* Colorado State University. https://writing.colostate.edu/guides/teaching/planning/introductions.cfm

Wroblewski, M. T. (2020, June 19). *Average salary of a marketing major.* Cron. https://work.chron.com/average-salary-marketing-major-27656.html.

Wulf, K.M., & Schave, B. (1984). *Curriculum design: A handbook for educators.* Scott, Foresman.

Yilmaz, Y., Lal, S., Tong, X. C., Howard, M., Bal, S., Bayer, I., Monteiro, S., & Chan, T. M. (2020). Technology-enhanced faculty development: Future trends and possibilities for health sciences education. *Medical Science Educator, 30*, 1787-1796. https://doi.org/10.1007/s40670-020-01100-1.

Zemke, R., & Kramlinger, T. (1982). *Figuring things out: A trainer's guide to needs and task analysis.* Addison-Wesley.

Zippia. (n.d.). Instructional design manager skills. https://www.zippia.com/instructional-design-manager-jobs/skills/.